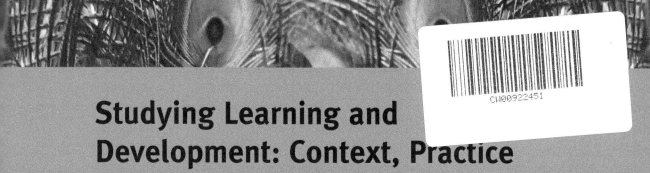

Studying Learning and Development: Context, Practice and Measurement

Edited by Jim Stewart and Patricia Rogers

The Chartered Institute of Personnel and Development is the leading publisher of
books and reports for personnel and training professionals, students, and all those
concerned with the effective management and development of people at work. For
details of all our titles, please contact the publishing department:
tel: 020 8612 6204
email: publish@cipd.co.uk
The catalogue of all CIPD titles can be viewed on the CIPD website:
www.cipd.co.uk/bookstore
An e-book version is also available for purchase from:
www.ebooks.cipd.co.uk

Studying Learning and Development: Context, Practice and Measurement

Edited by Jim Stewart and Patricia Rogers

Chartered Institute of Personnel and Development

Published by the Chartered Institute of Personnel and Development
151 The Broadway, London SW19 1JQ

This edition first published 2017

Designed and typeset by Exeter Premedia Services, India
Printed and bound by CPI Group (UK) Ltd, Croydon, CR0 4YY

British Library Cataloguing in Publication Data
A catalogue of this publication is available from the British Library

ISBN 9781843984146
eBook ISBN 9781843984603

Chartered Institute of Personnel and Development

151 The Broadway, London SW19 1JQ
Tel: 020 8612 6200
Email: cipd@cipd.co.uk
Website: www.cipd.co.uk
Incorporated by Royal Charter.
Registered Charity No. 1079797

Contents

List of figures and tables

Contributor Biographies

Phil Badley works a leadership coach and OD Consultant supporting senior leaders to change mindsets and behaviours to enable a cultural shift within organisations to deliver improved personal and organisational performance. He previously worked in senior leadership at board level within local government in a number of single-tier councils. He is a Fellow of the CIPD.

Tricia Harrison is the Professional Networking Co-ordinator at Liverpool John Moores University, with module responsibilities for International HRM/HRD, Organisational Behaviour, Strategic Human Resource Management and Leadership. Tricia's research areas are the development of professional practice, student employability, mental toughness and action learning. Previously, Tricia worked at Webster University, Geneva; Kingston University; and Bournemouth University as Senior Lecturer. Tricia also has extensive HR consultancy experience.

Dalbir Johal is an L&D professional with over 15 years' experience of organisation and leadership and management development and is a Chartered Member of the CIPD with a Masters in Strategic HRM and Change. As a qualified coach, Dalbir has a breadth of experience in the L&D field both in the public and private sector where she offers a solution-focused consultancy service from the identification and analysis of learning needs, to the design and delivery of a number of bespoke L&D solutions. In addition to her progressive career in industry, Dalbir is a lecturer and a module leader at Coventry University, delivering various modules on the CIPD postgraduate programmes. She combines her industry experience with the latest research and academia in L&D practice. She has led a number of postgraduate programmes and taught internationally. Dalbir has previously authored two CIPD academic books specialising in learning and development.

Wendy Marston is the Director of Positive Public Ltd, which provides strategic business support and advice to public service providers. Wendy has worked extensively as a Director at board level across Local Government and the NHS. Wendy's roles have primarily focused on business service redesign and managing major change programmes. Wendy has a particular interest in asset-based models working collaboratively with the workforce and external partners to develop 'what's strong' in an organisation rather than focusing on 'what's wrong'. Wendy's operational background is in leading the full range of business support services, including Human Resources, ICT, finance, performance management and organisation development.

Rachel Robins is a practicing Leadership and Behavioural Coach, Mentor and Mediator with a background as a Director of HR, Organisational Development and Improvement in the public sector. Her doctoral research area was in executive coaching in local government and she continues to research into the personal development of professionals. She is a Fellow of the CIPD and lectures on CIPD undergraduate and post-graduate programmes on leadership, development, strategic HRM, OD and HR professional practice.

Patricia Rogers, former Head of Human Resource Management and Organisational Behaviour at Coventry University, is now part of the Postgraduate Taught Strategy and Development Group responsible for the development of postgraduate taught strategies across Coventry University. Prior to coming to Higher Education, she was Head of Business School in Further Education and has held a number of management posts in industry. Patricia has edited the CIPD book *Developing People in Organisation*, with Jim Stewart, and jointly wrote the chapter *Improving Organisation Performance*, in the same book.

Raymond Rogers is a Senior Lecturer in the Faculty of Business and Law at Coventry University. He has over twenty years' industrial experience working in management and development roles particularly in the transport and engineering sectors. Ray has taught on the CIPD programmes at undergraduate and postgraduate level for ten years and has been involved in learning and development, management, statistics and accountancy linked to HRM/HRD. Ray has designed and delivered HRM/HRD courses in the Middle East.

Maureen Royce is the Associate Dean - Education for Liverpool Business School, LJMU and leads the academic HRM programmes both Undergraduate and Postgraduate. Maureen has considerable experience both in education and in HR where she currently advises not-for- profit organisations in HR strategy and policy. With a particular focus on inclusive education, Maureen has developed part time provision to enable greater diversity in HR programme areas and has promoted the embedding of diversity awareness and practice based diversity skills in the mainstream curriculum. In promoting inclusive education, the need to engage students in self development has been central to enabling students to become independent learners. In times of rapid change, Maureen believes that the ability to learn and grow as individuals forms an important part of the success of communities and organisations.

David Soehren is a Co-Director of Quantum Connections, an organisational behaviour consultancy and learning and development supplier. For the past 18 years, Quantum Connections has provided a wide range of services: organisational consultancy and improvement projects; leadership, management and graduate programmes; group and team facilitated workshops; executive and performance coaching; and employee performance development courses. Since 2011 David has been a Sessional Lecturer at Liverpool John Moores University within the Business School's Business Studies and Human Resource Management programmes. David has developed, managed and delivered a range of undergraduate and graduate modules.

Jim Stewart is Professor of HRD at Liverpool Business School and is former Professor of Human Resource Development at Coventry University. He was also previously Running Stream Professor of Human Resource Development at Leeds Business School where he initiated and led the DBA programme and established and was Director of the HRD and Leadership Research Unit. Prior to that appointment Jim was Professor of HRD at Nottingham Business School where he designed and led the MSc in HRD and was also Joint Course Leader of the NBS DBA. Jim is currently Acting Chair of the University Forum for HRD as well as holding the substantive position of Executive Secretary. He was appointed as CIPD Chief Examiner for Learning and Development in 2008 and is also a CIPD QA Visiting Panel Chair and an External Moderator. Jim is author and co-editor of over 20 books on HRD as well as of numerous articles in academic and professional journals.

Acknowledgements

We would like to thank our contributors for their sterling work in producing their chapters, and staff at CIPD Publishing for their patience and support. As always, thanks to our families for their understanding in accepting yet another book project taking our attention.

Walkthrough of textbook features and online resources

CHAPTER OVERVIEW

Concise chapter introductions outline the structure of each chapter and the topics covered.

LEARNING OUTCOMES

At the end of this chapter, you will be able to:

- summarise current practices, trends and emerging roles in learning and development
- identify the key knowledge, skills and behaviours required by learning and development professionals.

CIPD LEARNING OUTCOMES

At the beginning of each chapter a bulleted set of learning outcomes summarises what you can expect to learn from the chapter, helping you to track your progress.

 REFLECTIVE ACTIVITY 1.1

Who are your key stakeholders?

How would you describe your current relationship with each group?

How well defined are their needs?

What gaps do you have in your capability to deliver against identified need?

REFLECTIVE ACTIVITIES

These questions are designed to get you reflecting on what you have learnt and test your understanding of important concepts and issues.

CASE STUDY 5.1 SPECSAVERS: PASSIONATE ABOUT OUR PEOPLE

Supporting our staff to be the best they can be

We firmly believe in supporting and developing our staff so they can shine in their roles. Whether working with customers or supporting partners, our people are our ambassadors. It is, therefore, crucial that they are engaged and motivated in their work, skilled and

development at all stages, with the potential to take them on a full career journey from entry level to partner. Our learning and development portfolio covers all aspects of the Specsavers business, whether staff want to improve their customer service skills, brush upon their product knowledge or study for an accredited, professional qualification.

CASE STUDIES

A diverse range of case studies throughout the text will help you to place the concepts discussed into a real-life context.

 FURTHER READING

Baron, A. and Armstrong, M. (2007) *Human Capital Management: Achieving Added Value Through People* London: Kogan Page.

Bassi, L. Carpenter, R. and McMurrer, D. (2012) *HR analytics handbook*. McBassi & Company.

Burkholder, N.C., Golas, S. and Shapiro, J.P. (2007) *Ultimate performance measuring at work*. New York: Wiley.

CIPD (2014) *Managing the Value of your Talent: A new framework for human capital measurement*. London: CIPD.

Fitz-Enz, J. (2010) *The new HR analytics: Predicting the economic value of your company's human capital investments*. New York: American Management Association.

EXPLORE FURTHER

Explore further boxes contain suggestions for further reading and useful websites, so that you can develop your understanding of the issues and debates raised in each chapter.

ONLINE RESOURCES FOR STUDENTS

- A document containing self-assessment quizzes, and is available for each chapter.

ONLINE RESOURCES FOR TUTORS

- Lecturer's guide – including guidance on the activities and questions in the text.
- PowerPoint slides – design your programme around these ready-made lectures.
- Mulitple choice questions.

Visit **www.cipd.co.uk/tss**

Introduction

JIM STEWART AND PATRICIA ROGERS

OVERVIEW

This book is intended to support learning and teaching of the new CIPD Learning and Development (L&D) intermediate level qualifications. Those qualifications are composed of a number of modules, or units, which can be studied singly and lead to a CIPD 'award', or in combination to lead to a CIPD certificate or diploma qualification. These combinations may be offered by providers, such as universities or colleges, and those courses may lead to an award of the provider, which is approved by the CIPD. Certificate and diploma level qualifications both require successful completion of the three core units specified in the CIPD qualifications. This book is written to support study of those three core units. Certificate qualifications will require further study of two optional units and diploma qualifications study of an additional two optional units, making a total of five units for the certificate and seven units for the diploma. As there is a total of thirteen optional units, a series of e-booklets will be published by the CIPD to support learning and teaching of each of those. That series is edited by the same editorial team and has some of the same authors as contributors to this book. So, there is a coherent approach across all the new units.

This opening chapter provides an introduction to the subject and to the chapters of this particular book. We should perhaps say a brief word at this point on the use of terminology. Learning and development, HRD and training and development are used at times in this book. The terms HRD and training are used infrequently in the CIPD units, although they do occur in some of the indicative content specified in some units. The terms HRD, training and training and development can be assumed in this context to be synonymous with terms used more frequently in practice, such as learning and development, unless stated otherwise.

PURPOSE, AIMS AND OBJECTIVES

Our purpose in producing the book is clear and unambiguous; it is to help learning and teaching of the core units in the CIPD Level 5 qualifications in learning and development. Following good practice in supporting learning and teaching, we also list below some additional and more specific aims. These will hopefully help to guide you through the book and also provide a basis for assessing if the book is successful in achieving the overall purpose:

- to introduce and explore concepts associated with and relevant to the syllabus of the CIPD Level 5 Learning and Development core units
- to provide a practical and accessible exposition at intermediate level of key theories informing the professional practice of learning and development
- to provide a useful and useable resource to support the teaching and learning of learning and development as an academic subject at intermediate level
- to facilitate and support a critically informed examination of the theory and practice of learning and development.

It will be worth expanding on these aims. They suggest a clear connection with the CIPD syllabus for each of its intermediate level L&D core units, and this is deliberate. The book is intended to cover the ground indicated in the CIPD unit descriptors. However, this does not mean that those descriptors have exclusively determined the content, or that we have provided either *all* the information or *only* information relevant to each syllabus. The book has an openly declared purpose of preparing students for assessment. This purpose is achieved, however, by our interpretation, and that of our contributors, of the descriptors in relation to what we judge to be the *key* or *critical* concepts, and in terms of the understanding required to utilise and apply those concepts in professional practice. There will be varying views on what is *key* and what is *critical,* and so we acknowledge there will be varying interpretations. In addition, our content is limited to what can be included in a single book and single chapters. There are many examples of chapters here on topics which are the subject of whole books. So, again, the content is based on what we judge to be *key* and *critical.*

This raises a second important point about the aims of the book. While the final aim explicitly assumes a separation between theory and practice, we do not believe such a separation is either valid or useful. We share the CIPD philosophy that professional certification must mean the ability to practice in the profession. Therefore, a key purpose of the book is to help equip individuals to meet the expectations placed upon those performing specialist roles in learning and development in work organisations, and other contexts of professional practice.

A final point on the CIPD connection is to recognise that the book is intended to have relevance to and application in the study of L&D as a subject. This means that the relevance of the content is not restricted to the CIPD units but is intended to have value in any module concerned with learning and development. Particular chapters will, of course, have greater or lesser relevance to particular modules. In this book, each chapter is associated with a specific learning outcome of one of the CIPD intermediate L&D units. However, the book is also intended to support the teaching and learning of L&D as a subject rather than being restricted or exclusive to one specific syllabus or qualification.

Two more points are worth considering. First, we have attempted to create a resource which will be valuable both to those teaching and to those learning L&D. Although the book is written primarily for those learning to practise, we believe and hope that the content will include some insights and perspectives which will give pause for thought on the part of experienced teachers of the subject. The final point to make about the aims of the book is that we and our contributors wish to encourage alternative paradigms and perspectives to be applied to support critical thinking about the subject.

This statement and discussion of the aims of the book allows us to articulate some clear objectives. Again reflecting what is considered good practice in L&D, and indeed in teaching and learning practices in higher education, these are expressed in terms of what readers can expect to have achieved through using the book:

- to explain and analyse the organisational context of L&D practice
- to describe, compare and critically evaluate a range of theories, concepts and methods related to learning and development professional practice
- to identify, explain and critically evaluate the connections between L&D theory and practice
- to identify, collect, analyse, evaluate and apply data relevant to L&D professional practice.

READERSHIP

It will be clear by now that a primary readership for the book will be anyone studying L&D intermediate units as part of a CIPD qualification programme. This will include those studying in universities which provide their own qualification courses approved by the CIPD, as well as those studying for CIPD qualifications in other centres. However, the book has not been written exclusively for this audience and other readers are envisaged and expected. In fact, all those who 'study' L&D constitute the intended readership. It is, however, possible to identify some specific audiences.

It seems to be an increasing trend to include L&D in undergraduate studies. We have in mind all potential readers at undergraduate level, whether studying CIPD accredited or approved courses or not. As already stated, the book is concerned with application. Therefore, its value to undergraduate studies will require that students can relate personal experience of work organisations to the content. This experience does not have to be in professional roles. However, the book has not been written to consider the subject at a purely or exclusively conceptual level, and achievement of its aims and objectives assumes and requires regular interaction between reader and text based on personal experience.

While CIPD intermediate level equates to second or final year undergraduate studies, there are a number of postgraduate programmes where the book will be relevant. Perhaps the most obvious of these will be Diploma in Management Studies and MBA programmes which include human resource and/or L&D content, either as mandatory or elective modules. The book assumes no prior specialist knowledge or experience and therefore will be appropriate for and relevant to non-specialist readers. In addition, many universities offer well-established Masters' degrees in the professional areas of human resource management and human resource development. Some of these specialist programmes may require CIPD membership at the point of entry, and this book is aimed primarily at those studying for such membership. However, the book will be valuable for specialist and post-CIPD Masters programmes as some students on such programmes will not be specialist L&D practitioners and may not have studied the subject at CIPD level.

A final group of intended and expected readers is that of professional practitioners not involved in a course of formal study. The practice orientation of the book, already emphasised, provides sound reasons for the book's relevance to practitioners. It is not assumed that all readers will be students, and the content and design of the book does not require that to be the case. It can be read and used by practitioners who are not also, formally at least, students, and we hope the book reaches such a readership.

STRUCTURE AND CONTENT

The book follows a straightforward structure. Each chapter is focused on a single learning outcome of one of the CIPD core units. Chapter titles generally reflect the specification of the learning outcome in the title of the chapter. Thus, chapters of most relevance to a particular course and/or reader are easily identifiable. We have assumed that all courses of formal study will have all core units and so collections of chapters provide the resource for each unit. The order is that the first four chapters relate to 5LDP, the following three chapters to 5CLD and the final two chapters to 5DBC. However, we are not suggesting that is the only or even correct order of studying the units. The order of units is a matter of programme design and so will be variable. We do clearly suggest, however, that the chapters should be used to support learning and teaching of each unit in particular programmes and so not necessarily in the order they are organised in the book.

The order of units and chapters follows a straightforward logic. We begin in the first four chapters with the nature of professional L&D practice and the skills needed by individuals engaging in that practice. These chapters also include examining working with others and how to keep personal professional practice current. We then move on to more contextual factors such as organisation strategy and the influence and impact of that on L&D practice. The final two chapters have a common theme of accessing and utilising L&D information and data. This includes a chapter on using research projects to generate primary and original data. This logic is intended to provide one meaningful structure for those who will use the book as a whole in their studies, or who simply wish to further their understanding of all elements of L&D. The book's concluding chapter, as well as attempting to draw together some threads, speculates about future directions for the subject and the profession.

There is also a logic and common structure for chapters. Each substantive chapter (that is all except this one and the conclusion) has a set of common features. These include the following:

- introduction
- intended learning objectives
- main content
- in-text activities
- case illustrations and examples
- summary/conclusion
- case study with discussion questions
- suggested reading and resources.

The introduction sets the scene for the chapter and outlines its main purpose. This is then translated into a set of specific learning objectives. Readers are encouraged to check and assess whether these are achieved as they work through the chapters of interest to them. The main content of each chapter is interspersed with 'Reflective Activities'. These are designed and intended to encourage exploration and application of the concepts discussed in the main content. They are also, in some cases, sequential and cumulative; that is, in any given chapter, the third Reflective Activity, for example, will assume that the first and/or second activities have been completed. However, they are not sequential and cumulative in terms of the book, although the main content is intended to have that feature. Chapters adopt some variation in these activities with some including reflective questions as well as application tasks. All chapters require some form of reader interaction with the content and this interaction also commonly requires some interaction with others; for example, fellow students or work colleagues.

Completing the activities within each chapter is essential if the chapter objectives are to be achieved. It is possible to read the main content and ignore the activities. However, this will not serve or help to meet any of the purposes of the book. Many activities refer to 'your organisation' or 'an organisation you know/are familiar with'. This can be taken to mean any organisation; it is not necessary to be employed by the chosen organisation. As indicated above, many activities also refer to 'a colleague', sometimes with an instruction that this means a work colleague. In the absence of this instruction, 'a colleague' is meant to indicate someone with whom you are studying and who also carries out the activity. If either of these presents a problem (that is, you are not a student and/or you do not have work colleagues), then any other person can and will serve a valuable purpose. The important and critical requirement is that you *discuss* your responses to activities with some other person who will have views on the topic.

Each chapter closes with a conclusion/summary of the main arguments and an application case study. All case studies present actual scenarios experienced by professional practitioners. The intention is to encourage identification with the problems and issues encountered in professional practice. The purpose of the case studies is to at least facilitate discussion of applying the concepts examined in the chapter. They also serve the purpose of illustrating the practical implications of theoretical concepts. A final feature of some chapters, although not all, is 'illustrations of practice'. These are intended to give more life to the concepts being discussed. All forms of in-text activities serve a similar purpose and so those chapters not containing 'illustrations' should not be seen as less concerned with practice.

Given the points made about activities and case studies, it will be clear that they are an essential and integral component of the book. They are certainly important in achieving the objectives of the book and those of individual chapters. The book as a whole has a logical structure and sequence. But, particular parts and/or combinations of chapters may have specific relevance for particular courses of study or issues being faced in practice. So, within the context of our logic, we hope and intend that readers will make their own sense of the book as part of their sense making of the subject.

A FINAL THOUGHT

We have encouraged readers to evaluate the worth of the book and provided features such as intended learning objectives to help do so. This is because, like declaring learning objectives in the first place, evaluating the worth of investment in L&D is considered good practice. However, that element of good practice is harder to find being applied than other elements. Evaluation is clearly of relevance to all of the topics covered in this book and its constituent chapters. So, as a final introductory comment we as editors wish to encourage you as readers to have evaluation at the forefront of your mind as you read this book. Evaluate the book and its content, but also think about how you could and would evaluate the approaches, techniques and processes you read about if you applied them in your professional practice, either now or in the future.

DEVELOPING PROFESSIONAL PRACTICE IN LEARNING AND DEVELOPMENT

CHAPTER 1

The Knowledge, Skills and Behaviours Required of Learning and Development Practitioners

RACHEL ROBINS AND PHIL BADLEY

CHAPTER OVERVIEW

- Introduction
- Context for Learning and Development
- Frameworks for Learning and Development
- L&D knowledge skills
- Putting the data to work
- Designing effective learning
- How to evaluate learning
- Effective communication for L&D professionals
- Concept of CPD
- Summary

LEARNING OUTCOMES

By the end of this chapter, you will be able to:

- summarise current practices, trends and emerging roles in learning and development
- identify the key knowledge, skills and behaviours required by learning and development professionals.

INTRODUCTION

The world of workplace learning and development continues to change and mature. This brings with it not just challenges and exciting opportunities but also the need for learning and development (L&D) professionals to develop their knowledge and skills continually to meet the demands of stakeholders. The role of the L&D function is evolving due to a number of factors. These include continuing developments in the understanding of learning, advances in understanding of how people learn, and the application of emerging technologies to support learning. In addition, learning strategies and tactics must continue to be sensitive to fluctuating business strategies that themselves are subject to financial pressures.

This chapter examines the professional knowledge required of an L&D practitioner to be effective in contemporary workplaces. Our discussion starts with an identification of the different typologies of the role that includes a focus on the CIPD Profession Map from an L&D perspective. Other frameworks that contribute to an understanding of the multifaceted nature of the L&D role are also considered. The role is no longer limited to a provider of, or deliverer of learning. It cannot be seen in isolation as it must be integrated with other areas of people management practice. For example, with enhanced knowledge and skills, an individual might rightly expect an improved remuneration package, a revised performance agreement and raised expectations about future career progression. We then explore the knowledge and skills required of an L&D professional in a working environment.

Our discussion then leads to an analysis of how three of these L&D skills can be applied when faced with changing demands of different stakeholders. These skills are communication skills and styles; work-management behaviours, in particular self-management and –organisation; and working collaboratively with others. We conclude the chapter with an enquiry into the concept and the philosophy of Continuing Professional Development (CPD) and provide models and the theory that supports the requirement for the professional development of L&D professionals.

Throughout the chapter we include reflection points and activities for readers to inform their own CPD records and to plan future careers.

CONTEXT FOR LEARNING AND DEVELOPMENT

The context in which organisations operate reflects a range of issues – the economy, the influence of politicians and legislators, and the changing nature and expectations of society. When considering relevant learning activities, L&D professionals need to be mindful of these influences to ensure that knowledge and skills are relevant not just for current practice but support building capacity for the future.

The CIPD Research Report (2014) outlines the challenges for L&D in the future and challenges the function to be 'savvy, affecting and aligned, versatile and ubiquitous':

- Savvy, to not only be aware of an organisation's context and its business model but to understand nuances and consider potential implications for L&D. To use an example from the construction industry, L&D professionals would research emerging changes in building methods and techniques to ensure an organisation had sufficient numbers of staff with relevant knowledge and skills.
- Affecting and aligned, to be proactive and contribute to any required changes in organisational strategy and culture. For example, L&D professionals would respond to an upturn in the economy by liaising with colleagues to implement staff retention strategies.
- Versatile, and be able to react quickly to changing business scenarios and adapt to draw on different perceptions of the role. Having delivered learning, for example, L&D has a role to play in ensuring new-found knowledge and skills are consolidated on the job.
- Ubiquitous, to retain a presence and profile in an organisation so that learning is not an 'afterthought', but a key player in maturing strategies and tactics. L&D professionals need to have the credibility to be invited to strategy and change forums.

An effective L&D function will be at the heart of an organisation interpreting changing business needs and developing the capability of the workforce to enable the effective delivery of products and services to the market or client base. For many organisations the definition of workforce extends beyond managers and employees and can include apprentices, agency workers and volunteers.

The positioning of the L&D function in an organisational hierarchy can vary for a number of reasons. The size of a business has a significant influence. In many larger organisations, the L&D function is often positioned alongside, or within, the broader Human Resources function. The growth of internal expertise in Organisation Development (OD) also provides a synergy with the L&D function in some organisations. In examples, the linkages between organisational design activity and organisational development activity form part of the OD function. The CIPD Profession Map gives a detailed explanation of these elements. The need for skills development and improved employee capability provides a natural linkage between OD and L&D. In other organisational configurations, the function remains much closer to line management and is located within the structure of a plant, service or business function. The positioning of roles within an organisation will significantly influence the context and focus of operational roles within L&D, and the potential relationships with corporate or business-wide HR functions. For example, in a decentralised model the function is likely to be focused upon local operation business needs and be closely aligned with the day-to-day business operation. Dependent upon reporting lines within an organisational hierarchy, L&D professionals may not directly be line-managed within the broader HR function. This means that the HR function becomes a stakeholder that needs to be managed by the local HR/L&D teams situated within a business unit.

The type and seniority of job role within L&D will also have a significant influence upon the customer or end user of their service. In organisations with an L&D function there will be a range of operational duties and responsibilities usually based upon hierarchy within the team. Where the team is represented by a board or management team level manager from within an HR/L&D function, access to senior decision makers and to business-critical information about future direction and operational performance is accessible within the team structure. Where this is not the case it is important to establish an advocate for the function at senior level. In larger hierarchies, senior managers within L&D may well operate at senior level and oversee the leadership and operation of the function. In smaller organisations or functions the role may include involvement with direct users of the L&D service within the organisation.

Key stakeholders of L&D are:

- senior managers
- middle managers
- supervisors
- team leaders
- employees
- volunteers
- trade unions/employee representatives and union learning representatives
- HR/OD colleagues
- other internal expertise e.g. communications, IT, web developers
- employer/trade associations
- external L&D providers.

Each of these stakeholders is likely to have their own agenda and motivations, which sometimes conflict with that of others. This brings further complexity to the process of understanding business context and the drivers for change in forming learning outcomes and the wider learning environment. In some instances L&D expertise may be used elsewhere in the supply chain for the business. An example is the development of capacity and capability within the social care sector where support is provided from within some local councils to small businesses to ensure minimum standards of services are maintained in the provision of care services to older people in the wider population.

REFLECTIVE ACTIVITY 1.1

Who are your key stakeholders?

How would you describe your current relationship with each group?

How well defined are their needs?

What gaps do you have in your capability to deliver against identified need?

What is clear is that expectations of the L&D function are changing. The pace of change in organisations, the expectations for improvements in products and services; and reductions in operating costs/improvements in revenue and profitability mean that much more is expected from the function. This has implications at all levels of the profession which will now be considered.

This means that building effective working relationships with key stakeholders at all levels of the business is critically important for L&D professionals. There is a need for greater clarity of understanding about the changing nature of the organisation and its direction to enable employees to maintain the right skill base over time and to plan for future business scenarios. There is significant internal competition within an organisation for financial resources. However, L&D professionals are not always able to directly influence strategic spending decisions. This can lead to financial priorities not being directed to developing internal skills capability. A well-argued business case and an advocate at decision making meetings is therefore important.

The L&D function needs to improve its capability to develop good sources of information and a sound business rationale to attract the investment that is required to support longer term business objectives. A lack of organisational investment in L&D may cause operational delays, and reduce the performance and capability of employees. This can increase operational costs, and potentially the viability of the business and a loss in market share over time. However, reduced capability and employee performance may not immediately impact upon the business results due to time delays in a business reporting cycle. As a result, it may not be obvious at senior levels that business performance may stem from a lack of investment in L&D in previous business planning cycles. Hence the importance of the L&D function's capacity to build good business cases for investment at the right stages of business development.

Future investment in L&D interventions will benefit from the establishment of learning outcomes at the identification stage of the process and evidence gathering during and after the intervention, which is discussed later in this chapter, will help to evidence the benefits.

Figure 1.1 Current skills gaps

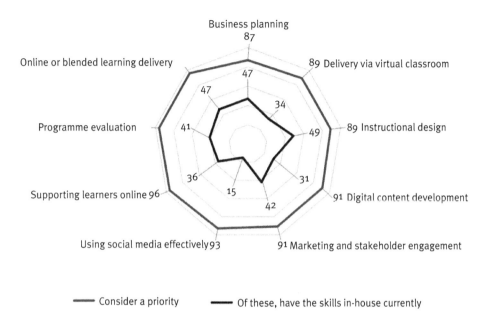

Source: CIPD research report – L&D evolving roles, enhancing skills Sept. 2015 (http://www.cipd.co.uk/hr-resources/research/l-and-d-roles-skills.aspx)

Figure 1.1 shows the gaps between current skill levels and business priorities. Clearly these gaps must close to enable the function to deliver against identified and agreed business need. This is particularly evident around the use and deployment of technology and social media within L&D. Whilst the use of digital learning as a training application continues to grow, and planning appears to be in place to increase the use of virtual classrooms and webinars, plans to implement mobile device-based learning need to be adopted more widely.

CIPD research indicates that up to 75% of HR and L&D professionals lack the capability to exploit new technology for L&D programmes. (*CIPD annual L&D survey 2015*). Further investment in learning technologies will be completely wasted if L&D teams cannot use and deploy them effectively. Our own practice experience shows that for many businesses the benefits of spending on technology for learning are not yet evident. Business cases need to ensure that such development fits within a blended learning approach and is directed towards improving organisational performance.

 REFLECTIVE ACTIVITY 1.2

How well do you understand your business? How do you keep up-to-date with the current direction and future trends?

FRAMEWORKS FOR LEARNING AND DEVELOPMENT

L&D ROLES AND TITLES

Whilst the titles of L&D roles may be similar across different organisations and sectors, the specific content of the work may well be different. Jobs in L&D that are publicly advertised over a period do evidence differences. Historically, many jobs were advertised for the generic job of 'trainer'. Increasingly, jobs are advertised for specific roles such as IT Trainer or Technical Trainer. A review of current L&D adverts shows a wide range of job titles which includes: Learning and Development Adviser, Learning and Development Consultant, Organisational Development Consultant, Learning Co-ordinator, Training Manager, Training Officer, Head of Content, Customer Service Coach, Digital Learning Specialist, Learning and Development Manager, Regulated Training Consultant, Training Design and Delivery Consultant, E-Learning Instructional Designer, Talent and Leadership Development Specialist, E-Learning and Resource Developer, Training Assistant, Instructional Designer, Management Trainer, On Boarding Induction Trainer, Online Learning Developer, Assessor, Global Head of Learning and Development. These titles give a useful illustration of the breadth and diversity of the L&D function within organisations from direct delivery through to the leadership and management of the function across the globe. In consequence, it is essential to refer to a specific organisational job description and person specification in a context to gain clarity about the nature of the role and the expectations of stakeholders in L&D.

Some organisations will have further specialisation within L&D in areas such as change management, leadership, diversity management, communications, and technology.

In some larger organisations the HR/OD function will also play an increasingly important role in coaching and supporting line managers, and also in procuring or delivering coach training and development. A coaching culture helps to ensure that team members can reach higher levels of performance, feel increased job satisfaction, personal growth, and career development. It is also interesting to note the growth in roles supporting technology-based learning programmes and virtual learning environments (VLE). They are increasingly used to support a blended approach to content delivery. Table 1.1 gives some examples of the key requirements of a number of these roles.

Table 1.1 Summary of key requirements for L&D roles

Typical role	Key requirements
L&D Management	Leadership experience and business acumen Strategic insight of business direction and capability Stakeholder management Lead L&D strategy and implementation Expert knowledge of theory, practice and its application in context, blended programme and digital applications Measuring impact and ROI Managing talent and career management programmes Implementing digital learning solutions
L&D Business Partner	Stakeholder management and engagement Advise business leaders from a base of expert knowledge of L&D approaches Strategic coordination and delivery of L&D interventions to improve performance and capability Management and monitoring of programme delivery and compliance Provide business consulting support

Typical role	Key requirements
	Knowledge of talent management Coaching line managers Management of teams and resources
Leadership/ Management Development Consultant/Adviser	Relationship management Analysis, design, commissioning, delivery of interventions Design of policy, practice and evaluation frameworks Programme management Succession planning and talent management Financial planning and management skills Knowledge of compliance and accreditation processes Team leadership, coaching and mentoring Budget management
Learning and Development Adviser	Identification of L&D needs Collation of data to inform priorities and resource requirements, and evaluation Co-ordinate the specification and commissioning of courses Oversee the production of products and materials Project management Delivery of programme content Development of content for VLE Budget monitoring Digital learning delivery
Trainer	Liaison with stakeholders and L&D colleagues re: business need Design of course material Direct delivery using blended approaches Design tests for understanding and compliance Maintain records and LMS systems Coordinator accreditation processes Digital learning delivery
Online Designer	Collaborate with subject matter experts on content development Conduct LNA Design and develop digital solutions and content Produce audio and video scripts and story boards Creation of documentation and materials Familiarity with digital production software and its capabilities Project management Stakeholder management VLE content management
Learning and Development Coordinator/ Assistant	Coordination of learning programmes Production and administration of literature and materials L&D programme content, and course administration, booking management etc. Administration of online assessments and report production Collating and analysing course evaluations Coordinating and updating VLE content Processing orders and invoices Records management Compliance reporting

REFLECTIVE ACTIVITY 1.3

How do the roles illustrated above reflect your own understanding of the L&D function in your organisation?

What skill gaps do you currently need to develop to help progress your career?

How would you describe your current role to a line manager within the business?

LEARNING TO BE A PROFESSIONAL

The CIPD is 'the professional body for HR and people development'. Its purpose is 'to champion better work and working lives by improving practices in people and organisation development for the benefit of individuals, businesses, economies and society'. As a professional body, the CIPD believes that great people management is not possible without a core or professional foundation. To support the professional development of its 140,000 members, CIPD has developed a Profession Map that identifies the activities, knowledge and behaviours required by the differing roles that are covered under the broad area of people management. The map is shown in Figure 1.2 and can also be found at http://www.cipd.co.uk/cipd-hr-profession/profession-map/.

Figure 1.2 CIPD Profession Map

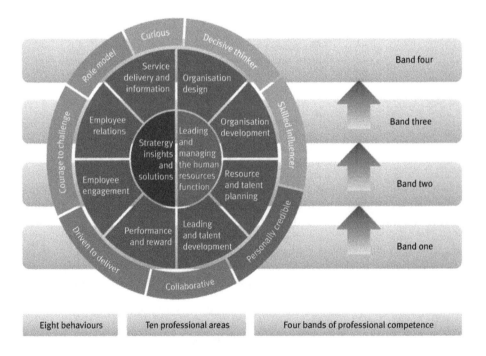

The map divides people management work into ten professional areas which have at the core:

- strategy insights and solutions, and
- leading and managing the human resources function.

These are supported by activities for:

- organisation design
- organisation development
- resourcing and talent management
- learning and talent development
- performance and reward
- employee engagement
- employee relations
- service delivery and information.

The level at which professionals operate for each of the areas is further divided into four bands that define practitioner career levels which broadly relate to the following level of role:

Band 1 – Administrator
Band 2 – Officer
Band 3 – Manager
Band 4 – Director

However, the exact nature of the role is likely to be different in changing contexts. The flexibility of the map allows the practitioner to focus on the areas most relevant to their role. Whilst the bands articulate the responsibilities for each of the levels, they are intended to be aspirational, so that professionals can identify areas of practice in which they will need to engage to progress to a higher level. We will consider in a later chapter how to use the Profession Map to plan and develop your career.

Learning and Development and the CIPD Profession Map

Every L&D professional will need to be competent in *Insights, strategies and solutions* to be able to respond to the implications for L&D of: the business and its structure and context; its vision and strategy; its products and services; and its financial performance. The second core area *Leading HR* is necessary so that skills of leadership, delivering value and evaluating the impact of L&D work can be demonstrated.

The areas of the map that most directly affect L&D include:

- *Learning and talent development* that specify standards for developing learning and strategy plans; designing learning solutions; delivering learning in different forms; managing talent and evaluating the impact of learning. Importantly, this area also includes the requirement for leadership development to ensure an organisation has the future capability to face the future with confidence.
- *Organisation Design*, to assess the current operating model and propose and implement alternative designs.
- *Organisation development*, to define a strategy, assess the people capability, build integrated OD interventions and manage change.
- *Resourcing and talent management*, to contribute to talent acquisition and development strategies, assess candidates and provide relevant onboarding activities.

As we identified in the chapter introduction, an L&D professional cannot ignore other areas of the map as the consequence of an individual having increased knowledge and skills has implications for:

- *Performance and reward* – to reflect increased competence and contribution.
- *Employee engagement*. Those who have received investment in development often have an improved psychological contract with their employers and strengthen their commitment to an organisation.

- *Employee relations.* In turn, happier and more committed employees tend to raise fewer disagreements.
- *Service delivery and information.* Being competent in a role enables staff to deliver superior internal and external service.

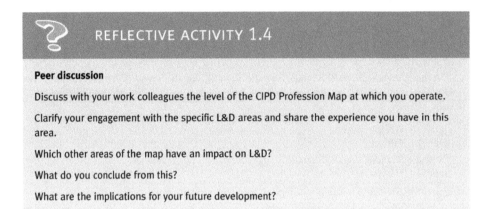

REFLECTIVE ACTIVITY 1.4

Peer discussion

Discuss with your work colleagues the level of the CIPD Profession Map at which you operate.

Clarify your engagement with the specific L&D areas and share the experience you have in this area.

Which other areas of the map have an impact on L&D?

What do you conclude from this?

What are the implications for your future development?

OTHER LEARNING AND DEVELOPMENT FRAMEWORKS

The most commonly used framework for learning is based on the historical four-part 'training cycle', a model of indeterminate origin, although a number of writers use it without a specific reference. It is shown in Figure 1.3. Although it has been used due to its simplicity and accessibility, it is generally used from a starting point of identifying needs and ending with evaluation. It is only focused on training as a form of learning, which is not always appropriate in current contexts.

From our introductory comments, it is clear that the role of the L&D professional is changing. Organisational practice is increasingly reducing its reliance on menu-based approaches for training courses, to deliver more tailored learning interventions based upon specific business needs. Different methods of learning delivery are being adopted and learners are being encouraged to assume greater self-reliance and responsibility for their learning. The rate

Figure 1.3 Systematic approach to training

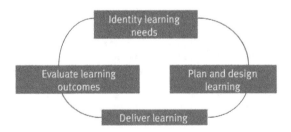

and range of these changes reflects the size and nature of an organisation, along with the context or industry sector in which it operates. The structural positioning of L&D within an organisation also varies depending upon local context and will influence expectations of the role and the activities undertaken. For all of these factors, the systematic approach to training has largely been replaced by other frameworks. The CIPD is not alone in wishing to articulate and clarify standards for L&D. The contribution of three other UK bodies will now be considered.

City and Guilds

City and Guilds (C&G) is a body that creates qualifications to help workers develop relevant skills for employment. For those who work in people development in the Further Education (FE) sector, such as college staff, C&G has three levels of qualification to support career development. The C&G website (http://www.cityandguilds.com/) identifies the focus and progression of these qualifications as

Education and Training – level 3 (6502)
    This covers the roles, responsibilities and relationships in education and training; inclusive teaching and learning approaches; assessment of learners; facilitating learning and development for individuals; facilitating learning and development in groups; and understanding principles and practices of assessment. This was formerly titled Preparing to Teach in the Lifelong Learning Sector (PTLLS).

Education and Training – level 4 (6502)
    This builds on the level 3 qualification and covers understanding roles, responsibilities and relationships in education and training; planning to meet the needs of learners in education and training; delivering education and training; assessing learners in education and training; and using resources for education and training. This was formerly titled Certificate in Teaching in the Lifelong Learning Sector (CTLLS).

Education and Training – level 5 (6502)
    The final level of qualification covers observation of performance in the work environment; examining products of work; questioning the learner; discussing with the learner; use of others (witness testimony); looking at learner statements; and recognising prior learning. This was known as the Diploma in Teaching in the Lifelong Learning Sector (DTLLS).

Lifelong Learning UK

Lifelong Learning UK (LLUK) has developed 13 National Occupational Standards (NOS) for L&D. These are grouped into four key areas and can be found at the following website http://webarchive.nationalarchives.gov.uk/:

Key Area A: Research learning and development needs

- Standard 1 Identify collective learning and development needs.
- Standard 2 Identify individuals' learning and development needs.

Key Area B: Plan and develop learning and development opportunities

- Standard 3 Plan and prepare learning and development programmes.
- Standard 4 Plan and prepare specific learning and development opportunities.
- Standard 5 Develop and prepare resources for learning and development.

Key Area C: Facilitate learner achievement

- Standard 6 Manage learning and development in groups.
- Standard 7 Facilitate individual learning and development.
- Standard 8 Engage and support learners in the learning and development process.
- Standard 9 Assess learner achievement.

Key Area D: Maintain and improve quality standards

- Standard 10 Reflect on, develop and maintain own skills and practice in learning and development.
- Standard 11 Internally monitor and maintain the quality of assessment.
- Standard 12 Externally monitor and maintain the quality of assessment.
- Standard 13 Evaluate and improve learning and development provision.

The Institute of Training and Occupational Learning

The Institute of Training and Occupational Learning (ITOL) (http://www.itol.org/) is a professional body for trainers and L&D professionals. It offers a range of advice and accessible learning to help a professional's progress for both new early career and the experienced professional seeking to further their career. As with CIPD, ITOL offers a membership grade to recognise qualifications and/or experience, and support ongoing professional development. Its qualification structure is not based on a hierarchy, but covers identified professional areas:

Introductory certificate

- Training and development
- Training delivery
- Coaching

Certificate

- Training and development
- Performance coaching
- Training consultancy
- Mentoring
- Personal coaching

Diploma

- Organisational learning
- Executive coaching
- Consulting excellence
- Professional facilitation
- Learning design and delivery
- L&D management

What is clear from a presentation of these approaches is the broad range of activities that fall within the remit of L&D. Each will require professionals to develop advanced knowledge and skills, an issue we shall cover in the next section.

L&D KNOWLEDGE AND SKILLS

THE ORGANISATIONAL CONTEXT OF L&D

In the HR Profession Map, the CIPD defines the purpose of the professional area *Learning and talent development* is to 'ensure that people at all levels of the organisation possess and develop the skills, knowledge and experience to fulfil the short- and long-term ambitions of the organisation and that they are motivated to learn, grow and perform'. However, current practice shows that the function is moving towards a business partner role. This is very different from a more traditional role based on the systematic approach to training shown in Figure 1.3. A business partner focuses on both improving individual and organisational performance and ensuring future capability. It is about seeking out and using an evidence base to gather insights into the strategic direction of an organisation, and then delivering innovative ways of improving organisational and people capability.

A challenge is for the function to recognise the need for such change. In some organisations it appears that organisational demand for business partner skill sets is outstripping the L&D functions investment in the capabilities of team members. As a result, some L&D professionals are not perceived as business partners as they do only deliver learning rather than implementing integrated solutions more broadly.

The role of L&D functions is also growing to accommodate responsibility for talent management. Talent management is a complex topic and can either refer to all members of staff with potential, or a restricted view that covers only those senior individuals who are considered to be in a position where they can make significant differences to organisational performance.

IDENTIFYING LEARNING NEEDS

The identification of learning and development needs within an organisation is based on an assessment of the levels of skills, knowledge, and attitudes of the current workforce, together with any anticipated gaps in employee capability to meet future business needs. Key stakeholders need to be consulted early in the process at the information gathering stages of the process. It is also important to validate the results of the training needs analysis (TNA). A TNA is effectively a stock take of current organisational capability. This analysis enables informed decisions about what learning provision is needed at organisational, team, and individual level.

At an organisational level it helps to identify the nature of the learning needed to ensure that employees have the right skills and knowledge to deliver the organisation's business priorities. Business performance is dependent upon having the right quality and quantity of skilled people. This information provides the foundation for L&D professionals to evaluate effectiveness and demonstrate the impact of investing in L&D to the organisation.

At team level it helps to identify operational changes, and new projects that require different ways of working or reorganisation. Restructuring of roles and tasks may also necessitate changes in roles requiring the performance of different tasks or responsibilities that require input and support from the L&D function.

For individuals, linking their own personal learning and development needs to those of the business is often carried out as part of performance review. Learning opportunities help to build employee capability to progress career goals and business contribution. The L&D function can then interpret and prioritise these identified needs against the wider business strategy. The process must relate to business strategy, and its aim is to produce a plan for the organisation to make sure there is sufficient capability to sustain business performance and meet its statutory requirements e.g. in the UK the Data Protection Act 1998, Health and Safety at Work Act 1974.

Data is available from many sources including business plans, work standards/ governance, job descriptions, and person specifications. Interviews with line managers or other key players are primary sources of information on changes to work organisation and can expand and interpret priorities and plans. Other potential sources are questionnaires and surveys of managers, employees and customers.

Data from management information systems or virtual learning environments will also provide key data, e.g. information on existing competence frameworks and analysis of levels of competence achieved, performance management and appraisal data.

An analysis of this data will follow the usual cycle of gather data, analyse, commission, evaluate, review, reanalyse.

Much of this data will be sensitive, particularly where individuals' knowledge and skills gaps are exposed, so confidentiality must be respected in accordance with local policies and practices in respect of data security.

In addition there are times when, for commercial reasons or reasons of security, for example, a major change is planned that senior management wish to keep confidential. In these situations learning professionals need to build trusted relationships and persuade senior management that the confidential planning of learning and development interventions can contribute to the success of the change.

Figure 1.4 The value of learning – a new model of value and evaluation (CIPD 2014)

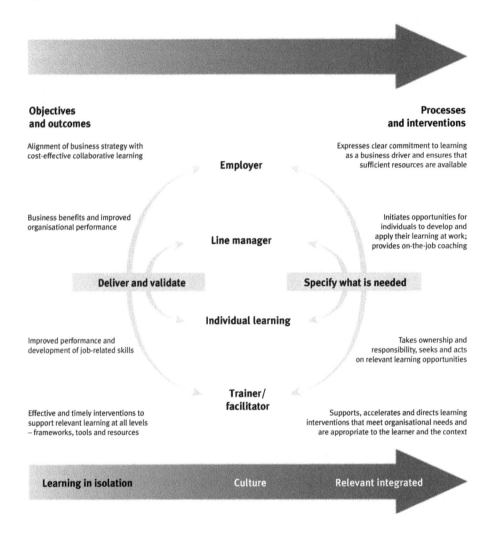

Creating an effective plan and programme for a learning and development strategy is critical in ensuring that the resources for L&D align with business needs. Our own research suggests that organisations may need to improve data gathering processes to make more informed choices about resource allocation. A number of examples show that practitioners do not always manage to engage line managers in sufficiently detailed conversations to develop a tailored L&D plan. This causes some L&D functions to continue with a menu driven approach to learning based upon historical need in the absence of more timely information. Other examples have shown that the growing pressures upon L&D to reduce operational costs places further pressure upon available resources to capture and analyse data to inform L&D plans. Figure 1.4 shows the cyclical nature of the process of aligning skills and capabilities with the direction of the business and the interventions of the L&D function.

In some circumstances, such as an organisational or project-based skills audit, a learning needs analysis may be a one-off exercise rather than an ongoing operation (for example via annual performance appraisal) or a combination of approaches. A further example is when a new business idea or market is being explored to establish the current skill base. Any shortfall against the expressed need, and the approach to addressing how the need can be met in the short, medium and longer term, should be considered.

AN ALTERNATIVE APPROACH TO ASSESSING LEARNING NEED

Financial pressures and changing demands for improving performance put pressure on the L&D function to find better ways to align employee capability with the needs of the business. Assessment of learning needs must be thorough and evidence-based. This can take significant time and effort from within L&D and line managers to achieve. Often, in a rapidly changing business environment, processes need to be agile and more responsive to need. The CIPD has developed an approach in conjunction with the University of Portsmouth call 'RAM' (relevance, alignment, measurement). The RAM approach helps to focus analysis on the key business and organisational outcomes in the following ways:

Relevance: how does the current learning provision meet new opportunities and challenges for future business need?

Alignment: dialogue with key managers and other stakeholders are critical to establish what they are seeking to deliver and how the L&D function can help them achieve it. Alignment of all elements of the Workforce Strategy (WFS) is also critical. Key strategies such as reward, organisational development, learning and development, engagement and other aspects of the management of human resources must be integrated with business strategy.

Measurement: it is also critical that the HR and L&D functions measure and evaluate the interventions effectively and consistently. Our own research suggests that there is a weak evidence base within HR and L&D at the moment for the evaluation of L&D. A mix of evaluation methods are used, such as return on investment (ROI) and broader measures of expected change and improvement, such as return on expectation and the linking of L&D outcomes to key performance indicators (KPIs).

More information is available on this approach on the CIPD website via the factsheet on measuring and evaluating learning outcomes. (http://www.cipd.co.uk/hr-resources/factsheets/evaluating-learning-talent-development.aspx).

PUTTING THE DATA TO WORK

Collating relevant information from the needs analysis will allow the presentation of data to key stakeholders. This usually takes the form of a report on overall learning needs for the department or organisation. Discussing its content with senior managers will provide guidance on which gaps are most business critical; and allow priorities to be identified and agreed against the available resources.

Once priorities and budgets are agreed, the L&D team will be able to set plans for learning interventions, and can plan the implementation against available budget and urgency of the training need for the organisation. This should cascade down into individual learning plans identified as part of the appraisal/personal development planning process.

Our research suggests that the following priorities emerge most regularly from gathering information on development needs for L&D teams:

- leadership skills
- management skills
- interpersonal/soft skills
- professional skills
- change management skills
- project management skills.

As organisations seek to build flexible and more agile structures, the needs for skills development in the themes indicated above become an important component in embedding a different organisational culture. Operational leaders are increasingly expected to demonstrate greater self-sufficiency in their day-to-day role. In turn, the role of a manager is also developing to recognise the importance of improving employee engagement, particularly for innovation and improvements to efficiency. Engagement generally leads to an improvement in customer satisfaction and therefore ultimately to organisational success.

UNDERSTANDING LEARNERS AND THEIR MOTIVATIONS

Adult learners' expectations of the learning environment are changing as a consequence of the knowledge society. The introduction of technologies into the workplace and in wider society places new pressures upon individuals to keep up to date. L&D professionals may typically take an overview of the skills, knowledge and attitudes required to perform a role to a good standard. It is also important that L&D professionals have an understanding of the psychological aspects that underpin adult learners. Research undertaken by Bloom *et al* (1956) identified that adults learn through a combination of three principle domains:

- cognitive domain (intellectual capability; that is, knowledge, or 'think')
- affective domain (feelings, emotions and behaviour; that is, attitude, or 'feel')
- psychomotor domain (manual and physical skills; that is, skills, or 'do').

L&D professionals will be familiar with knowledge, attitude and skills, however, reference to the original work by Bloom may help with understanding of the theory. Knowledge enables individuals to build a 'store' for later recall and application, using personal judgement in a context.

The affective domain relates to 'attitude' and is likely to be interpreted today as a person's values and beliefs. In practice, for an L&D professional this is related to a person's openness to listen and engage with new concepts, methods and ideas. Increasing confidence and competence gives the learner greater capacity to develop and filter content and make informed decisions about how to apply the learning in practice.

The psychomotor domain relates to an individual's practical skills and is associated with muscle memory. For example, when using a bank's cash point, most of us may be able to remember a PIN by hand movements rather than being able to state aloud the number.

Within an organisational setting, the purpose or need for the learning and development will impact upon the learner. An example is the need to achieve accreditation for a course, for example a CIPD Level 5 qualification. For the individual following a career path with the HR profession, being assessed as competent will be a significant achievement and enable further progression within an organisation. This requirement has the potential impact upon basic, psychological and self-fulfilment needs for the individual. Each learner will have different needs at different stages of the development cycle.

This brings us to an understanding of a framework known as the conscious competence learning model, shown in Figure 1.5. It is important when designing a learning intervention that L&D professionals understand where learners are on the continuum. This is because if the awareness of skill and deficiency is low or non-existent, then the learner is at the unconscious incompetence stage and is unlikely to see the need for learning.

Figure 1.5 Five stages of competence

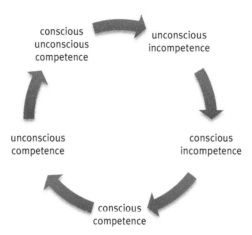

Establishing awareness of a development or training need (conscious incompetence) prior to attempting to impart or arrange training or skills necessary to move learners from stage 2 to 3 is crucially important. If an individual cannot see the reason and benefit of engaging in learning, then an intervention will fail to bring about the intended results. Individuals only fully engage with development opportunities when they are aware of their own need for it, and the personal benefit they will derive from achieving it. It is therefore important that L&D professionals ensure that they take learner motivations into account in the specification, design and delivery of interventions.

DESIGNING EFFECTIVE LEARNING

Understanding how people learn is obviously an important dimension to the effective practice of learning and development professionals. Perhaps the best-known model of the learning process is the one developed by David Kolb in 1984. Kolb's experiential learning theory is concerned with the learner's internal cognitive processes and that learning involves the acquisition of abstract concepts that can be applied flexibly in a range of situations. 'Learning is the process whereby knowledge is created through the transformation of experience' (Kolb 1984).

The model was originally developed to understand problem solving, which is really just another way of defining learning and has four stages, shown in Figure 1.6:

1   Concrete Experience – a situation is experienced by a learner.

2   Observation and Reflection – the learner reviews what occurred in the situation.

3   Conceptualisation and generalisation – the learner tries to make sense of the situation.

4   Experimentation – the learner then applies what has been learned in a new and testing new ideas.

Figure 1.6 Kolb's learning cycle

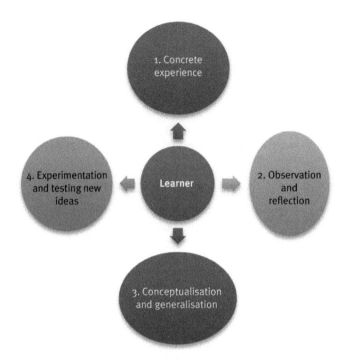

It is more helpful to see the model as a spiral rather than a cycle where new experiences bring new learning and greater understanding leading to further experimentation that is repeated over time. It is also important to note that a full and rich learning experience involves each of the stages rather than emphasising one particular area.

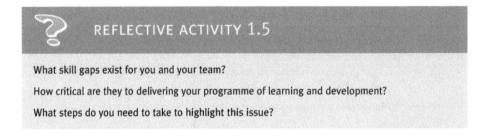

REFLECTIVE ACTIVITY 1.5

What skill gaps exist for you and your team?

How critical are they to delivering your programme of learning and development?

What steps do you need to take to highlight this issue?

TECHNOLOGY ENABLED LEARNING

Organisational demand to have the right capabilities in place to respond at speed in the global market place is putting pressure upon the way that L&D functions think about creating the right learning environment. There is a need for continuous learning. Increasingly, learners are not waiting for formal input from training programmes, but are looking at a multitude of sources for knowledge.

The 70:20:10 model (Lombardo and Eichinger 1996) highlights learner preferences in the ratio between the hands-on learning (70%), learning from others (20%), and expert input (10%). In adult learning, this emphasises the desire to seek new learning experiences and experiment with them in practice as a self-directed learner. As technology advances, hands-on learning is likely to mean greater engagement through blended learning. Figure 1.7 illustrates a range of blended learning inputs available to develop a learner's capability.

Figure 1.7 Blended learning inputs

The balance between face-to-face and online learning is beginning to change. With the increasing capability of smartphones and the rapid expansion of the use of tablet computers, learners increasingly expect to seek and access information online. They also expect to be able to work seamlessly across multiple devices. Personalisation of learning environments is also expected to be on a par with other applications like Facebook. L&D professionals must be able to keep up to date and 'savvy' with what technologies are available and how to use and apply them in context.

Learning is increasingly taking place in the workplace through problem solving, watching, trial and error, and imitating. The growth of social and community learning via watching online content, and sharing e-books, video, podcasts, blog articles, slideshares, webinars and online networking is changing the way that L&D functions need to manage the learning environment within the business setting.

Technology also provides an opportunity for L&D to design and enable learning to meet the changing demands of organisational design. Employees are becoming more dispersed and agile in the way that they are expected to work. Teams work across locations with increasing mobility, and have less time available to learn due to operational pressures. This causes businesses to want more online delivery and in a shorter time. This in turn causes the content of learning inputs to focus upon the minimum knowledge required, and allows the learner further access to content based upon personal need.

The development of massive open online courses (MOOCs) designed for online study by larger groups of employees also provides further opportunities for engagement across different geographical locations within national, or multinational organisations. These platforms are increasingly being used by further and higher education establishments as part of a blended approach.

The L&D professional needs to understand this technological environment, experiment with it in the context of emergent development needs within the business, and commission or develop content that maximises the potential for learning across the organisation.

REFLECTIVE ACTIVITY 1.6

What is your current level of understanding of advances in learning?

How well is your team investing in developing its future capabilities to meet future business need?

How well is talent currently being developed within your organisation?

What role will a VLE play in the delivery of employee development in your organisation in the future?

HOW TO EVALUATE LEARNING

Understanding the impact of learning and development within an organisation is important. It contributes to understanding what is helping to improve employee performance, helps to shape future programmes, and provides evidence to justify investment in L&D. There is growing evidence (CIPD 2015) that more attention is being paid to ensure effective and efficient ways of evidencing the return on investment of L&D interventions. However, competition for time and resources and the impact of other business initiatives can mean that L&D functions do not always undertake structured evaluation.

Many organisations have used measures such as return on investment (ROI) evidence to decide the viability of a course of action. This has not always been true for L&D. The consequence of this is that L&D runs a risk of failing to be able to develop and secure business cases for investment that are vital to the development and growth of business capability. The CIPD Learning and Talent Development survey (2015) demonstrates that evaluation of L&D is considerably more common and in greater depth in organisations where L&D is aligned with the business strategy.

It is important to consider the purpose of an L&D intervention at the outset. Here are some outcomes to consider, depending on the objectives of your learning and development intervention:

- increased employee retention
- increased production
- employee survey to measure engagement and morale
- reduced waste
- increased sales
- higher quality ratings
- increased customer satisfaction
- fewer staff complaints.

The evaluation criteria need to be able to evidence the benefits gained as a result of the investment in L&D. Most organisations carry out evaluation at some level. The following list shows a range of measures used to assess effectiveness:

- learner reflection and feedback
- manager reflection and feedback
- general HR metrics e.g. absence, retention, performance, Investors in People standard
- strategic business measures e.g. profitability, revenue generation, market growth, values and behaviours, customer satisfaction
- stakeholder feedback.

The CIPD survey (CIPD 2015) suggests that this information is primarily used to update or revise the L&D intervention, with only around half of L&D teams sharing the results with other parts of the business. Evidence shows that the three main barriers to better evaluation are as follows:

- The urgency of the next *business priority* causes employees to reschedule the priority of an evaluation exercise. Consequently it may not be completed.
- The ability to capture information in an efficient and effective way from learners and their managers is also an issue. *IT capability* seems to vary as not all LMS systems can deliver the information in a reportable format.
- As a result the *quality of the dat*a collected along with its analysis within the L&D function can fall short of expectations.

A frequently used model for L&D evaluation is Kirkpatrick's four levels of evaluation model. (Kirkpatrick 1979). The model seeks to measure:

- reaction of student – what they thought and felt about the training
- learning – the resulting increase in knowledge or capability
- behaviour – extent of behaviour and capability improvement and implementation/ application of new knowledge and skills back on the job
- results – the measurable effects on the business that result from improved performance.

Table 1.2 illustrates how the model can be used in practice.

Table 1.2 Kirkpatrick levels of evaluation

Level	Description	Example	Benefit
Reaction	Immediate reaction of participants on a programme	Course evaluation sheet, telephone or face-to-face follow up against a template Feedback questionnaire via an online LMS	Low cost, simple to administer Provides basic data
Learning	Assessment of pre and post capability of the learner	Output from a PDR/ Appraisal Pre and post assessment questionnaire Online assessment tool Observation of practice	Quantifiable data can be evidenced and show level of improvement Allows comparison of individual performance against a standard
Behaviour	The application of learning in the role	Line management supervision process Feedback from peers and customers Improved outcomes and work performance	Evidences the impact of development over time on the employees' performance and capability
Results	Demonstrates impact on business performance	Achievement of high level of performance against plan	Enables resources to be targeted more effectively within the business to

Level	Description	Example	Benefit
		Development of capability with a talent pool Bottom line improvement in business results	maximise impact on improvements in employee performance Organisational impact is more difficult to evidence

The initial stages of the model are used most frequently for data gathering and evidence of evaluation. It can be more time-consuming and expensive to measure behaviours and results over time, and it may not always be practical for all organisations and situations to gather data at this level. This may be because LMS systems have historically been seen as extensions of the L&D function as a record-keeping and course-logging database. The systems are not always readily accessible to the line manager or employee. However, the online capability of some systems is beginning to change this into an opportunity for L&D to connect more effectively with learners and their managers through more integrated business systems.

Historically, there also tended to be more of a focus upon the employee benefit of the learning and transference back to the role, rather than the business impact and benefit of the investment in the learner. There is an increasing emphasis within organisations upon being able to evidence the benefits of investing in L&D. This suggests that L&D professionals need to think more creatively at the initial stages of identifying the business benefits of programmes and agreeing operational measures with line managers that they agree to monitor and report back on as part of their own personal performance measures. This is likely to improve the organisation's capability to evidence the results stage of the Kirkpatrick model, and consequently provide the business case for future investment in L&D.

EFFECTIVE COMMUNICATION FOR L&D PROFESSIONALS

Communication is a two-way process of giving and receiving information through any number of channels. Whether one is speaking informally to a colleague, addressing a conference or meeting, delivering a learning and development event or writing a newsletter article or formal report, the basic principles set out in Table 1.3 apply.

Table 1.3 Basic principles of communication

Know your audience	Think about who are you communicating with, and what will engage them with your message. Take another look at the list of stakeholders previously identified to help you think through who you need to communicate your message.
Know your purpose	Even the simplest communication has a purpose. Make sure that you are clear about the message you are conveying. 'What's in it for me'?
Know your topic	Research your subject matter. Be clear about the structure and content that you need to share.
Anticipate objections	Be clear about how much people already know. Think through the possible reactions or actions that people may take. Prepare to answer with facts in a confident and authoritative way to overcome objections. Be aware that there will always be an objection at some point. Objections can bring out new and important areas for debate. You also need to have the confidence to politely close a conversation down.

Present a rounded picture	Think about the key elements of the topic and note the pros and cons of your message and present a realistic picture of the theme. Set realistic expectations of what is required.
Achieve credibility with your audience	Use the opportunity to build upon your relationships with your audience. Use the right language in context for the audience that you are addressing. In presentations also take time to consider the venue, the timing and the environment. Think about how you can manage and control these factors, and what you can do to mitigate environmental factors.
Follow through on what you say	Ensure that you have a 'call to action' to enable people to respond in an appropriate way. Be realistic in your own capability. Do not over-promise. Do follow through on your actions.
Communicate a little at a time	Pace and content are critically important. Be as clear and concise as you can be to hold the attention of the audience.
Present information in several ways	Be aware that we need a mix of visual, auditory and kinesthetic methods to present information effectively. Use language to engage across this spectrum and consider which are most appropriate for a given situation.
Develop a practical, useful way to get feedback	Practice makes perfect. Use the opportunity for rehearsal in whatever form of communication. Invite colleagues, peers, your manager and customers to give you feedback both in your preparation, and after the event.
Use multiple communication techniques	Consider how to best engage the interest of your audience in terms of the medium that you choose. Follow through and follow up using channels that you know will attract a response from your intended audience.

BARRIERS TO EFFECTIVE COMMUNICATION

David McClelland (1988) built on the earlier work of Abraham Maslow's (1943) theory of needs by identifying three motivators that he believed we all have: a need for achievement, a need for affiliation, and a need for power. People will have different characteristics depending on their dominant motivator. McClelland believed that these motivators are learned and largely dependent on our culture and life experiences.

These characteristics are illustrated in Table 1.4:

Table 1.4 McClelland's motivators

Motivator	Descriptor
Power	Seek status within a group. Motivated by a sense of power. They have a need to be seen as influential and make an impact. They have a tendency to dominate, need to lead, and to push their ideas within a group.
Affiliation	Team players motivated to interact with others. Seek to build friendly relationships. Keen to be liked and popular.
Achievement	Need a sense of accomplishment. Motivated to achieve realistic goals and show advancement in their work. Keen to receive feedback on progress and achievement.

McClelland's theory (1988) can help you to identify the dominant motivators of people and help to inform the way to communicate with them to help influence how you set learning goals and provide feedback, and how you motivate and reward team members.

You can also use these motivators to craft, or design, the learning content and environment for learning to more effectively engage with learners who will have the full range of motivational drivers described above.

When you communicate, it needs to engage with all three of these drivers to capture the potential motivations in a group. So, for instance, someone motivated by achievement needs to be offered challenging, but not impossible opportunities in the development programme. They thrive on overcoming difficult problems or situations, so make sure you keep them engaged in this way by ensuring that the content and style of delivery challenges learners with this preference. People motivated by achievement work very effectively either alone or with other high achievers. When providing feedback to them as learners, give them a fair and balanced appraisal. They want to know what they're doing right and wrong so that they can improve.

People motivated by affiliation work best in a group environment, so try to integrate this message into the communications and design of the programme. They don't like uncertainty and risk, and this may inhibit their ability to learn. When providing feedback to them as learners make it personal to them. It's important to give balanced feedback, but start by emphasising their good points in progress and your trust in them, and they are more likely be more open to developmental feedback.

Learners motivated by a high need for power work best when they're in charge. Because they enjoy competition, they do well with goal-oriented tasks and learning challenges. So evidence this opportunity in the learning. They may also be very effective in negotiations or in situations in which another party must be convinced of an idea or goal. When providing feedback to them as learners, be direct with these team members, and keep them motivated by helping them further their learning opportunities.

COLLABORATIVE WORKING BEHAVIOURS

As the role of L&D professionals develops towards a more generic business partner or internal consultant with broader business related skills, it becomes increasingly important to develop effective working relationships with key stakeholders across the business.

Identify your key stakeholders

Key stakeholders of L&D will include:

- senior managers
- middle managers
- supervisors
- team leaders
- employees
- volunteers
- trade unions/employee representatives
- trade unions/learning representatives
- HR/OD colleagues
- other internal expertise e.g. communications, IT, web developers
- employer/trade associations
- external L&D providers

Take time to understand their situation and their motivations in the role. Help them to identify where the development needs lie within their area of responsibility, and their own level of confidence in being able to deliver the required levels of performance. Develop an empathetic and trusting relationship with them over time. The more you invest initially in building the relationship, the stronger will be your capability to open up a meaningful dialogue about business challenges.

Being collaborative, a CIPD professional behaviour, is essential for an L&D professional. Firstly you need to establish with whom you may need to collaborate on a regular basis from the list above. Each of the relations identified in Figure 1.8 can be seen as key relationships for the L&D practitioner.

Figure 1.8 Collaborative working relationships

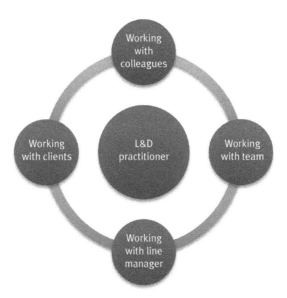

Although these four relationships are very different, in many ways you will need to employ the same skill set in order to maintain them as effective and healthy. To maintain collaborative relationships they need to be managed. You need to take time to understand and value others, both their opinions and beliefs. This can be achieved and improved by using the appropriate and frequent communication to build and maintain these relationships. This will require your time and it does need to be planned. Do not rush these conversations, but spend time actively listening to these stakeholders, together with other relationship building techniques, this will be time well spent and will benefit you in the future when you may require an insight into their thinking and actions.

During your working day you will always be part of a team, so team collaboration will always be essential and key to effective delivery in L&D. This is dealt with in more detail in Chapter 3.

WORK-MANAGEMENT BEHAVIOURS

Manage your time and priorities

Maintaining clarity about your purpose, objectives and deliverables within the role is critically important. Giving a focus to your priorities and meeting the expectations of key stakeholders is often a constant process of rationalisation and rescheduling. This needs order and discipline in your approach to work.

Sometimes the needs of different customer groups will conflict. This is usually where the role of hierarchy and authority within the structure of L&D will play its part. It is important to be clear about when the potential for conflict requires support to ensure that L&D provision stays within agreed policy, and that business priorities continue to be met.

ROLE MODEL BEHAVIOURS

Table 1.5 Extract from CIPD Professional Role Model behaviour criteria

Band 1	Band 2	Band 3	Band 4
Has a deep sense of own core values and operates within personal boundaries	Has a deep sense of own core values and operates within personal boundaries	Skilled at managing any conflict between personal values and those of the organisation	Skilled at managing any conflict between personal values and those of the organisation
Consistently acts according to organisational and legal principles and agreed processes	Encourages others to act in line with organisational standards and frameworks	Sets out the standards and values for managers and peers and holds people accountable for their actions	Challenges leader and organisation actions when inconsistent with espoused values, beliefs and promises

The CIPD defines a role model as someone who consistently leads by example and acts with integrity, impartiality and independence, balancing personal, organisation and legal parameters. It is therefore important for an L&D practitioner to be aware of their own behaviour at all times. However, the saying 'Nothing worth having was ever achieved without effort' by Theodore Roosevelt is very true. Acting as a role model requires you to recognise you are always on show and act as you would expect others to at all times. You will note from Figure 1.9 that the CIPD framework has four bands for each behaviour to signify the development of the behaviour through experience as you progress through your career.

It is important that, in line with the professional behaviours, you also exhibit professional management skills such as self-management and organisation techniques in the workplace. A well-organised L&D practitioner should be skilled in being able to clarify their work tasks and requirements with their line manager or client, in order to plan and organise their work. This organisation will allow them to set and manage their priorities, closely monitoring all delivery timescales. If these skills are practiced to a high level then they will have the ability to honour commitments and meet required deadlines. These skills will be discussed in further detail in Chapter 3.

There are also contra-indicators identified by CIPD for being a role model that should *not* be demonstrated in the workplace:

- does not lead by example or stand by own principles or espoused beliefs
- is preoccupied with own agenda rather than the needs of the client or organisation
- acts inconsistently or overlooks inappropriate behaviour with regard to the company's processes, values and expected behaviours
- enforces organisational and HR processes without considering impact on individuals and the interaction with personal values.

Deliver on your promises

Be clear about what you can and cannot provide to stakeholders. It may on occasions be tempting to over-promise, but if expectations are not met, future relationships will be undermined. Be open and honest about what is possible to build more realistic expectations of what can be achieved within available resources. Involve L&D colleagues for help with requests that fall outside of your remit. It is however, important to retain ownership of the issue to sustain the relationship with the stakeholder. Understand the policies, procedures and practices of your function and how they fit with business need. You may have service level agreements or contracts in place that guide the services that you provide. Delivering on promises and keeping customers informed is a good way to build sustainable and trusted relationships with stakeholders.

Equally important are the contra-indicators identified by CIPD for collaborative behaviour that should *not* be demonstrated in the workplace:

- consistently works in isolation, pursuing own solution without involvement of appropriate stakeholders
- fails to build contact with people beyond own work area
- shows little consideration or respect for other colleagues
- withholds relevant information, expertise or knowledge from others
- does not contribute willingly to the team and adopts a passive role
- fails to listen, showing little interest in the views of others
- fails to recognise the value of diversity
- does not understand the importance of relationships and so fails to nurture them.

 REFLECTIVE ACTIVITY 1.7

Consider the list of contra-indicators above and discuss how you can ensure that you do not exhibit these behaviours.

CONCEPT OF CPD

In this final section of the chapter we will consider in greater detail the importance of CPD to professionals of many disciplines, not only L&D. CPD is an activity by which professions ensure that their skills and knowledge remain up to date and relevant in response to changes in the business and professional environment. Engaging in CPD is a hallmark of the reputation and quality of a professional practitioner. Lifelong learners are able to provide stakeholders with relevant and up-to-date advice.

CPD is a process that operates by the individual reflecting back on current capabilities before looking forward to plan future development. This process allows individuals to start from the present position towards the future. The process can add energy and direction to work and learning, and more importantly our own continuous improvement (Megginson and Whitaker 2011).

REFLECTIVE PRACTICE

There are several models and approaches to CPD that will be discussed in a later chapter. For now, all approaches commence with a reflection on development undertaken, practice and performance from previous experiences. Reflective practice and the ability to undertake personal reflection in an honest and open way is a key element of CPD and a skill which improves with practice. An understanding of the learning that you have achieved, the quality of the practice that you have delivered and the value of the experiences you have had during the last year, will contribute to becoming a better learner in the future. The process allows you to understand how you learn best. Reviewing your practice can help you to understand what works best and by reviewing your performance you will be able to see what improves your performance and what may be the barriers to achieving the level you seek.

HOW PRACTITIONERS ENSURE THEIR SKILLS, KNOWLEDGE AND BEHAVIOURS REMAIN RELEVANT

As we have seen throughout this chapter, the skills, knowledge and behaviours of the L&D professional are broad and varied. L&D professionals need to be business focused, highly knowledgeable and have effective professional behaviours drawn from the CIPD Profession Map. While organisations have a responsibility to develop their employees we also know that a professional has responsibility for their future development. It is an important trait of the L&D professional to undertake CPD. Engaging in a range of learning experiences helps to ensure a professional's competence over the course of a career. This may also include formal education to supplement and enhance such occupational learning. We have also noted through our experience of working in organisations that those who take a planned approach to knowledge and skills development tend to progress their careers more quickly and in a direction of their choosing. Planning CPD in advance means that development is more likely to be relevant to a professional's working life.

Ultimately, the success of personal development will rest on the practitioners taking personal responsibility for their own learning, development and performance. This ownership and the associated skills to implement it separate those 'who will' from those 'who just think about it'. Taking responsibility, owning the process, and ensuring plans are put into actions are the elements that will set the professional apart from the rest and will equip them for high performance in their current role, the next role or career progression.

WEBLINKS

HR profession map. Available at: http://www.cipd.co.uk/cipd-hr-profession/profession-map/profession-map-download.aspx [Accessed 26 October 2016].

L&D: new challenges, new approaches. CIPD research report. Available at: http://www.cipd.co.uk/hr-resources/research/l-and-d-challenges-approaches.aspx [Accessed 26 October 2016].

ITOL website. Available at: http://www.itol.org [Accessed 26 October 2016].

Institute of Leadership and Management website. Available at: https://www.i-l-m.com/about-ilm [Accessed 26 October 2016].

Talent management: an overview. CIPD factsheet. Available at: http://www.cipd.co.uk/hr-resources/factsheets/talent-management-overview.aspx [Accessed 26 October 2016].

Learning and development 2015. CIPD survey report. Available at: http://www.cipd.co.uk/hr-resources/survey-reports/learning-development-2015.aspx [Accessed 26 October 2016].

L&D: evolving roles, enhancing skills. CIPD research report. Available at: http://www.cipd.co.uk/hr-resources/research/l-and-d-roles-skills.aspx [Accessed 26 October 2016].

The value of learning: a new model of value and evaluation. CIPD report. Available at: http://www.cipd.co.uk/NR/rdonlyres/94842E50-F775-4154-975F-8D4BE72846C7/0/valoflearnnwmodvalca.pdf [Accessed 26 October 2016].

Evaluating learning and development. CIPD factsheet. Available at: http://www.cipd.co.uk/hr-resources/factsheets/evaluating-learning-talent-development.aspx [Accessed 26 October 2016].

REFERENCES

BLOOM, B.S., ENGELHART, M.D., FURST, E.J., *et al.* (1956). *Taxonomy of educational objectives: the classification of educational goals.* Handbook I: Cognitive domain. New York: David McKay Company.

CIPD (2015) *Learning and development 2015* [online]. Survey report. London: CIPD. Available at: www.cipd.co.uk/hr-resources/survey-reports/learning-development-2015.aspx [Accessed 26 October 2016].

KIRKPATRICK, D.L. (1979) Techniques for evaluating training programmes. *Training and Development Journal.* Vol 3, No 6, pp44–53.

KOLB, D.A. (1984) *Experiential learning: experience as a source of learning and development.* New Jersey: Prentice Hall.

LOMBARDO, M.M. and EICHINGER, R.W. (1996) *The career architect development planner.* Minneapolis: Lominger.

MASLOW, A. (1943) A theory of human motivation. *Psychological Review.* Vol 50, No 4, pp370–396.

MCCLELLAND, D. (1988) *Human motivation.* Cambridge: Cambridge University Press.

MEGGINSON, D. and WHITAKER, V. (2011) *Continuing professional development* (2nd ed). London: CIPD.

CHAPTER 2

Planning to Meet Personal Learning and Development Needs

MAUREEN ROYCE AND WENDY MARSTON

CHAPTER OVERVIEW

- Introduction – Creating awareness of self-assessment
- The role of self-assessment in developing performance
- Using self-assessment to identify development needs
- Using knowledge to map development against performance-related criteria
- Summary

LEARNING OUTCOMES

By the end of this chapter you will be able to:

- undertake a self-assessment positioning relating to personal attributes and characteristics
- co-ordinate sources of knowledge in self-assessment to map development needs
- produce a map to link individual assessment to work, behavioural and professional criteria.

INTRODUCTION

Personal and professional development depends to some degree on individual learning but the way in which learning can be integrated into different aspects of life requires self-evaluation. Self-assessment involves developing an understanding of the complex array of factors influencing life choices and development. In improving performance through self-assessment, a broad view should be taken on the where learning might occur. We do not have to be in a formal teaching environment to enhance personal learning and performance and Lave and Wenger (1991) identify that learning can occur through many channels. The 'Towards Maturity' CIPD report (2014) takes this thinking a stage further, recognising the range of activities and approaches to learning and seeking to understand how these approaches can be used most effectively to develop tools for improving practice and learning. This chapter looks to guide self-assessment in a systematic way to encourage the harnessing of learning opportunities. Once identified as having development potential, learning opportunities can be built into the everyday behaviours with the aim of improving performance overall. In recognising the people and interventions which have a positive impact and those which may distract or have a negative impact, individuals can make choices to enhance their own performance through self-assessment. This chapter seeks to ask questions and create a sense of priority so that development needs are tailored to circumstance rather than being generically assigned. This focus on personalisation of learning means that the mapping to development areas and commitment to action take into account individual characteristics and environment and so are more likely to be undertaken.

The mapping of the various elements allows for the creation of a performance plan using a self-development analysis chain. Personal development depends on considerable effort and potential evaluation of competing choices by individuals and this section will consider the tools available to prepare for these choices and how to reflect on our own motivation, personality and disposition to create a development pathway that will work with, not against, our natural preferences and work/home environmental factors. In understanding the elements contributing to performance we may find that we have a fragmented approach and may lack an honest assessment of the time spent and the value of the outcome. Self-assessment is self-reported so it is perfectly possible for delusion about the time and effort and likelihood of carrying out plans to be incorporated. A plan is drawn up but may never be activated to the point where there is a change in performance behaviour. Biased self-reporting at the planning stage does not build confidence in the possibility of success. By reviewing key elements of performance mapping ahead of overall mapping, there is an opportunity to adjust expectations in line with reality. This chapter takes a holistic view of self-assessment in line with personal characteristics and personal environmental conditions to support a more resilient and realistic approach to self-assessment and the subsequent setting of personal development plan goals.

THE ROLE OF SELF-ASSESSMENT IN DEVELOPING PERFORMANCE

The management of performance is often considered to be cyclical. An example of this would be Torrington and Hall (1995), who use a three-part model – planning performance, supporting performance and reviewing performance. This chapter looks at the planning stage and, in particular, the understanding and information an individual needs to hold about themselves in order to make progress. Heisler *et al* (1988) talk about the need to energise and set behavioural expectations. This ability to understand where the support, knowledge, time and environment to support performance development comes from will help in the setting of realistic and achievable goals and continuous professional development aspirations. Paul Matthews (2014) discusses the need to change the way we change in the report 'Hacking HR to build an adaptability advantage' and recognises that personal change needs to occur continuously with change driven from the bottom up by individuals motivated to change and develop performance. Understanding positioning on a personal basis and building in behaviours to support knowledge development and change facilitates proactive learning.

Developing strong performance behaviours requires active engagement rather than passive reporting of achievements. An example of this might be a 'to do' list created with the contents already partly achieved, part of the self-deception we sometimes practice on ourselves. De Wall (2013) discusses the idea of having a 'drive for performance' in individuals looking continually at improvements. In order to have this drive, De Wall (2013) identifies the need for individuals to have a thorough understanding of their priorities, needs and wants ahead of discussing how to develop this into a plan of action. The individual self-assessment tables in the chapter will support in identifying these priorities and understanding the priorities at any given point in time.

INDIVIDUAL CHARACTERISTICS IN PERFORMANCE

Motivational assessment

Motivational behaviour in personal development may be linked to drivers, needs, emotions and may vary from individual to individual. An understanding of why an individual might wish to embark on a programme or series of events leading to personal development activity helps to secure the value of the involvement because development in any area of life may result in sacrifices needing to be made in another. Additionally, what motivates one may alienate another (Harlen and Deakin Crick 2003) so this is a highly personalised assessment but is one that ensures that the learner has thought carefully about the consequences of embarking on a programme of development prior to commencement. Maclennan (2008) recognised that in order to develop as individuals and to develop learning, students had to actively engage with the process, whether that be informally in a discussion, formally in a class or through individually focused reading. As part of self-development, learners should be aware of their motivational state – why they are motivated to develop themselves in some way but also understand which of the ways in which development can take place is likely to motivate rather than alienate.

Table 2.1 Map One: Pre-development assessment of motivation to engage

Drivers	Why are you driven to succeed in your personal development journey? Is it linked to progression at work? To better prospects? Or is this linked to personal satisfaction and interest in a topic to add value to our health and well-being?
Needs	What is it that you need to gain from the development activity? Does it fit with the needs of the organisation as well?
Emotions	Is self-development crucial to my sense of self-worth or confidence? Will self-development help my social confidence?

When considering motivation, goal orientation will be a primary consideration. Part of achieving success in self-development will be linked to the attractiveness of the goal and the importance attached to achieving mastery of the new skills or knowledge. Once an individual has assessed the underlying motivation behind a goal, the objective becomes easier to define. With clarity of objective comes an appreciation of the journey needed to achieve this objective. Increased competence comes to be expressed in terms of self-defined improvement. Because the motivation is self-defined then more positive attitudes are developed which reflect the position of the learner who is less likely to handicap themselves with self-defeating behaviours. The value of the outcome to an individual will determine effort also (Huczynski and Buchanan 2001). Motivational triggers for informal learning driven through self-assessment are identified by Tews *et al* (2016) as relating to a requirement to adapt quickly to a dynamic business environment. Molloy and Noe (2010) recognise the motivational value of informal learning from an employee perspective as successful careers require personal initiative and self-assessment beyond the range of the organisation. Although the identification of key engagement links may be helpful, ultimately there may be no conclusive answer with regard to what exactly motivates an individual to perform well (Houldsworth and Jirasinghe 2009). Furthermore, motivation can change very quickly (Hutchinson 2013) and people respond differently to the same motivational tools (Beech and Chadwick 2014).

Personality and emotional assessment

Personality traits influence the way in which we see the world. An appreciation of the role that personality plays in self-assessment supports analysis. In conducting a self-assessment, the extent to which we are self-aware and can use self-knowledge to direct our thinking helps to move to a consideration of which developmental initiatives will be best suited to us. Personality may well have an impact on successful performance but it may be only one of many factors related to individual performance. There is some doubt about the accuracy of personality testing so self-application of tests without expert interpretation may be misleading (Buchanan and Huczynski 2010) and, further, may not guarantee the intended behaviour (Williams 2002). Akhtar *et al* (2015) consider that an overall assessment of broad personality 'type' may be too generalised to help with an assessment of performance impact and that it may be necessary to assess each variable of personality.

Environmental assessment

Using self-assessment to develop and improve performance is the sign of an engaged practitioner but part of our self-knowledge is the recognition that stressors or burnout (Timms *et al* 2012) can lead to detachment if the stress involves a long-hours work culture or an overly high workload. In the final stages of mapping, a review of our operating environment and resilience will support a realistic assessment of the capacity an individual has to manage an increased focus on personal development.

Within their 2014 report '*Getting smart about Agile Working*', CIPD recognised the importance of using virtuality and outcome-based indicators of achievement, both of which are supported by the development of a robust self-assessment capacity combining self-knowledge with the motivation for personal development.

Using knowledge of self to aid self-assessment

In addition to understanding assessing motivational position, learners need to understand the features of their environment that will also impact on self-development. This requires an ability to assess the impact of physical, mental and societal well-being levels. Barriers to learning can take many forms and a strong self-assessment will recognise that as well as motivational and personality-related influences, the environment and support will play a considerable role, too. Knowledge of such barriers and supporting issues may not immediately be evident in a work-based or learning-based environment, so self-assessment becomes a crucial part of identifying the type of development intervention likely to be most resilient in the personal environment. Digitally enabled learning is perceived as a way of creating flexibility of place, time and pace but isolation and a view that digital learning can be non-interactive (Sambrook 2003) means that the learner has a role in identifying and assessing the tools most suited to personal circumstances and attributes. Self-assessment using the tools of identifying emotional intelligence will support clarity in choosing the right path for self-assessment. Autonomy can have a significant impact on an individual's level of motivation as it can make them feel empowered to make the changes required to progress. The autonomy in self-assessment can in its own right be a powerful motivational tool that can motivate an individual to operate to the best of their ability. This can be supported by DeCharms (1984) who claimed that motivation can be enhanced through encouraging workers to exert personal control over their role, and to take responsibility for it. Developing this, Maricutoiu *et al* (2016) advise that depersonalisation of job roles and associated stress can be moderated by interventions which include personal accomplishment. In achieving goals, within a self-managed environment there is an additional gain in reducing the risk of emotional exhaustion. Tews *et al* (2015) recognise the enormous diversity of learning opportunities available in both corporate and personal life and the self-assessment exercises in this chapter support the creation of a personal chain linking elements together in a holistic rather than piecemeal way which will enable the identification of gaps and lost opportunities as well as a route map for more strategic personal development. Within level 5, CIPD expectations include a generic understanding of what is required to be an effective and efficient HR professional with the emphasis on the ability to create a CPD plan. The mapping exercises within the chapter are designed to assist with creating a framework of opportunity and personal preference to support the development of CPD.

USING SELF-ASSESSMENT TO IDENTIFY DEVELOPMENT NEEDS

Gaining confidence from the insights gained from an analysis of personal motivational and personality-led preferences, learners can move towards an identification of the form of development which will be most effective in supporting their development. The identification of preferred methods of learning will take into account the environment and constraints identified in the previous section.

Using the information gained in the earlier sections, reflect on which of the interventions might be most effective. Use a scoring system in terms of level of preference 1–5 or a simple traffic light system – green for preferred, amber for would work, red for unlikely to be successful. The organisation of personal development preferences in this way can help both the individual and the organisation make the most effective use of their time and resources.

Mapping will create an information flow allowing for identification of potential but currently unused development interventions. As individual circumstances change, the 'fit' with interventions will also change and updating of mapping will allow an updated review of developmental opportunities to occur. In identifying the development opportunities in this way, the gaps between what is currently being utilised in development terms and what might be available (Jafari *et al* 2009) can be articulated.

Although knowledge mapping is used across organisations, the applicability to individual learning and development is acknowledged by Driessen (2007) and others. Ellinger (2005) identifies contextual factors working to facilitate informal learning. These factors included commitment to learning (motivation), tools and resources (environmental analysis), relationship with people (emotional and environmental analysis) and creation of webs of relationships (emotional and environmental analysis).

Table 2.2 Map Two: Analysis of suggested development interventions and their fit with personal attributes

	Fit with motivational analysis	Fit with personality analysis	Fit with environmental analysis	Fit with emotional analysis
On the job training				
Secondment				
Mentoring – being a mentor				
Mentoring – having a mentor				
Peer-to-peer discussion				
Access to in-house experts				
Interim roles				
Coaching – becoming a coach				
Coaching – having a coach				

	Fit with motivational analysis	Fit with personality analysis	Fit with environmental analysis	Fit with emotional analysis
Voluntary roles to build skills				
Academic course				
Formal training programme				
Online training				
Digitally enabled knowledge gathering from websites				
Social networking via LinkedIn or similar				
Knowledge gathering through Twitter or similar				
Webinars				
Podcasts				
Blogs				
Attending conference				
Attending professional CIPD event				
Discussion-based workshop				
Guided reading with forum support				
Personally directed reading/research				
Teaching				

Table 2.3 Example map for an individual motivated by broadening relationships and building networks

	Fit with motivational analysis	Fit with personality analysis	Fit with environmental analysis	Fit with emotional analysis
On the job training				
Secondment				
Mentoring – being a mentor				
Mentoring – having a mentor				

	Fit with motivational analysis	Fit with personality analysis	Fit with environmental analysis	Fit with emotional analysis
Peer-to-peer discussion		x		
Access to in-house experts			x	
Interim roles				x
Coaching – becoming a coach				
Coaching – having a coach				
Voluntary roles to build skills	x			
Academic course				
Formal training programme				x
Online training				
Digitally enabled knowledge gathering from websites				
Social networking via LinkedIn or similar	x			
Knowledge gathering through Twitter or similar				
Webinars				
Podcasts				
Blogs				
Attending conference				x
Attending professional CIPD event	x			
Discussion-based workshop	x			
Guided reading with forum support				
Personally directed reading/research				
Teaching				

Table 2.4 Example map for an individual motivated by self-directed informal and personalised learning

	Fit with motivational analysis	Fit with personality analysis	Fit with environmental analysis	Fit with emotional analysis
On the job training				
Secondment				
Mentoring – being a mentor				
Mentoring – having a mentor				
Peer-to-peer discussion				
Access to in-house experts				
Interim roles				
Coaching – becoming a coach				
Coaching – having a coach				
Voluntary roles to build skills				
Academic course				
Formal training programme				
Online training	x			
Digitally enabled knowledge gathering from websites	x			
Social networking via LinkedIn or similar				
Knowledge gathering through Twitter or similar	x			
Webinars			x	
Podcasts			x	
Blogs				
Attending conference				
Attending professional CIPD event				
Discussion-based workshop				

	Fit with motivational analysis	Fit with personality analysis	Fit with environmental analysis	Fit with emotional analysis
Guided reading with forum support				x
Personally directed reading/research		x		
Teaching				

Through the analysis, a personalised pathway can be developed allowing for a structured self-assessment tailored to individual needs.

STRUCTURING SELF-ASSESSMENT

A structured self-assessment can support the development of a coherent plan by developing an honest view of the underlying motivational triggers encouraging an individual to take the time for self-reflection. Moreillon (2016) highlights the effectiveness of reflection on the applicability of Twitter for both networking and knowledge within a librarian context and notes how respondents view their professional standing as being improved through the use of social media. In coding the suitability of development interventions to individual preferences, a reflection on experience of applicability will help to test the effectiveness of each method.

RECOGNISING BIAS IN SELF-ASSESSMENT

Part of the recognition process is to work with a framework to create an honest and questioning appraisal that would include recognition about why previous efforts in a particular segment of performance may have been less successful. Harrison (2013) provides useful guidelines for thinking about questions to avoid bias and self-denial (Smart and Creelman 2013) about what might need to change.

Avoiding self-delusion, bias in terms of our self-assessment involves investigation. A framework based around the work of Harrison (2013) could help individuals to think through and identify the areas of bias most frequently applied to our own self-assessments, which prevent a progression towards stronger performance. It involves confronting the areas we might most often seek to avoid – having a difficult conversation with yourself.

Table 2.5 Map Three: Avoiding self-delusion

Question	Self-assessment	Impact on personal performance Honest assessment of position
Capability	Skills assessment Relevance of skills Updating of skills Knowledge based capacity	Based on performance reviews, informal feedback and peer discussions, knowledge in relation to discussions taking place within the wider world of HR or on LinkedIn or within the CIPD discussions and blogs.

Appropriate and inappropriate behaviours	Time management networking Knowledge management Reflection	Mapping of experiential and knowledge opportunities within the working week acknowledging where opportunities were lost. Identifying time-wasting distractions and focusing on knowledge and confidence-boosting activities
Deadlines	Impact on self Impact on others Impact on reputation Impact on performance	What deadlines have you successfully met – reflect on the positive outcomes Honestly appraise those you have failed to meet and reflect on how different behaviours could positively impact on this. What forms of support or learning could make a difference?
Norms and rules	Operating culture Well-being – personal rules Flexibility – family and other commitments	What time frames are part of my own and family well-being?
Engagement	Resilience Frequency of engagement with knowledge sources Engagement with networks	Are you trying to engage with knowledge or networks in a way that is simply unsuited to you? Go back to map 2 and check alternative options

Source: adapted from Harrison 2013

MITIGATING BIAS – TAKING A BROADER VIEW

By seeking reassurance in comparisons with others rather than striving for personal excellence we may hold ourselves back and fail to make the effort required to create change. Map Three can be revisited and updated to see where the personal successes and blockages lie. Mohammadyari and Singh (2014) identify a willingness to access content using a range of sources and devices, which may be owned either by themselves or their organisations, as being crucial to improving both digital literacy and performance.

Aguinis (2007) counsels about the need to understand individual differences, to recognise that we each see the world through a different lens and to avoid being frustrated if feedback comes from a very different perspective to that of oneself. Balancing the views of others with your own voice involves using your inner coach to guide you to set developmental goals which take into account your own self-assessment but also the feedback from your networks and colleagues. Knowledge mapping can be considered a process of discovery and analysis which allows for a visualisation of the most relevant features associated with self-development (Jafari et al 2009).

NETWORKING

Networking involves making use of opportunities to engage with other individuals who might be able to help and support you in your personal development. This section will look at face-to-face networking (social media networking is considered separately). Networking opportunities are sometimes highlighted as such, perhaps at the start or end of an event or presentation or sometimes an activity might be badged as 'for networking'. Networking can be a relaxed and enjoyable way of developing support for some individuals while others will be much less comfortable with making contacts with new people in a more casual environment. Reviewing the response you have to networking will help to identify how best to approach building networks to support your performance.

Table 2.6 Map Four: Networking

Aspects of networking I am comfortable with	Aspects of networking I am uncomfortable with
Benefits of face-to-face networking	Costs of face-to-face networking

Using the self-evaluation in Table 2.6, consider how valuable the networking process might be compared with the time and the level of effort you would put into this. Then consider how comfortable the process feels so that a view of the value of networking can be established. If the perceived 'cost' of networking is too high, then alternatives to face-to-face networking such as use of social media might provide alternatives.

THE VALUE OF MENTORING AND FRIENDSHIP GROUPS TO SHAPE DEVELOPMENT

There is considerable evidence to link performance development to feedback, particularly from trusted networks. In alignment with Deci's Cognitive Evaluation Theory (1975), Weiner and Mander (1978) emphasise the importance of feedback in personal motivation. Feedback allows us to see personal performance through the lens of others and reflected through different experiences and backgrounds. The feedback allows us to shape our self-assessment more accurately and Vallerand and Reid (1984) highlight the importance of positive feedback in facilitating motivation. Over time mentoring and friendship groups tend to develop cultures (Moreillon 2016) and norms develop concerning the use of the medium for either professional, serious or social comment. Understanding how to use these networks, particularly remote networks, effectively can aid not only the ability to access knowledge but also the ability to question and gain support from fellow professionals.

Figure 2.1 Personal stakeholder map

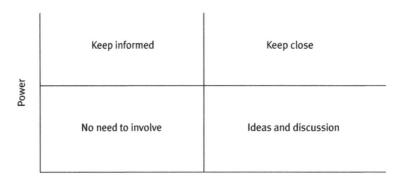

In a work-based environment, personal stakeholders are a valuable source of advice, learning and influence. Stakeholders do, however, need to be managed.

The matrix above can be used to effectively organise your stakeholders into four key groups, depending on their level of interest in you and your personal/professional development, and their level of power and influence to be able to help you reach your goals.

For example, you are keen to take on additional responsibility for a service change project in which you have recently become involved. You know you can support the senior responsible officer (SRO) to engage and involve front-line staff in developing service options. Your stakeholder map might look something like this:

- **Keep close** and manage well your relationship with the SRO; preparing for, and contributing to project meetings and offering to take on additional specific actions linked to staff engagement (for example facilitating a staff workshop) to prove your capability and capacity.
- **Keep informed** those colleagues and stakeholders who are influential as part of the wider change project to ensure you are kept abreast of key developments. You will be able to share your thinking too in order to promote understanding and make sure you are aware of any interdependencies across the project work streams that arise.
- **Involve your peers and mentors in discussion to shape your ideas.** This is essential to any well-formed proposal and will increase your confidence that a variety of viewpoints have been thought through and included as appropriate.
- Finally, there are bound to be colleagues that you feel there is **no need to involve** at this time, although the landscape may change quickly depending on how service options progress, so be aware of how power may shift over time.

USING KNOWLEDGE TO MAP DEVELOPMENT AGAINST PERFORMANCE-RELATED CRITERIA

KNOWLEDGE CREATION AND UPDATING

The rate of pace of change in organisations and in society creates an environment where individuals must continue to update and create new knowledge in order to engage and be effective in their organisations and in their wider life also. Because time is in short supply, individuals will look to find ways of developing knowledge that fit around their already busy schedules. Whether attending CIPD branch events, reading *People Management* magazine, going on bespoke training or simply listening to those who already have the knowledge in their immediate environment, both formal and informal methods of knowledge creation can be actively integrated into personal development plans. McLellan (2008) felt that, as a tutor, she was the most active learner in her class as she prepared everything whereas the students received. To make a knowledge-gaining experience active, learners have to do something with the knowledge they have acquired. It may be that they file it for future use, or discuss with a set of behaviours or skills that might enhance their own development, or seek to take the knowledge further, to expand what they have learned. Perhaps the key element here is to track times where knowledge, experience or networking has been expanded so that patterns can be detected and a more strategic use of time management can be planned for the future. Collaboration is a significant part of the skills and behavioural requirement at level 5 and the usefulness of any of the activities undertaken needs to be evaluated and weighed against the time and sacrifice in terms of personal and family well-being.

Table 2.7 Map Five: Consolidating the knowledge

Sources of knowledge in personal development	Taking action	Consolidating the knowledge
Twitter over a morning cup of tea	Noting areas of professional or organisational interest	Following up references

The map in Table 2.7 can be used to show sources of knowledge and to track how this knowledge is used in personal and professional development.

Gaining and using professional knowledge is integral to personal and professional development. There will never be a time when you are 'fully developed'; learning is truly a lifelong endeavour. There are a variety of formal and informal ways and means to keep up to date in whatever field in which you are currently working or studying. For the examples given below, assess the ease of access to the method concerned and the quality of the learning you have undertaken.

Table 2.8 Map Six: Updating your knowledge

Keeping up to date	Ease of access?	Quality of learning?
Policy and practice journals will keep you up to date with the latest research and thinking and critical evaluation of key topics.	*E.g. Online alerts to office email. Circulation of key policy documents. Availability of summary documents.*	*E.g. Being able to pick and choose your topic areas. Finding completely new areas of interest to pursue.*
Social media as an increasingly important source of knowledge in real time. LinkedIn Twitter Blogs Professional site blogs Webinars Podcasts	*E.g. Separation of work and life media – has this been possible or desirable?*	*E.g. Tends towards snippets of information rather than in-depth analysis.*
Professional networks can be developed and	*E.g. Takes effort to set up and maintain*	*E.g. Proving to be a good source of*

Keeping up to date	Ease of access?	Quality of learning?
maintained through attending local, regional and national forums when possible.	*personal relationships. Access can then be both ad hoc and in the form of organised get-togethers.*	*personalised information and advice.*
Mentoring as an invaluable aid to learning and development; someone who can guide and advise you on issues and also link you into wider networks that share your interests.	*E.g. Matching with a mentor you can form a long-term relationship with.*	*E.g. Making sure you put in the effort and thought to get the very most out of the relationship.*
Daily newspapers can add valuable analysis and provide viewpoints on political, social, economic and environmental policy that can spark ideas.	*E.g. Readily available from local outlets in hard copy and available online.*	*E.g. Care required on understanding reporting bias.*
Conferences and seminars are used by all industry sectors to give and receive information.	*E.g. Cost of attendance and location.*	*E.g. Carefully looking at the agendas to make sure the topics covered are of interest and relevant to learning aims.*
Secondment opportunities, where you undertake a different role in the same or partner organisation for a short period of time, can be available and beneficial to gain knowledge and different perspectives across and between sectors.	*E.g. Availability in organisations can vary.*	*E.g. Making a substantial contribution to wider knowledge and experience.*
Academic qualification is of course an option throughout your career. Increasingly, employers need to see a track record of experience and delivery linked to formal study so be balanced in your approach. It's always a good idea to seek advice	*E.g. Online qualifications, location and distance of on-site campus courses.*	*E.g. Grade achieved or aiming for.*

Keeping up to date	Ease of access?	Quality of learning?
from a senior officer in your organisation before embarking on a course of study to make sure it will enhance your prospects by being relevant.		

It is best to use a mix of these at any one time and some may suit your current environment better than others, so be flexible and reflect on your approach regularly.

This activity needs to be planned in as part of working life, not as an add-on if and when you have the time, otherwise opportunities for progression may be lost. The extent to which digital knowledge and support plays a role in mapping for 5 and 6 is likely to grow and with it a need to include personal digital development into the knowledge requirements.

Greene (2014) suggests that, despite conventional wisdom that students are digitally literate, there is evidence to suggest that some may struggle to appropriately vet, understand and use the wide array of information available from the Internet. Additionally, uncritical consumption (Eysenbach *et al* 2002) remains an issue for personal development as online information may be both inaccurate and misleading.

Examples of social media sites and services include (but are not limited to):

- popular social networks like Facebook and Twitter
- professional social networks like LinkedIn
- photographic social networks like Flickr and Instagram
- sharing and discussion sites like Reddit.

Table 2.9 Map Seven: Social media sites and personal digital literacy

Sites I already use and gain benefit from	Sites I feel would be advantageous to use	Action needed to improve social media to support my development

Available on mobile devices and PCs, such sites are an ever-increasing part of our personal and professional lives. Being 'connected' in real time to events both locally and globally is rapidly being used as a key tool to improve our ability to gain and use knowledge. Moreillon (2016) recognised that being part of a 'connected' community offers support in differing ways. The online community streams can offer advice or respond to specific questions and can be directed specifically to a pertinent issue. Online communities also behave like communities of practice (Wenger 1998) bringing together expertise, interest and the opportunity to interact with those who hold knowledge and expertise in an area of interest to the learner.

Using social media in a professional capacity has many benefits including opportunities for research, raising awareness of topical issues, engaging with the public and other stakeholders, and of course the chance to establish a wider and more diverse professional network. A key development skill is identified by Greene (2014), who acknowledges the importance of critical thinking in assessing the reliability and suitability of information.

A note of caution: most organisations will have a Social Media Policy that you should follow. Take care not to post any information that unintentionally may be seen as either sensitive, i.e. breaching data protection laws, or potentially damaging to a company's reputation. Most organisations now hire social media experts as part of their communications team who use data monitoring software to flag key terms.

REFLECTIVE ACTIVITY 2.1

What learning and development activities are you doing at the moment? Are you getting the very most out of them? What could you do better or differently? Use these initial thoughts as you progress through the next section.

KNOW YOURSELF – CREATING AN INDIVIDUAL MAP TO SELF-DEVELOPMENT

During this chapter, various aspects with the potential to impact on the success of self-development have been considered. By combining the self-assessment preferences an individual map can be created which will allow individuals to track their development activities and to recognise opportunities when these present themselves.

Figure 2.2 Self-development analysis

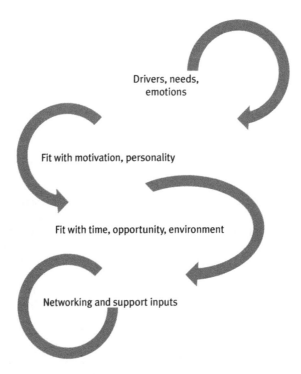

The self-development chain creates a reference piece where learners can check and reflect that the development they are considering or undertaking is a good fit for their individual needs and requirements. Sometimes, the strongest development can come from learning through informal workplace relationships, networks or skills acquired through volunteering. By working through the chain, thoughtful reflection is encouraged so that the personal development routes achieve the best outcomes.

Table 2.10 Tools to support your self-assessment: self-development analysis chain

Elements of the chain	Elements these contribute to self-development	How the self-development enhances performance
Drivers, needs, emotions	*Need to develop professional identity – self-confidence provided by formal qualification*	*Clarity about underlying emotions and how to use these positively to achieve success*
Personality and motivation		*Ability to work with motivational triggers and build these into planning Understanding the personality traits which would support me or potentially act as barriers to achievement and recognise these in developing plans*
Fit with time, opportunity, environment	*Work opportunity for funding or time support to achieve Identification of pockets of time to achieve self-development goals*	*Opportunity cost of development – what could be done instead and is this an acceptable trade*
Networking and support	*Work colleagues or friends who understand your objectives Support from external groups such as CIPD and networking provided Family and friends' support (link to creating time)*	*Extending your network into the digital world to increase both knowledge and support*

USING SELF-ASSESSMENT TO CREATE CPD

The self-development chain and supporting tools prepare the ground for the creation of CPD plans that will be robust and resilient. The resilience comes from the self-assessment which means that individual factors such as time, motivation, support and the ability to identify what needs to be changed in order to achieve the desired development have already been considered. Tews *et al* (2016) suggest that experience sampling assists with the understanding of learning experiences as they occur in the day. Using the chain as a framework, consideration could be given to the form in which engagement with learning takes place at home and at work in both formal and informal circumstances.

SUMMARY

Ultimately, the key skill is the ability to have an open and honest dialogue as part of self-assessment avoiding bias and self-delusion. Aguinis (2013) advises on how to be your own coach and in doing so brings together a number of the framework areas discussed in this chapter. Aguinis (2013) places particular emphasis on the establishment and maintenance of trusting relationships and lines of communication. Honest self-assessment involves dialogue with peers and network colleagues to ensure that the view we have is shared with others. Ultimately, there is an importance to acknowledge that change is driven by self and that the responsibility lies with the individual and not with organisations, supporters, managers or family members. Molloy and Noe (2010) discuss the importance of informal learning for the upkeep of knowledge and current skill sets. Viewing self-assessment through the lens of individual responsibility is essential if change and performance improvement is to result.

REFERENCES

AGUINIS, H. (2013) *Performance management.* 3rd ed. New Jersey: Pearson.

BUCHANAN, D.A. and HUCZYNSKI, A.A. (2010) *Organizational behaviour* (p. 794). Pearson.

BEECH, J. and CHADWICK, S. (2014) *The business of sport management.* Pearson.

DECHARMS, R. (1968) *Personal causation.* New York Academic Press.

DE WAAL, A. (2013) *Strategic performance management: a managerial and behavioral approach.* Palgrave Macmillan.

DRIESSEN, S. (2007) A framework for evaluating knowledge-mapping tools. *Journal of Knowledge Management* Vol 11, No 2, pp109–117.

GREENE, J.A., YU, S. and COPELAND, D. (2014) Measuring critical components of digital literacy and their relationship with learning. *Computers and Education.* Vol 76, pp 55–69.

HARLEN, W. and DEAKIN CRICK, R. (2002) A systematic review of the impact of summative assessment and tests on students' motivation for learning. In: *Research Evidence in Education Library.* London: EPPI-Centre, Social Science Research Unit, Institute of Education, University of London.

HOULDSWORTH, E. and JIRASINGHE, E. (2009). *Managing and measuring employee performance.* London: Kogan Page.

HUCZYNSKI, A. and BUCHANAN, D. (2001) *Organizational behaviour: an introductory text (Instructor's Manual).* Financial Times/Prentice Hall.

JAFARI, M., AKHAVAN, P., and AMIRI, R. (2009) A framework for the selection of knowledge management techniques. *Journal of Knowledge Management Practice.* Vol 10, No 1.

LAVE, J. and WENGER, E. (1991) *Situated learning: legitimate peripheral participation.* Cambridge: Cambridge University Press.

MARICUTOIU, L., SAVA, F. and BUTTA, O. (2016) The effectiveness of controlled interventions on employees' burnout. *Journal of Occupational Psychology.* Vol 89, No 1, pp1–27.

MOHAMMADYARI, S. and SINGH, H. (2015) Understanding the effect of e-learning on individual performance: *The role of digital literacy computers and education*. No 82(2015), pp11–25.

MOLLOY, J. and NOE, R. (2010) 'Learning' a living: Continuous learning for survival in today's talent market. In KOZLOWSKI, W and SALAS, E (eds). *Learning, training and development in organisations* (pp 333–361) New York: Routledge.

MOREILLON (2016) Storytime for Learning in a Digital World. *Knowledge Quest*. Vol 44, No. 3.

TEWS, M., NOE, R., SCHEURER, A. and MICHEL, J. (2016) The relationship of work family conflict and core self-evaluations with informal learning in a managerial context. *Journal of Occupational and Organisational Psychology* (2016) Vol 89, pp 92–110.

TIMMS, C., BROUGH, P. and GRAHAM D. (2012) Burnt out but engaged: the co-existence of psychological burnout and engagement. *Journal of Educational Administration*. Vol 50, No 3, pp327–345.

TORRINGTON, D. and HALL, L. (1995) *Personnel management: human resource management in action*. Europe: Prentice-Hall International.

VALLERAND, R. J. and REID, G. (1984) On the relative effects of positive and negative verbal feedback on males and females intrinsic motivation. *Canadian Journal of Behavioural Science*. Vol 20, No 6, pp94–102.

WENGER, E. (1998) *Learning in doing: social, cognitive and computational perspectives*. Cambridge: Cambridge University Press.

WILLIAMS, R.S. (2002) *Managing employee performance: design and implementation in organisations*. London: Thomson Learning.

CHAPTER 3

Working Collaboratively as a Member of a Team or Working Group

Tricia Harrison and David Soehren

CHAPTER OVERVIEW

- Introduction
- Groups and teams
- Working with others
- Meetings
- Techniques for influencing, persuading and negotiating
- Assertiveness
- Managing relationships
- Presentation and report writing
- Summary

LEARNING OUTCOMES

By the end of this chapter you will be able to:

- explain the concept of group dynamics
- discuss political behaviour in organisations and how this can impact on the achievement of organisation and L&D objectives
- have the knowledge to successfully manage meetings
- apply different methods for influencing, persuading and negotiating with others in different contexts.

INTRODUCTION

Team working is both challenging and exhilarating as it is only partially dependent on self. Not only is teamwork dependent upon the individuals involved, it is also highly influenced by other internal and external factors such as financial budget, culture, etc. Quite frequently collaboration and teamwork are used interchangeably, however, there is a difference and this is where the chapter begins. Following this there is a critical evaluation of group dynamics and components of effective as well as ineffective teams.

This chapter then moves into the practical activity of how to conduct and manage meetings and later in the chapter presentation and report writing. Research by Bulut and Culha (2010) identified the essential nature of the L&D and HR practitioner's role in the management of training opportunities and employee commitment. Key skills of influencing, persuading, negotiating as well as assertiveness, are essential to perform the role and to form positive and sustaining work relationships.

GROUPS AND TEAMS

Often the terms 'teams' and 'groups' are used interchangeably. In order to understand how to work collaboratively with others as a member of a team or 'working group', it is important to understand the difference between the two terms. Not all groups are teams but all teams are groups. To start, we will look at the general conditions that make a group and then look at the differences between groups and teams in the work environment.

GROUPS

A group is defined as a collection of individuals who are co-ordinated or who co-ordinate their individual efforts and share some common interests or purpose with others. Members of a group share common beliefs, principles and interactions regarding a common outcome. Bratton (2015) defines groups as comprising at least two people, who continually interact with each other, have something in common, and recognise that they are members of the group.

People within groups share information and resources in order to enable other individual members to achieve their tasks. At an identity level, group members see themselves as individual members in a larger group working together and contributing towards a common purpose. A group:

- is a collection of individuals who are organised
- shares a common interest or purpose
- is made of individuals responsible for their own task
- interacts, communicates and/or shares resources with other group members
- member sees themselves as part of a group.

Figure 3.1 Examples of groups

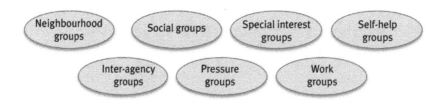

Informal and formal groups

Groups can be informal or formal. Individual members of informal groups often have the ability to walk away from the group either when their service or input becomes unnecessary, or when they no longer feel that they are gaining from being a member of the group. Formal groups are assembled, organised and structured. Individuals are brought into formal groups to fulfil a role within the group. When individuals leave the role, others may be brought in to replace them. Whether informal or formal, the success of the group is often measured by its final results.

Work groups

In work groups, individuals interact primarily to share information. This may be to help make decisions but the sharing of information is primarily used to help each group member to perform within their area of responsibility. For the rest of this chapter we will refer to 'working groups' as formal groups within organisations comprising of more than three individuals working together for a common purpose.

Group dependency level

In organisations, groups can operate at three levels of 'individual dependence', meaning the level that individuals are dependent on others to fulfil their task.

Dependent level groups are often centred on a single managerial role, usually a manager or supervisor. The manager plays the part of boss and/or controller. Individuals within the group have their own role and responsibilities but the manager is accountable for each group member's performance. At this level the manager is responsible for solving problems and making decisions. Working with the manager, the individual is dependent on the manager to co-ordinate and control the conditions for individual performance.

Independent level groups, like dependent level groups, each group member has a defined role and level of responsibility. It is different from a dependent level group in that the management role tends to control less and focuses more on directing group members on achieving their individual assignments. Individual accountability of performance shifts from the manager role to the individual. At this level group members become more responsible for communication, co-ordination and control within the group. Lawyers, Sales Representatives and Teachers are examples of independent level groups as they serve a common outcome but work independently of each other.

Interdependent level groups, individual group members rely on each other to complete their tasks. They have a shared responsibility for the successful completion of goals and outcomes. This shared responsibility creates the need for group members to increase their level of co-ordination with one another. Members of interdependent groups freely share information, resources and create the conditions that help other members of the group to achieve their individual contributions to the group's final results.

Figure 3.2 Teams are a type of work group

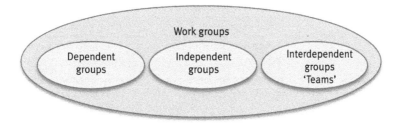

Groups that are operating at the dependent and independent levels may be may be highly efficient and effective at achieving results, but the term 'Team' is used to describe a group that operates at the *interdependent* level.

TEAMS

A team is described as an assembled group of people interdependently working together with the purpose to achieve mutual goals within a specified period of time. Team members have an understanding of the collective accountability for the group task, and are supportive of the collective efforts of individual team members. Katzenbach and Smith (2005) state that teams differ fundamentally from working groups because they require both individual and mutual accountability. Simply stated, a team is more than the sum of its parts.

The purpose of assembling a team is to complete more complex tasks than what would be possible for an individual working at a dependent or interdependent level. Maximising this interdependency of group members creates conditions for synergy, creativity, joint accountability and innovation.

Differentiating characteristics of teams

- Individuals positively impact, influence and support each other's performance.
- Individuals are mutually committed to each other.
- Individuals share a joint accountability for the achievement of group goals.
- A team's strength depends on the individual members' sense of group purpose and interconnectivity.
- Overall success depends on a functional interpersonal dynamic.
- Team members use their individual strengths to achieve group results.
- Team members are aware of and utilise the strengths of other team members.
- A member's absence can seriously hamper the abilities of other team members to perform effectively.

Generally, it is much easier to form a group than a team. Table 3.1 shows the general difference between groups and teams. Note that there may be slight differences between dependent and independent levels of group function.

Table 3.1 General differences between groups and teams

Key areas	Groups	Teams
Description	A collection of individuals who work together and share information to complete individual task	Group of individuals having a collective identity joined together to accomplish a joint goal/task
Number of leaders	One	One or more
Dependence	Dependent/Independent	Interdependent
Success	Success is based on each individual's contribution	Success is dependent on the entire group's contribution
Goal emphasis	Individual goals	Team goals
Outputs	Produce individual work products	Produce collective work products
Individual focus	Concerned with one's own outcome and challenges	Concerned with outcomes of everyone and challenges that face the team
Process	Come together to share information and perspectives Discuss, decide, delegate to individual member	Frequently come together for decision-making, discussion, problem solving and planning Discuss, decide to do collectively
Accountability	Manager	Individual and mutual accountability

Key areas	Groups	Teams
Responsibility	Individual responsibility	Shared responsibility
Role description	Roles and responsibilities are defined based on tasks to be completed	Roles, responsibilities and tasks are defined to help team to achieve its objective
Roles	Identify every person's role in task	Identify every person's role and task in regards to helping the collective effort of the team Each person can often switch and allocate parts of their tasks to others
Best case scenario	Win/lose situations are common	Aims for a win-win
Trust	Trust may or may not be important to perform individual task	Trust is very important to perform group task
Communication	One- or two-way	Honest and open multi-way communication
Personal development	Training focuses on improving individual task performance	Members are encouraged to continually develop skills and share best practice for the development of others
Conflict resolution	Conflict is resolved at management level	Team members realise conflict is normal and sees it as opportunity for new ideas and creativity Team members work to resolve conflict quickly and constructively

Source: Developed by authors from a variety of sources

In the work environment, many people will use the terms groups and teams interchangeably; be careful not to make assumptions when you hear them being used, check your understanding of the use of the terminology. No one description of groups and teams will work all of the time in all contexts. Nor will always working in team be the best option. The reality is that, depending on the group objective, managers may need to move between different levels of dependency and group structures. The challenge facing managers, L&D and HR professionals is in having the flexibility of awareness and the capability to use appropriate personal, managerial and development skills that are required to support groups in achieving their specific tasks and objectives, whilst reflecting the need of dependencies within those groups.

 REFLECTIVE ACTIVITY 3.1

Group or team?

Critically compare your work group. Describe the group based on dependencies. Would you describe it as a group or team? Justify your answer.

COLLABORATION

The environment in which organisations operate is constantly changing. This creates situations that affect organisational goals. Traditional work groups may not have the skill set, resources, technology or flexibility to achieve them. In this case other forms of working environments or group structures are needed. The term collaboration has become a buzzword. Like 'teams' and 'groups' its meaning can sometimes be diluted and signify different things to different people. According to the *Oxford English Dictionary*, the Latin root *collaborare* means to 'work together'. Most definitions of collaboration are a simple variation of the action of working with someone to produce something. Collaboration must mean something more than what our above description of 'groups' already accomplishes.

Michael Schrage (1995) in his book *No more teams!*, suggests that collaboration is a process of value creation which traditional structures of communication and teamwork cannot achieve. Unlike teams that come together to achieve a joint goal, individuals or groups that collaborate come together to achieve a special project or common vision. When organisations need to create something new, collaboration becomes necessary when the need for interdependency is so great that without a shared vision, it cannot be achieved. Unlike teams, which work towards achieving a common objective, collaborators often have conflicting interests and objectives.

Organisations may choose to collaborate with other organisations or create the conditions for intra-organisational collaboration between groups and teams. Resources and information are shared between the collaborating parties but so are the risks. When collaboration works, there are many benefits for all parties:

- builds a better understanding of complex problems
- builds a better understanding of stakeholder's expectations
- promotes problem solving
- creates win/win scenarios and joint gains
- fosters action
- fosters innovation
- promotes change.

Although there are many benefits when working collaboratively it can be very difficult to achieve. Collaborative projects require stricter governance to account for shared risks. Collaboration can be time-consuming and, over time, managers may see resources dedicated to these projects better used in core business activities. Competing objectives can be hard to resolve and a high level of trust must be maintained of each party's capability, competence, engagement and commitment to the overall success of the project. Other forces such as political pressures, both from within and outside the organisation, may also affect successful collaboration. For this reason, it is important to be aware of the forces that may impact on group performance, especially in a collaborative environment.

WORKING WITH OTHERS

Understanding the forces that affect how groups perform is important when we want to know how we can manage or contribute to the group's success. Originating from the Greek *dýnamis* 'power' and *dynamikós* 'powerful', Group dynamics is the study of the processes and forces that affect how group members interact with each other (*intra*group dynamics), or between groups (*inter*group dynamics). Kurt Lewin (1946) is credited for coining the term 'group dynamics'. The study of group dynamics emerged to explore the nature of groups, their laws, establishment, development, and interactions.

Good dynamics improve individual performance in groups and a team's ability to achieve objectives. Individuals have a clear understanding of expectations and are motivated to perform. They feel a part of something larger and contribute accordingly. In teams, group members trust one another, they work towards a collective decision, and they hold one another accountable for making things happen. Research has also shown that when a team has a positive dynamic, its members are nearly twice as creative as an average group (Diehl and Stroebe 1987). In a collaborative environment, good dynamics reduce risks to all parties by creating a culture that promotes individual accountability and commitment to maximise each party's benefit realisation.

Poor dynamics prevent individuals and teams from achieving their objectives. In groups with poor dynamics performance can be reduced due to: inappropriate group structure; poor leadership; ineffective processes and functioning methodologies; poorly defined goals; and negative individual behaviour.

Understanding group dynamics is important for managers in general and for the development of L&D strategy and interventions. Often, dynamics are the root cause of performance issues. Once addressed, management practices can be developed to get the best from individuals and improve overall team performance. There are many theories, models and tools available that help towards understanding the elements that affect team dynamics. They explore the variety of organisational, contextual and individual psychological issues that affect performance. The main theories, models and tools are grouped bellow as contextual (the surrounding area in which groups operate) and psychological (predicting human behaviour by understanding psychological processes) models in Tables 3.2 and 3.3.

Table 3.2 Contextual models to understand group dynamics

	Definition	Examples
Culture	The sum of attitudes, customs, and beliefs that distinguishes one group of people from another	Hofstede (1991) O'Reilly, Chatman, and Caldwell (1991) Deal and Kennedy (1982) Schein (1992) Handy (1993) Johnson *et al* (2013)
Management processes	The methods that aid the structuring, investigation, analysis, decision making and communication of business issues	Performance management Appraisals Reward/recognition Situational leadership
Team functioning methodologies	The stated or common way in which a group works or operates	Project management Business process reengineering Collective problem solving Running meetings Information sharing Communication
Organisational structures	How activities such as task allocation, co-ordination and supervision are directed toward the achievement of organisational goals	Hierarchical Functional Matrix Network Cross-functional teams
Stakeholder models	Any person, organisation, social group, or society at large that has a stake in a business's activity	Stakeholder theory Governance structure Customer forums Feedback Representative groups

Source: Developed by authors from a variety of sources

Table 3.3 Psychological models used to understand group dynamics

	Example	Focus
Group dynamics	Lewin	Considers how people interact and the common perceptions that arise within a group.
Psychoanalysis	Freud Bion	Concerned with the (natural) defensive behaviours of team members.
FIRO/Human elements	Schutz	Considers the compatibility between people using behaviours of inclusion, control, openness, and how those behaviours relate to inner feelings of significance, competence and likeability.
Group development	The Tuckman model	Stages of group development
	Social Exchange theory	Individuals form relationships based on the implicit expectation of mutually beneficial exchanges based on trust and felt obligation. Thus, a perception that exchange relationships will be positive is essential if individuals are to be attracted to and affiliate with a group.
	Social Identity theory	Suggests that individuals get a sense of identity and self-esteem based upon their membership in salient groups. The nature of the group may be demographically based, culturally based, or organisationally based. Individuals are motivated to belong to and contribute to identity groups because of the sense of belongingness and self-worth membership in the group imparts.
Trait based theories	Myers Briggs disc	Consider how the different personality traits of individual group members affect their interactions and team performance.
Team roles	MTR-i Belbin	Examines how individuals assume different 'team' roles.

Source: Developed by authors from a variety of sources

HOW DO INDIVIDUALS CONTRIBUTE TO POOR DYNAMICS?

There are many forces affecting group dynamics that may be outside a group member's circle of influence or control such as process, set methodologies and organisational structures. However, individuals within groups do have influence and control over how they engage and work together. The most common behaviours that individuals exhibit that contribute to poor dynamics are as follows.

The **'Yes' person** wants to be seen to agree with a leader, and therefore holds back from expressing their own opinions and stops others from making new contributions.

Blocking behaviour disrupts the flow of information in the group. Types of blocking roles individuals can take are:

- The *Aggressor*: this person often disagrees with others, or is inappropriately outspoken.
- The *Negator*: this group member is often critical of others' ideas.
- The *Withdrawer*: this person doesn't participate in the discussion.
- The *Recognition seeker*: this group member is boastful, or dominates the session.
- The *Joker*: this person introduces humour at inappropriate times.

Free riding or social loafing – When group members take it easy, they may work well on their own but provide limited contributions to the group.

Evaluation apprehension – When people hold back their opinions when they feel that they are being judged excessively harshly by other group members.

Groupthink – Janis (1982) described the phenomenon that occurs when the desire for group consensus overrides an individual's desire to present alternatives, critique a position, or express an unpopular opinion.

Weak leadership – creates conditions for lack of direction, infighting, or a focus on the wrong priorities.

PROACTIVE LEADERSHIP

Reactive leaders frantically cope with the ever-changing pressures of task allocation, reduced resources and the demand for increased performance. As they react to their environment they find themselves running to put out one fire, only to be confronted with another. Proactive leaders anticipate issues, are organised and able to plan accordingly. Proactive leaders are able to manage their time and think long-term allowing them to make the best decisions, prioritising and implementing tasks. They are good listeners and communicators. Group members feel as if their opinions matter and are valued. They inspire others through their interpersonal skills and as a role model. They face issues calmly and are good at solving problems, seeking advice from both within and from outside the group. Above all proactive leaders develop group members' skills and use their strengths, not because they are nice (although they may be) but because they see it as the best way to achieve organisational objective. Strong proactive leadership is needed in all aspects of management but is especially crucial in the creation and development of effective groups and teams.

TEAM ROLES

Although we list Belbin's team roles in the psychological models table, the Belbin model (1993) it is not a psychometric but is based on many years of observable behaviour regarding the team roles that individuals may take depending on the group's make-up, individual preferred working style and the task at hand. For managers, understanding group members' ability to engage in different roles can help in the formation and development of groups and teams, identifying good team role balance and the creation of personal development plans. For more information regarding the nine team roles, visit www.belbin.com.

TUCKMAN

Bruce Tuckman (1965) identified four stages of group development: Forming, Storming, Norming, Performing. Tuckman states that the stages are necessary and inevitable in order for the team to grow by: facing up to challenges, tackling problems, finding solutions, planning work, and to deliver results. Later, Tuckman and Mary Ann Jensen (1977), added a fifth stage called Adjourning. Table 3.4 shows how proactive leaders can influence group development from one stage to another whilst considering dependencies and general issues.

Table 3.4 Tuckman's group development

Stage	Indicators	Issues	Leadership activities
Forming Dependent on leader for guidance and direction	The group is getting used to the lay of the land. Initial low-level boundary testing. Some initial confusion as to how the group will work together.	*Will I be accepted?* Why are we here? Tentative disclosure. Low group cohesion. May be high levels of excitement or apprehension. Low performance.	Set team purpose. Set clear objectives for the group. Set clear objectives for the individuals. Set clear role descriptions. Create conditions for group members to get to know each other.
Storming Independent	Individuals see themselves as part of a group. Group members become more comfortable with challenging boundaries.	*Will I be respected?* Challenge to authority. Challenge to direction. Challenge each other. Turbulent dynamics may impact group performance.	Set clear process and structures. Build trust. Remain positive. Remind group of its purpose. Resolve conflicts positively, recognising it is a natural process.
Norming Interdependent	A consensus is created as to how the group will operate. Commitment and unity are strong. Feeling of togetherness forms. Trust develops.	*How can I help the group?* Groupthink. Accept blind spots. Group members may cover for poor performers.	Shift to responsibility and accountability to group members. Continue to develop team strengths. Address weaknesses. Rotate roles to create a flexible group.
Performing Interdependent	High level of trust exists within the group. Acceptance of different view. Emergence of synergy.	*How can we do better?* Processes may become routine. Ways to improve may ignored.	Delegate. Coach. Mentor.

Stage	Indicators	Issues	Leadership activities
Adjourning	Disbanding of the group as its purpose has been achieved.	*What is next?* Insecurity. Vulnerability.	Celebrate. Reward achievements. Support.

Source: Developed by authors from a variety of sources

Although the Tuckman model is highly regarded, there are other models that also look at group development. The Drexler/Sibbert Team Performance model (Grove 2016) explores seven steps to create high performing teams (1. Orient your team members, 2. Build trust, 3. Clarify team goals, 4. Gain commitment, 5. Implement, 6. Rock the high performance, 7. Renew the team). These are similarities to Tuckman's stages but it explores those points where blockages stop groups from achieving high performance. You can find more information on this model at www.grove.com. In their paper *Creative leadership processes in project team development: an alternative to Tuckman's stage model,* Rickards and Moger (2000) explore how creative leadership is applied to 'weak' and 'strong' performance barriers.

MEETINGS

Meetings are a fact of business life as people come together to make plans or take decisions. This section will provide critical guidance on how to make the most of people's time in meetings. The value of achieving purposeful meetings when you consider the employment staff costs and numbers often involved cannot be underestimated. It is suggested that in the US $37bn (Meeting King 2015) is wasted every year on unnecessary meetings but there are also emotional costs that cannot be measured as easily.

The ability to conduct effective meetings is particularly relevant to L&D professionals, who frequently need to gather multi-source feedback from colleagues and other staff members. For example, trainers will regularly be involved in the identification of training needs. Meetings are frequently used in the process of identifying learning needs analysis (Harrison and Auluck 2014). However, much of the data collected for learning needs analysis may be sensitive, relating to the Knowledge, Skills and Attitudes (KSA) issues of an individual employee. Consequently, any learning needs analysis system must accommodate the need for respect, confidentiality and ethical application. Therefore, it is important that Trainers develop assertiveness as well as positive influencing, persuading and negotiating skills. They also need to be mindful of costs as Beevers and Rea (2010, p73) suggest: 'Few, if any, organizations have unlimited training budgets. Time spent clarifying learning needs and priorities help ensure limited resources are used to maximum effect.'

RUNNING SUCCESSFUL MEETINGS

You may recall personally the feelings of frustration from attending poorly planned meetings that can appear to waste time. This is because bad meetings can be draining for the individual. Likewise, though, good meetings can create energy, enthusiasm and motivation. Chairing meetings is frequently challenging and a good Chair needs to demonstrate a broad spectrum of skills, including: influencing, active listening, decisiveness, adaptability, assertiveness and impartiality. These skills will be covered in the section that evaluates the competencies needed to work in teams.

We have chosen to deploy an acronym to plan, organise and capture the components of a successful meeting. There are three parts to the process – ARP:

A – **Aspiration**
R – **Results**
P – **Principles**

Aspiration concerns the purpose of a meeting and agenda setting. The purpose of the Results section is to define and achieve an agreed output. The practical organisation such as choice of media, timing and who needs to be in the meeting will form part of this section. The Principle section is about achieving mutually respected outcomes. It relates to expectations about the values/ethics/behaviours, including skills in order to achieve this. Overall, ARPs remind the organiser of the key message that planning is at the heart of every successful meeting.

Before ARPs are discussed in greater detail it is relevant to highlight the often espoused belief that 'no idea is a bad idea'. The inference being that everyone should be free to share their thoughts. However, whilst this may be true in the majority of circumstances and especially in creative settings, pragmatically this may not always be possible. For example, on occasions boundaries such as financial constraints may make some ideas impossible to implement.

REFLECTIVE ACTIVITY 3.2

Personal experience of meetings

In small groups share with one or more others an experience of a meeting that you attended and feel could have been improved in some way. Discuss what happened and what could be improved.

ASPIRATION

Every participant needs a clear understanding of the purpose of the meeting, most likely achieved through the production of an agenda, so that they can come prepared to be able to fully contribute. It is also important to choose the most appropriate type of meeting to fit the purpose and achieve the preferred outcome.

Types of meeting

Following a synthesis of a number of sources we would suggest that the majority of meetings can be classified into four different types: Decision making, Information Giving/Sharing, Information Gathering and Problem Solving. The authors have used a classification system in order to assist with determining the most appropriate type of meeting to be deployed.

To help the meeting co-ordinator two dimensions are included in this classification system: Involvement and Structure, as per Figure 3.3. The Involvement axis measures the degree of involvement of participants needed either before or during a meeting. This could be determined by asking questions such as 'How much freedom is there for the participants to change decisions'? The structure axis is concerned with the degree of structure needed before and during the meeting. Although all meetings will need a structure, we suggest that the extent of this will depend on the type of meeting. For example, one consideration is whether the meeting objectives are more likely to be achieved through a formal, logical and mechanistic structure or allowing more freedom.

Figure 3.3 Types of meeting – degree of involvement and structure

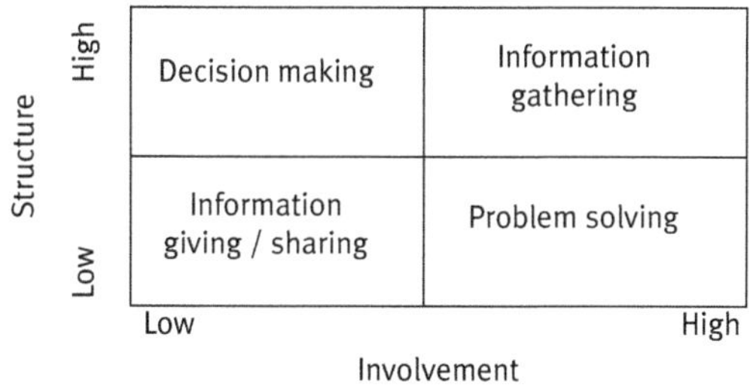

Information giving meetings

Information giving/sharing meetings tend to be the most straightforward type. It is where one or more people share ideas. In the case of training this could be one person sharing their knowledge with others, such as how to manage a task. Traditionally, those in attendance at this type of meeting are passive listeners, the information tends to be factual and the meeting fairly formal. The aim of the meeting is to convey a specific message and for members to understand this. This does not mean that there is no room for discussion, but this would be within a relatively defined contextual setting. Visual communication, such as slides, are useful to help convey the message.

Low structure/low involvement. This type of meeting could be conducted with low to medium degree of structure either formally or informally. Generally, it is the responsibility of one person to organise and, therefore, the involvement of others to make change is constrained.

Information gathering meetings

The purpose of this meeting is to gather information. This section will use the example of identifying learning needs, adapted from one of the authors' chapter (Harrison and Auluck 2014) owing to it being a core role of a trainer. In practice this stage of evaluating learning needs is often characterised by a 'diagnostic' element underpinned by a process of information gathering and analysis (Leat and Lovell 1997, Iqbal and Khan 2011).

High structure/high involvement. It is important to have a clear structure and clarity of process. The participation of others is essential and therefore this is high involvement.

Problem solving/creativity meetings

The main purpose of the problem solving/creativity meetings are to enable experienced and knowledgeable people to generate ideas. A variety of techniques such as quality management type tools (Total Quality Management Weekly 2015), and brainstorming can be usefully deployed. In the context of problem solving the concept that no idea is a bad idea works well. However, this is not always the case owing to other resource implications.

Low structure/high involvement. This type of meeting can tolerate a low to medium structure to accommodate creative ideas. High involvement of individuals is essential to create momentum.

Decision-making meetings

It can be useful to hold a separate decision-making meeting with this as a core purpose. For example, it can be more efficient for key stakeholders with authority, whose time is most costly to the organisation. There are different types of group decision-making processes, and care should be taken to choose a process that best matches the situation. A decision-making process could involve evaluating options, ranking preferences, and voting. In the context of training this could be used to sign off budgets, make final decisions on management training programmes etc.

High structure/low involvement. There is a clear agenda to this meeting, which will have a high structure. It is likely that the participation of members will be limited to those who have the power to make the final decision.

RESULTS

This concerns the desired outcome of the meeting. Prior to the meeting the organiser should have a plan of what is to be achieved from the meeting. For example, a team may wish to create an action plan, determine key responsibilities or define research areas. Essentially the practical aspects of organising the meeting will help to achieve the results.

There are many practical aspects to organise a meeting such as:

- organising a joint agenda by encouraging participant contributions
- allocate times to the agenda items
- adhere to proposed timings
- agree start and finish times
- stick to start and finish times
- create an expectation that participants will come prepared to contribute
- make known on the agenda the priority items – use a classification system.

A further aspect of the practical section is the choice of media. Advancements in technology have contributed to changes in the nature, processes and methods of work. With the global shift from an industrial-based workforce to a more knowledge-based workforce (Drucker 1998), combined with a global talent base, it is likely that discerning skills to hold e-meetings will be essential.

Traditional face-to-face meetings are being replaced with telephone, video conferencing and other electronic mechanisms such as MeetingBurner, which is one of the fifteen methods acknowledged by Fance (2015).

There are a variety of media tools that can be webcast, whereby live or delayed sound is delivered over the Internet. Users will frequently have a camera on their laptop so that they can not only communicate but also share information such as spreadsheets or PowerPoints. Frequently, online tools such as Outlook are used to organise meetings, too.

With globalisation and the increased use of online meeting and web conferencing tools there are other considerations. Online tools such as 'Every Time Zone' (Every Time Zone 2015) can be usefully deployed when organising meetings across time zones. World Time Zone (World Time Zone 2015) works in a similar way but it is possible to type in specific places.

 REFLECTIVE ACTIVITY 3.3

Media tools

There are tools for synchronised communication (everyone at the same time), such as Sqwiggle or webcast, and for asynchronous communication (everyone at their own pace), such as Trello and Hackpad. In the latter form of communication people can work at their own pace and leave questions for others. Using the Web explore these tools and identify other options.

PRINCIPLES

This is the widest reaching area and possibly something that is overlooked, although, like culture, it is frequently binding (Bratton 2015). Ethics/values relate to the behaviour of the participants: how they treat and respect each other. For example, there may be a rule that laptops will be down and mobiles turned off.

If you search for how to conduct meetings on the Internet, there is no shortage of advice and therefore it is strange that many people can still recall attending ineffective meetings. One significant reason is the varying psychological components involved. Also, in meetings of more than three people individuals can behave differently (Belbin 1993). It is important therefore to verbally agree principles of behaviour or conduct that team members will abide by. For example, members arriving on time and being in the present, that is, not answering telephone calls or checking messages. On occasions this may require the co-ordinator to manage egos and control airtime of more vocal members.

Ultimately, the necessary skills to organise and manage meetings are underestimated. Skills such as diplomacy, open-mindedness, objective and non-judgemental listening are all needed to successfully chair a meeting, notwithstanding good organisation skills to set up and monitor outputs. Another aspect that has been largely under researched and overlooked is the impact of emotion. According to Feng and Maitlis (2014) much of the research has focused on the emotional displays of one person, typically the meeting co-ordinator, and less on team members. However, emotional displays can have powerful effects on group dynamics and processes such as decision making.

 REFLECTIVE ACTIVITY 3.4

Mini case study: global meetings

Joe Money is an International Manager who regularly holds international meetings. In this case example, he chaired one of the meetings that involved 50 employee representatives from all the major European countries. The purpose of the meeting was to share information and the meeting lasted two hours. The organisation uses webcast. With this tool it is possible to see the names of people in the call, to share and edit work. Participants were invited to the call using Outlook calendar. This tool is a very efficient way to organise and manage meetings. There are a number of potential issues, however, that the organiser needs to be aware of, such as time zone issues. For example, in this case, there is a three-hour time difference between Moscow and Siberia. Also, the varying accents of the participants can be problematic so the organiser uses the skill of summarising in writing regularly throughout the call. A further issue is that participants do not have access to any potential emotional dilemmas, for instance, in this call, there were representatives from Russia and the Ukraine.

Question

In groups of three or four identify the elements of ARPs in this case study. Discuss the challenges of conducting meetings with time zone differences such as China and the USA.

TECHNIQUES FOR INFLUENCING, PERSUADING AND NEGOTIATING

This section will highlight the core techniques needed not only to chair meetings but also to successfully work in teams.

When considering the role of a trainer it is likely that influencing techniques are routinely deployed. This is because the role is largely dependent on working and encouraging others. On some occasions people, for example Senior Management, may need to be persuaded of the benefits of training. At other times skills will be needed to negotiate with line managers who need to balance operational concerns and training.

INFLUENCING

One definition of influencing is *'the power to change or affect someone or something without directly forcing it to happen and without apparent effort'*. In his book on persuasion and influence, Professor Robert Cialdini (1984) gives rules (scarcity, reciprocity, authority, similarity, commitment and consistency) that govern how we influence and are influenced by others.

Scarcity

The rule of scarcity will influence the perceived value of something. For example, if people are told that there is only one place left on a training course they will more likely be interested. This is because the course is then perceived as being sought after – it must be valuable as others want it. Price also works in this context. If something is expensive, buyers tend to assume it is high quality and in demand.

Reciprocity

The basis of this rule is that people will feel compelled or obligated to give something back if they are given something. Salesmen are taught to offer a three-year warranty first because then when customers are offered a one-year cheaper option they are more likely to purchase it. Providing training support for a challenging member of staff could encourage a manager to support a training function's request.

Authority

People are more likely to take advice from those that they perceive to be experts, possibly, one reason for the increase in occupations who wish to be deemed professions. Attaining the CIPD qualification is one way of gaining knowledge and making others aware through, for example, a plaque on the wall. The reason why people tend to obey authority is deep-seated and learned from parents, school etc.

Similarity

People tend to like people who they perceive to be more like than dissimilar to them (Jeffery 2014), for example, in terms of background, experience, interest. Trainers will frequently be working with an age-diverse population so one tip is to try to find something in common with the person. Remembering and using people's names is helpful too.

Commitment and consistency

People prefer those who keep their promises. Stickability, doing what someone says they will do, is highlighted in Mental Toughness (Clough and Strycharczyk 2012). People who stick to what they say they are going to do are more likely to behave consistently, which is often associated with honesty and fairness. Therefore developing personal commitment will not only help the person influence others but will also help them develop resilience that is particularly useful in times of adversity.

PERSUASION

A working definition of persuasion is when someone induces someone else to do something through using reasoning or argument. Effective persuasion is similar to influencing, recognising in particular the role of commitment and consistency. According to (Kunnanatt 2008) the elements that enable someone to persuade another person are largely emotional, such as being sincere and honest. In order for someone to be persuaded they must make a change in their attitude, belief or value. Therefore, they must believe that it is the right thing to do. In essence this fits with the concept Emotional Intelligence that was developed in the 1990s (Goleman 1996, Goleman 1998) who claimed that the concept of 'rational' intelligence ignores emotional competencies. EI is the ability to identify, integrate, understand and reflectively manage one's own and other people's feelings.

Figure 3.4 Emotional Intelligence

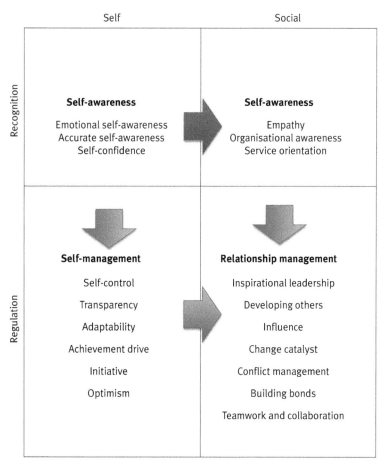

Source: Adapted from Goleman *el al* (2013)

There are four dimensions of EI as shown in Figure 3.4. Self-awareness concerns the ability to recognise and understand one's own emotions, as well as understanding the effect that these moods have on others. Social awareness is the ability to understand the view point of others and those around us. Self-management concerns the ability to control disruptive thoughts and feelings, whilst relationship management is how an individual effectively manages relationships and builds networks.

The purpose of a negotiation is normally to work out a deal that is suitable for both parties. It is a process that will often involve a degree of compromise in order to reach an agreement, whilst aiming to avoid disputes. It is also important to recognise that negotiation occurs in a formal and informal way, frequently on a regular basis. The challenge is that individuals have their own personal view of the preferred outcome that can differ quite considerably. However, by adopting sound principles such as fairness, mutual understanding and a commitment to maintaining a healthy long term relationship, it is possible to achieve a mutually satisfying outcome.

In order to be successful in negotiation a structured approach can help. The following stages of a negotiation are useful in practice:

Preparation

This stage involves analysing:

Goals – What do both parties wish to get out of the negotiation? If the others' wants are unknown it is necessary to try and second-guess them.

Options – Consider all options and alternatives. Weigh up the strengths and weaknesses of possible alternative options. What are the preferred outcomes?

Relationships – Identify the depth of the relationship, including perhaps historical landmarks. Also, is there a preference to sustain a long-term relationship and the possible consequences of not doing so? In terms of the trainer it is frequently the case that the relationship will need to be sustained so it is important to maintain a balanced position.

Compromise – Consider the possible consequences of each action.

Discussion

There are fundamental key skills of listening and questioning that are needed as both parties put forward the position as they view it. This is when the adage 'there is a reason why there are two ears and one mouth' is important. During the discussion it is essential to articulate and recognise the preferred goals of each party.

Win-win outcome

In order to gain a win-win outcome both sides must feel that they have gained something, despite sometimes this being different to their original intentions. The perceived gain is important to maintaining future positive relationships. If a win-win is not possible then a compromise can be a positive alternative.

Agreement

Preferably agreements should be placed in writing so that both sides have clarity of the outcomes.

People can think that they are assertive, however, it is not always easy to identify truly assertive behaviour. This is because sometimes there is a fine line between aggressive or passive and assertive behaviour. The background to this behaviour lies in what is commonly known as the fight or flight instinct (Lavoie 2016). In many ways passive is the opposite of aggressive behaviour as highlighted in the following definitions:

Aggressive Behaviour

This is when people behave in a way that means they get what they want but at the expense of another's feelings, wants and needs.

Passive Behaviour

This is when people behave in a way that means they end up doing what someone else wants, regardless of their own feelings, wants and needs.

Assertiveness is different as it is a response and is about balancing the needs of others and one's own rights. Figure 3.5 illustrates the individual nature of passive, aggressive and assertive behaviour. Furthermore, the arrows indicate movement and flow between the styles. However, the evidence of innate passive or aggressive behaviours results in the need of individuals to make a choice to behave in an assertive manner. Individuals need to learn how to behave in an assertive way, the benefits of which can help people achieve internal psychological health as well as improve relationships with others.

Figure 3.5 Drivers of assertiveness

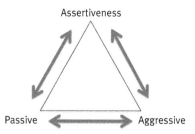

One of the issues is that when learning from a textbook, it is possible to overlook the fact that the definitions tend to represent behaviour at one (normally the extreme) end of a continuum. For example, the extreme end of aggressive behaviour maybe typified by a person shouting and looking angry. It can seem obvious that the person is more interested in their opinion and desire to dominate the situation. However, someone could behave aggressively but in a quiet, controlled, albeit manipulative manner. This type of behaviour often typifies bullies who are less overt but have the same aim: to get their own way.

If someone behaves in an assertive way during or following communication with another individual both will feel satisfied as the outcome of assertive behaviour is a win-win situation. The person being communicated with will know that they have been listened to, that their voice has been heard. Listening is an essential skill for virtually all communication and takes priority in the method explored in the next section.

Simple assertiveness techniques

Three of the most simple assertiveness techniques that can be used to deal with the majority of situations will be included:

Say 'no'

Many people find saying 'no' the most challenging word to say. This is frequently owing to anxiety about the possible response or fear of causing upset to someone else. However, despite these reservations often people prefer a straight answer as they then know where they stand in the situation. It can also save time, avoid conflict and be more respectful.

The broken record

This is a technique that is often used by children. One of the authors recalls a conversation that their child was having with their friend in the backseat of the car. The child's friend asked 'How many times does it take before your mum says yes?' My child pondered this and replied 'Dad about four and Mum about seven!' The child had learned that by asking the same question a number of times they would eventually get the answer they wanted. The broken record technique involves repeating the message. It is a technique frequently used in journalism. The disadvantage of this method is that it can be exasperating for the parties involved.

Fogging

Fogging is more likely to be used when someone is behaving aggressively. In fogging the purpose is to find minor points of agreement. The result is that the person can get distracted and find it difficult to disagree when the individual is agreeing with them, even if it is in a small way. An example of fogging might be:

Comment: You are always late.
Response: Yes, occasionally I am late. However, I am also frequently the person who is last in the office at night.

 REFLECTIVE ACTIVITY 3.5

Assertiveness role plays

In small groups role play one of the following situations. Try and use different ends of the continuum in your role play.

- 'Why didn't you give me more notice?' Asked in an irritable tone of voice (**AGGRESSIVE**)
- 'I'm terribly sorry, I don't think I can today, I'm behind with my work and I've promised to go over to Michael's. Also, I normally call in at my Dad's house on a Tuesday . . .I'm awfully sorry' and you feel guilty afterwards. Or say 'Oh all right, if you feel like doing it now. . . .' (**PASSIVE**)
- 'I can't manage today, there is a very important meeting – I'll pop in tomorrow and we can arrange a definite time then.' (**ASSERTIVE**)

If you prefer to use visual situations, follow the link to ten assertiveness scenarios https://www.youtube.com/watch?v=Ymm86c6DAF4.

Additional sources for developing assertiveness are available on sites such as YouTube. Consider the impact of body language and assertiveness in the following YouTube clip: https://www.youtube.com/watch?v=TdU2l0i2Wh0 or communication and assertiveness: https://www.youtube.com/watch?v=9zbt_9R8GrM.

MANAGING RELATIONSHIPS

People are bombarded with stimuli that need to be processed in some way. Perception helps us to do this. Perception is defined by Bratton (2015:125) as *'the process of selecting, organising and interpreting information in order to make sense of the world around us'*. On the one hand perception helps the brain to remain stable but on the other hand can cause individuals to unfairly judge others. One of the most common perceptual errors, stereotyping, will be explored as this is particularly relevant to working in groups.

As the neurological processing involved in perception is undertaken by a human who has feelings and emotions, it is different to that of a computer. Hence, two people may appear to experience a similar event but may recall or think of it very differently. The reason for this may include prior experience, circumstances, expectations or personality. As there is a significant number of stimuli to process, perceptual error can be a regular occurrence. One common perceptual error is stereotyping, developed by Lippmann (1922), where people are placed in a category – for example, ALL French people strike regularly. According to Jeffery (2014) this can be caused by unconscious bias.

Theory of unconscious bias suggests that when an individual meets or sees someone they will place them in one of two categories: in-group (people like them) or an out-group (people they find threatening). People then use the out-group to stereotype which leads to bias (Jeffery 2014). The physical process stems from the use of the amygdala, which is a set of neurons that form a region in the medial temporal lobe, roughly in the centre of the brain. The role of the amygdala is to isolate the emotion linked to an idea. It looks for the neural pathway that leads to the right association and we can use a default pathway. However, when the brain is overloaded, or when we depend on impulse, we do not use the part of the brain that controls for bias.

In the workplace, the differences in roles, responsibilities and rewards associated with being either an employer or an employee mean that there are perpetual challenges. Nevertheless, perceived unfair treatment can lead to disharmony and, at an extreme level, industrial action.

Despite the issues with perception it is an essential human dimension, helping people to make judgements, despite extensive quantity of individuals. Ultimately, perception helps to protect individuals from suffering mental illness, maintaining the balance of the brain.

 REFLECTIVE ACTIVITY 3.6

Team perceptions

In what ways can the individual perceptions of the team members affect those within and outside the team?

POLITICS AND POWER

Political awareness is an important ability for all employees to possess. The ability to know the right person to talk to, to agree or disagree with, even the right meetings to attend is important when navigating through an organisational environment. Some people in organisations have greater influence and authority, often deemed as power. Effective managers need to be aware of the sources of power within their organisation and be able to work within and through this.

According to Raven (2008) individuals with authority draw their power from the following:

- **Reward** power – control over finance and other valued resources
- **Coercive** power – those who have the capacity to manipulate and dominate others
- **Legitimate** power – provided from formal, hierarchical position
- **Referent** power – given by others because someone is liked and has developed personal influence
- **Expert** power – one of the basis of all professions is knowledge. People with knowledge who are perceived to be an expert by others.

In order to achieve organisational objectives it is necessary to understand those who have power in the organisation. Effective networking is based on one's ability to identify and influence those with authority.

Negative organisational politics are behaviours that individuals and informal groups engage in in order to protect their self-interests at the expense of others and/or the organisation. These behaviours usually manifest when people either no longer trust that they are valued or are looking for an increased level of authority, influence or power. There are many ways that these behaviours manifest such as the political techniques and tactics listed below:

- gatekeeping
- controlling the agenda
- game playing
- building coalitions
- exchange of favours
- rituals and symbols
- using policies and procedures as a tool
- grapevine communications.

Addressing these behaviours head-on with integrity and true power is fundamental if group and organisational goals and objectives are to be achieved.

REFLECTIVE ACTIVITY 3.7

Politics and power

1 Discuss the types of power and how they can be both positive and negative.

2 Have you seen the effect that negative organisational politics can have on people and on organisational objectives?

3 Have you had an experience of negative organisational politics? If so what was your reaction?

4 How might you address negative organisational politics?

5 Are we inadvertently engaged in negative organisational politics?

BUILDING AND SUSTAINING POSITIVE RELATIONSHIPS

Creating and maintaining healthy productive relationships both within and outside the L&D function is important to enable the HR professional to move freely, both vertically and horizontally, through organisational structures. Not all ideas, processes and training initiatives will be openly accepted by those that you engage. Depending on the perceived value added that you might provide, managers may seem reluctant to release people resources as this may impact on short-term group goals.

Developing relationships and your network will help to move through, reduce or even remove the barriers that you may encounter. Good relationships presuppose trust and integrity in what you have to offer. Good networks help you where you may not yet have an area of influence. Having a good network moving up the organisational hierarchy also adds credibility and your perceived 'expert' power. The relationships also provide a conduit for feedback and the intelligence that may help you achieve your objectives.

Building and sustaining these relationships may be as important as the skills, services and processes that you present. A Personal Network Map (Figure 3.6), based on the concept of a sociogram, is a pictorial representation of your network. It is similar to a stakeholder map (sometimes called an influence map in project management) in that it shows the importance of each contact, the type of relationship of the contact and the amount of influence that you or they have on others. This will help to pinpoint where you may need to develop your network and influence. After all, who you know is as important as what you know.

Figure 3.6 Personal Network Map

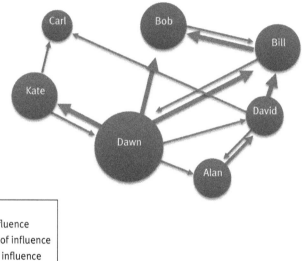

Key
Circle size = overall influence
Line direction = effect of influence
Line size = strength of influence

 REFLECTIVE ACTIVITY 3.8

Personal Network Map

Think of a situation where you need to influence others.

Can you directly influence them?

List everyone who is directly or indirectly involved in the situation.

What influence do they have in the situation?

What relationships do you need to develop or utilise?

RELATIONSHIPS AND CONFLICT

There will be times that we all encounter a difficult person or functional conflict. How we handle this barrier should be seen as an opportunity to develop your relationships. It is very easy to confront this type of barrier with the same energy or react in a way that will cause further difficulties in the future by breaking the relationship. The TKI Model or Thomas-Kilmann Conflict Mode Instrument (Kilmann and Thomas 1977) helps individuals to identify conflict styles and develop strategies to defuse conflict, creating more productive results. The model explores five conflict modes within two axes (co-operativeness and assertiveness). Each of the modes sits within the two-dimensional axis shown in Figure 3.7.

Figure 3.7 Thomas-Kilmann Instrument (TKI)

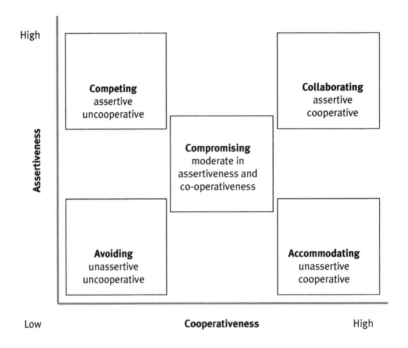

Source: CPP TKI

Avoiding *is both unassertive and uncooperative:*

- You side-step the conflict without trying to satisfy either person's concern.
- You withdraw from the conflict or attempt to sweep it under the carpet.

Forcing/competing *is assertive and uncooperative:*

- You impose your solution on the problem, satisfying your own concerns at the other person's expense.

Accommodating *is unassertive and co-operative:*

- You attempt to satisfy the other person's concern at the expense of your own.
- You concede the issue without a fight, to preserve harmony.

Compromising *is intermediate in both assertiveness and co-operation:*

- You use bargaining or negotiation so that each party trades some concessions for some gains.

Collaborating *is both assertive and co-operative:*

- You work together to find an outcome that meets the clearly stated needs of both parties as far as possible.

Kilmann and Thomas found that we all have the ability to use all of the modes but we use some modes more often based on temperament and personal predisposition. Using this model helps navigate individual conflicts and provides a tool to help facilitate functional or intergroup conflicts.

REFLECTIVE ACTIVITY 3.9

TKI

How often do you demonstrate each mode?

What situations are best for each mode?

How do we deal with others when they demonstrate each mode's typical behaviour?

How can you use this information to plan for a difficult situation?

PRESENTATION AND REPORT WRITING

Two of the core skills needed in working with others is presentation and report writing. Effective presentation skills will be considered initially, followed by report writing.

PRESENTATION SKILLS

Effective presentations skills are important to enable the communication of accurate messages. Most people worry about standing up in front of people. This is a natural fear but one that can be overcome with preparation and practice. The key is to gain experience. We would strongly advise that learners, rather than shy away from presenting, take every opportunity to practice and gain experience. Eventually, the individual will build up resilience that will help them to feel more in control and more confident.

The following is a step-by-step plan of action to develop a presentation:

1   Clarify the purpose of the presentation (audience).

2   Research and collate the content (use total quality techniques mentioned in meetings section).

3   Structure the content into a logical order (sections, headings, order).

4   Decide how to present the information (style, accessories, equipment, video).

5   Prepare presentation (wording, structure, opening, middle, close).

6   Practise and rehearse (get feedback, clarify).

7   Plan the venue, control the environment.

8   Do a 'dress rehearsal' if warranted (predict questions).

9   De-stress and prepare yourself – confidence and control.

Learning theory from the work of Buzan and Buzan (2010) found that people remember more when points are repeated or stand out because they are different. They will also remember less from the middle of the learning event, and more from the beginning and end. Therefore, remember to always use the following guidelines:

- **OPENING** – Tell them what you are going to tell them.
- **MIDDLE** – Tell them.
- **CLOSE** – Tell them what you told them.

The opening should grab the audience's attention, for example by using intriguing data or a caption. It must also introduce the topic and purpose. The close should also be designed to catch the audience's attention and follow logically from the opening. Another important aspect of the close is to thank the audience.

There are greater opportunities to use technology, such as Prezi, in presentations and communication generally as discussed later in this chapter.

REPORT WRITING

A good report will be clear, concise, complete and correct. In essence, it will:

- tell the reader, that is, answer the question posed
- be easy to understand
- be easy to read.

In order to produce a good report the authors have produced recommended steps to be taken before, during the writing process and at the end (see Table 3.5). The steps encourage the writer to maintain a focus on the purpose of the report and requirements of the reader.

Table 3.5 Steps in the report writing process

Timing	What/Who	Reflective questions
Before	Reader	Who is he/she? What does he/she want? Why should he/she read it?
	Writer	Why am I writing this? What do I know?
	Material	Where is the information? Who can help? How do I put it together?
	Style	Active/passive
	Structure	Think of the reader. Write so that it follows his/her requirements.
Writing	Language	K.I.S.S. (Keep it simple, stupid) phrases Jargon – will everyone understand?
	Presentation	Neat, clean, well laid out e. g. spelling, punctuation
During	Revision	24-hour rule (ask a friend to read it)
	Final check	

It is notoriously difficult to notice mistakes in your own work. We therefore recommend that the writer waits 24 hours before checking their personal work or, better still, asks someone else to read it.

A simple report structure includes:

- executive summary (if lengthy report)
- aims and objectives/introduction
- main body/findings

- conclusions
- recommendations
- appendices.

A simple business case includes:

- executive summary
- introduction
- problem statement
- analysis of the situation
- options and benefit analysis
- recommendations
- conclusion.

The introduction should clearly outline the purpose of the report. The findings should be factual and evidence based. The conclusion can contain opinion. In the recommendations section there should be no new information added.

USING TECHNOLOGY TO COMMUNICATE AND INCREASE COLLABORATION

Presentations and reports are important forms of communication. As we move forward into the digital age we are becoming more reliant on technology to communicate. Although the quality of the content may not be improving, our ability to instantly share ideas, influence others and work with group members who are no longer sitting next to us is. We can communicate with our smartphone, which allows us to call, text, send emails and make video calls wherever we are. The Web provides simple tools to collaborate on documents such as Google Docs and Dropbox and there is an industry devoted to Cloud Collaboration platforms. Microsoft recently bought Yammer for $1.2bn to make its product SharePoint more marketable. The only constraint on the use of this technology is the restrictions put in place by organisations who are concerned about commercially sensitive data being leaked or lost. Finding the right technology solutions to increase collaboration is becoming a key strategic issue for the HR professional and organisational security teams.

SUMMARY

This chapter provides an overview of the essential skills required to manage and work within a team, as well as to work with others.

Although many reference books will use the terms teams and groups interchangeably the difference is summarised in Table 3.1. The primary difference is the interdependency level and all that this involves in group situations. Understanding group dynamics is essential in both being a part of and managing groups and teams in order to improve performance.

In many bureaucracies, political skills at all levels of a hierarchy are evident to a greater or lesser degree. The chapter highlights the relevance of this for HRD practitioners who are frequently working in roles where they need to influence others. The power skills identified by Raven (2008) are useful in political behaviour. However, assertiveness, persuasion and negotiating skills also play a necessary and critical role.

The meetings section is essentially practical in nature, providing guidance on how to conduct meetings from a local and international perspective. The process of ARPs as recommended in the chapter was developed through anecdotal evidence gathered from practitioners, primarily employed in multinational organisations. Adopting the skills suggested will significantly help the productivity of a department and the wider organisation, owing to the financial costs in terms of time when more than one employee is working together.

Paramount to all the topics and skills is the need for managers and the HRD practitioner to be able to adjust the practitioner's style according to the individual and situation.

REFERENCES

BEEVERS, K. and REA, A. (2010) *Learning and Development in Practice.* London: CIPD.

BELBIN, R. M. (1993) *Team roles at Work.* Oxford: Butterworth Heinemann.

BRATTON, J. (2015) *Introduction to Work and Organizational Behaviour.* 3rd ed. London: Palgrave.

BULUT, C. and CULHA, O. (2010) 'The effects of organizational training and organizational commitment', *International Journal of Training and Development.* Vol 14, No 4, pp309–322.

BUZAN, T. and BUZAN, B. (2010) *The Mind Map Book: Unlock Your Creativity, Boost Your Memory, Change Your Life.* London: Pearson.

CIALDINI, R. (1984) *Influence: The Psychology of Persuasion.* New York: William Morrow & Co Inc.

CLOUGH, P. and STRYCHARCZYK, D. (2012) *Developing Mental Toughness.* London: Kogan Page.

DEAL, T. and KENNEDY, A. (1982) *Corporate Cultures – The rites and rituals of corporate life.* USA: Addison-Wesley.

DIEHL, M. and STROEBE, W. (1987) 'Productivity loss in brainstorming groups: Toward the solution of a riddle', *Journal of Personality and Social Psychology.* Vol 53, No 3, pp497–509.

DRUCKER, P. (1998) 'Management's new paradigm', *Forbes*, Vol 162, No 7.

Every Time Zone (2015) [online]. Available at: everytimezone.com/#2015–11–3,155,cn3 [Accessed 2 September 2016].

FANCE, C. (2015) *Online Meeting and Web Conferencing Tools – Best Of* [online], Available at: http://www.hongkiat.com/blog/online-meeting-tools/ [Accessed 11 November 2016].

FENG, L. and MAITLIS, S. (2014) 'Emotional Dynamics and Strategizing Processes: A Study of Strategic Conversations in Top Team Meetings', *Journal of Management Studies*, Vol 51, No 2.

GOLEMAN, D. (1996) *Emotional Intelligence.* London: Bloomsbury.

GOLEMAN, D. (1998) 'What makes a leader?', *Harvard Business Review*, pp93–102.

GOLEMAN, D., BOYATZIS, R. and MCKEE, A. (2013) *Primal Leadeship: Unleashing the Power of Emotional Intelligence.* Boston, MA: Harvard Business School Press.

Grove (2016) *Drexler/Sibbet Team Performance Model* [online], Available at: http://www.grove.com/ourwk_gm_tp.html [accessed 3 May 2016].

HANDY, C. (1993) *Understanding Organisations.* 3rd ed. London: Penguin.

HARRISON, P. and AULUCK, R. (2014) Identifying Learning Needs. In STEWART, J. and CURETON, P. (eds). *Designing, Delivering and Evaluating L&D: Essentials for Practice.* London: CIPD.

HOFSTEDE, G. (1991) *Cultures and organizations: Software of the mind.* London: McGraw-Hill.

IQBAL, M. Z. and KHAN, R. A. (2011) The Growing Concept of Training Needs Assessment: a review with proposed model, *Journal of European Industrial Training.* Vol 35, No 5.

JANIS, I. L. (1982) *Victims of Groupthink.* Boston, MA: Houghton Mifflin.

JEFFERY, R. (2014) The Neuroscience of Bias: Diet cola makes you (even) more racist. *People Management.* No 22, pp22–26.

JOHNSON, G., WHITTINGTON, R., SCHOLES, K., ANGWEN, D. and REGNER, P. (2013) *Exploring Strategy Texts and Cases.* 10th ed. London: Pearson.

KATZENBACH, J. and SMITH, D. (2005) The Discipline of Teams. *Harvard Business Review.*

KILMANN, R.H. and THOMAS, K.W. (1977) Developing a Forced-Choice Measure of Conflict-Handling Behavior: The 'Mode' Instrument. *Educational and Psychological Measurement.* 37, pp309–325.

KUNNANATT, J. T. (2008) Emotional intelligence: theory and description. *Career Development International.* Vol 13, No 7, pp614–629.

LAVOIE, S. (2016) *Walter Cannon: Stress and Fight or Flight Theories* [online], Available at: http://study.com/academy/lesson/walter-cannon-stress-fight-or-flight-theories.html [Accessed 3 May 2016].

LEAT, M. J. and LOVELL, M. J. (1997) Training Needs Analysis: weakness in the conventional approach. *Journal of European Industrial Training.* Vol 21, No 4, pp143–153.

LEWIN, K. (1946) Action research and minority problems, *Journal of Social Issues.* Vol 2, No 4, pp34–46.

LIPPMAN, W. (1922) *Public Opinion.* New York: Free Press.

Meeting King (2015) [online], Available at: meetingking.com/37-billion-per-year-unnecessary-meetings-share/ [Accessed 3 November 2015].

O'REILLY, C., CHATMAN, J. and CALDWELL, D. (1991) People and Organisational Culture: A profile comparison approach to assessing people-organisation fit. *Academy of Management Journal.* Vol 34, No 3, pp487–516.

RAVEN, B. (2008) The Bases of Power and the Power/Interaction Model of Interpersonal Influence. *Analyses of Social Issues and Public Policy.* Vol 8, No 1.

RICKARDS, T. and MOGER, S. (2000) Creative Leadership Processes in Project Team Development: An Alternative to Tuckman's Stage Model. *British Journal of Management.* Vol 11, No 4, pp273–283.

SCHRAGE, M. (1995) *No More Teams!* New York: Bantam Doubleday Dell Publishing Group.

Total Quality Management Weekly (2015) *Total Quality Management (TQM) Tools* [online]. Available at: Totalqualitymanagement.weebly.com/tqm-tools.html [Accessed 3 November 2015].

TUCKMAN, B. (1965) Development sequence in small groups. *Psychological Review.* No 63, pp384–399.

TUCKMAN, B. and JENSON, M. (1977) Stages of small group development revisited. *Group and Organizational Studies.* 2, pp419–427.

World Time Zone (2015) [online], Available at: www.worldtimezone.com [Accessed 2 September 2016].

CHAPTER 4

Applying CPD Techniques to Devise, Implement and Review a Personal Development Plan

RACHEL ROBINS

CHAPTER OVERVIEW

- Introduction
- The importance of CPD for professionals in a changing environment
- Using reflective practice to enrich your CPD process
- Stages of the CPD Cycle
- CPD Learning Logs
- Sustaining the motivation for CPD
- Summary

LEARNING OUTCOMES

By the end of this chapter you will be able to:

- undertake a self-assessment of L&D capabilities to identify development needs
- select a justified option for professional development
- produce a plan to meet development objectives
- reflect on performance against the CPD plan, identifying any further learning needs and revise the plan accordingly.

INTRODUCTION

Continuing Professional Development (CPD) is an essential activity in order to be a credible professional and this is the case especially when that professional is employed in Learning and Development (L&D). CPD can assist in career development and help professionals achieve a high professional standard required by employers today. It can ensure that you keep your skills up to date and prepare you for your next role.

In this chapter I propose a rationale for CPD for the L&D practitioner, illustrating why professionals require evidence of their professional development and what it adds to their ability to deliver a quality service for their employer. This will also include analysing the role of reflective practice and how it contributes to the completion of an effective CPD log. There are of course many different approaches to reflective practice that have been developed over a number of years and the chapter will explore these approaches and how they can be used by L&D practitioners to achieve a deeper and more engaged understanding of our own learning and its effectiveness.

The effectiveness of our learning becomes increasingly more important in the current turbulent times of change in our environment. More recently, these have been brought about by issues such as financial instability, company mergers, greater use of technology by consumers and employees and the flexibility demanded by both customers and the workforce. This list that illustrates the need for CPD to be effective and conducted in an efficient way, could almost be endless as organisations try to come to terms with changing environment, changing employee and customer expectations, and a national skills shortage in many disciplines.

There is of course not only an obligation for CPD to be undertaken as part of the employer/employee relations, but also a much wider obligation. There are many professions (for example, the Law Society and the General Pharmaceutical Council in the UK) that require their members to undertake a defined number of CPD hours hours in year in order to continue practice. CIPD, the professional body for the L&D practitioner, has a policy on CPD (CIPD 2015a) that contains essential principles. A key element of the principles is that, as a member of CIPD you will regularly invest time and learning as a key part of your professional life and that this is not an optional extra. There is therefore not only an obligation for the profession to ensure that there is a framework and requirements for CPD for its members but also an obligation from L&D practitioners to engage in CPD to ensure that they continue their personal development.

Later in the chapter we will consider the implications of the commitment to lifelong and self-managed learning and the options for professional development that are available. This will include identifying the sources of information that are available to practitioners about their personal effectiveness which is a key element reflective practice and the use of CPD. The chapter will then conclude by illustrating how to design a meaningful personal development plan and identify several examples of what these can look like.

There is a clear process to guide you through stages required to ensure that your CPD plan is effective. The more often you complete your CPD records, the easier it will become and you will find your confidence being boosted by having a visible record of your achievements and clear plans for the coming year. The reflection you undertake during the compilation of the plan will improve your creativity in tackling new challenges throughout your career.

THE IMPORTANCE OF CPD FOR PROFESSIONALS IN A CHANGING ENVIRONMENT

The philosophy of continuous professional development is that there is a process by which individuals take control of their own learning and development, by engaging in an on going process of reflection and action. It is based on the notion that each of us has the responsibility for developing ourselves rather than transferring this responsibility to our manager or anyone else in the organisation.

According to Megginson and Whitaker (2011) what makes CPD different from other types of training and development is:

1   The learner is in control.

2   CPD is a holistic process and can address all aspects.

3   We are regularly looking forward to how we want to be, reflecting on how we are, and working from our present position towards the future direction.

4   CPD works if you have the support and financial backing of your employer, but it can also work even if the employer is indifferent or hostile. It must be learner driven.

Development will occur through a myriad of experiences, both formally and informally such as: discussions, mentoring, online learning, workshops, debate with colleagues and work shadowing others. All of these and more can enable you to improve what you do and the way you do it. Identifying your CPD needs can occur as a planned process or instinctively as a response to current gaps in skills or knowledge. Proactive planning is a key characteristic of professional practice.

The CIPD Research Report, *L&D Evolving roles, enhancing skills* (CIPD 2015b) describes the environment of the L&D professional as fast-paced and ever-changing and therefore the professional needs to constantly expand her/his knowledge and skills base in order to build both organisational and individual performance. Interestingly, the report also found that although L&D professionals are constantly championing the importance of having and retaining up-to-date skills and capabilities, they do not always take their own advice consistently. The authors of the research believe that in the current volatile work environment the L&D professional needs to be agile, adaptive and ambidextrous to drive performance and stay relevant, continually aligning their work to the needs of their current situation. If L&D professionals are to be prepared for the future, then there is a requirement not only to concentrate on other colleagues' development but also to give the same concentration to their own development. Therefore, the challenge for the L&D professional is to focus their role on the current skills required, and shape their own professional development to meet these.

The CIPD Learning and Development Annual Survey Report 2015 (CIPD 2015c) identifies that due to current business transformational changes, a core skill for L&D professionals in future will be the ability to diagnose and solve problems for the organisation. Key capability gaps that currently exist for L&D professionals are analytical and technological skills. The workplace of today is constantly changing and therefore the L&D professional needs to learn continuously to meet the needs of a turbulent, transforming world.

The benefits of CPD as defined by CIPD in *Fresh thinking on CPD: the value of what you do* (CIPD 2015d) cover personal and employer interests and should be of interest to all HR professionals. The benefits are:

- building confidence and credibility; you can see your progression by tracking your learning
- earning more by showcasing your achievements; a handy tool for development
- achieving your career goals by focusing on your training and development
- coping positively with change by constantly updating your skill set
- being more productive and efficient by reflecting on your learning and highlighting gaps in your knowledge and experience.

With such clear benefits stated, there is a compelling argument for the personal investment a professional would make in the time spent on CPD.

However, the commitment to CPD is not a 'one-off' event. CPD is a cyclical activity shown in Figure 4.1. Before examining each stage of the cycle, we must first consider each stage in turn.

USING REFLECTIVE PRACTICE TO ENRICH YOUR CPD PROCESS

Reflective practice enables us to examine our own world of work, our practice and indeed ourselves. When we look back over our experiences, we are able to identify what was effective and what might be improved when we next encounter a similar situation. Rudyard Kipling (1902, p83) offers us questions that encourage us to examine our practice:

I keep six honest serving men

They taught me all I knew

Their names are What and Why and When

And How and Where and Who

If we ask Kipling's questions of ourselves in relation to our practice and learning we can add to the richness of our understanding. Understanding 'What', 'Where' and 'Who' can help us to identify the content and context of our learning. Understanding 'Why', 'How' and 'When' we learn will ensure we make the most of every opportunity in the future.

Figure 4.1 Stages of reflective practice

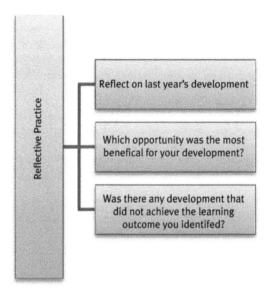

In Table 4.1, stages in reflective practice are presented. It focuses particularly on positive experiences that you had rather than dwelling on weaknesses.

The outcome of your reflection can be recorded in your personal development record.

Table 4.1 Development record example

Development record				
Name				
Covering the period from:	This year		To:	Next year
Key Dates	What did you do?	Why?	What did you learn?	How have/ will you use this? Any further action required?
23 March	I managed a new project for the first time	I had not led on a project before but recognised I needed the experience so took the opportunity.	A greater understanding of working to tight timescales and a better understanding of the different roles and styles that come together in a project to make it successful.	I have been able to transfer the new skills I learned on project management into my current role

CIPD MODEL OF REFLECTIVE PRACTICE

The CIPD professional view of reflection is that CPD should become a routine part of working life and that it is instinctive. This is certainly true if you are employed as an L&D practitioner. You should see learning as an intrinsic part of your job, and that you do not have to interrupt your work to do it. You should behave routinely to plan, record and reflect on your learning and see more opportunities for personal development in your daily life.

If you regularly practice reflective learning the world becomes a richer, more stimulating place because you increasingly see opportunities to extend your learning experiences. The CIPD Reflective Learning guide poses six questions to structure your reflection.

Figure 4.2 CIPD reflection stages

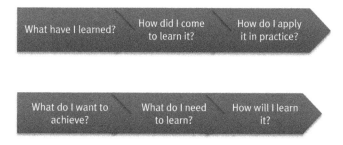

REFLECTIVE ACTIVITY 4.1

Apply these questions to your practice:

What are the implications for your own CPD?

Answering these questions will ensure you think through your learning opportunity and understand how this has improved you as a learner and as a practitioner.

ALTERNATIVE MODELS OF REFLECTIVE PRACTICE

There are many models of reflection. Essentially, they are all based around the one idea of thinking about an experience, thinking about why it is as it is and then deciding what you have learned from it, and then what to do next time. However, a variety of authors have worked on these ideas and devised models that either ask questions or have a cyclical approach.

You may find that using one model more than another gives you focus on your development. It is hard to confront a blank piece of paper or your blank mind and know where to start so a model can help you. All have ideas in common and all are cyclical in nature so that when you reach the end of a cycle you can start again.

Three of the most popular other models are by Johns (1994), Driscoll (1994) and Gibbs (1988). They all have benefits and disadvantages so you need to try them out to see what suits you. All models ask you to consider similar issues, what happened, what was important about it, why it happened as it did and what, if anything, you would do next time. The most important point to take from a model is what can you learn from it, and how does this affect your future practice?

Driscoll

Driscoll's (1994) model is a simplified version of that by Boud, Keogh and Walker (1985). It is limited to just three questions: 'What?' 'So what?' and 'Now what?' as shown in Figure 4.3. It does look deceptively simple but it is best suited to the more experienced reflector who needs or likes less direction.

Figure 4.3 Driscoll's model of reflective practice

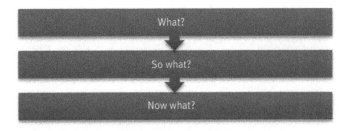

An adapted list of Driscoll's model questions

WHAT – the first question is to ask is what was the situation or occasion in detail, by returning to the situation. So here is an example of questions you may ask:

- What is the purpose of returning to this situation?
- What exactly occurred in your words?

- What did you see? What did you do?
- What was your reaction?
- What did other people do?
- What do you see as key aspects of this situation?

SO WHAT – the second question is to ask of the situation or occasion in detail, by understanding the context of the situation. Here are some questions you may ask:

- So what were your feelings at the time?
- So what are your feelings now? Are there any differences? Why?
- So what were the effects of what you did or did not do?
- So what 'good' emerged from the situation?
- So what troubles you, if anything?

NOW WHAT – the third question is to ask of the situation or occasion in detail, by thinking through what the future outcomes could be. Here are some questions you may ask:

- Now what are the implications for you, your colleagues?
- Now what needs to happen to alter the situation?
- Now what are you going to do about the situation?
- Now what happens if you decide not to alter anything?
- Now what might you do differently if faced with a similar situation again?

Johns

An alternative reflective model was developed by Johns (1994). In a short version of this model you take a real situation you have been in and answer as many questions as you can. This does not have to be in order and some questions might not seem relevant immediately.

1   Describe the event of incident. Keep this short and include the important aspects rather than every detail.
    - What happened, when, where, who?
    - Causes. Why? What factors contributed?
    - Context. What are the significant background factors?

2   Reflection on the incident:
    - What were you trying to achieve?
    - Why were the various actions taken?
    - What were the consequences of these actions for you?
    - How did you feel?
    - How did others feel about it?
    - How do you know how they felt?

3   Influencing factors:
    - What internal factors influenced decision-making?
    - What external factors affected your decision-making?
    - What sources of knowledge influenced or should have influenced your decision-making?

4   Could you have dealt better with the situation?
    - What other choices did you have?
    - What would have been the consequences of these choices?

5 Learning
- How do you feel about this experience?
- How has this experience changed your ways of knowing? That is, what knowledge do you now have or did you use in these areas?

Gibbs

A very popular model of reflective learning particularly in the field of nursing is that developed by Gibbs (1988). It is shown in Figure 4.4 and is often used by students as a framework in coursework assignments that require reflective writing.

Figure 4.4 Stages in Gibbs' model

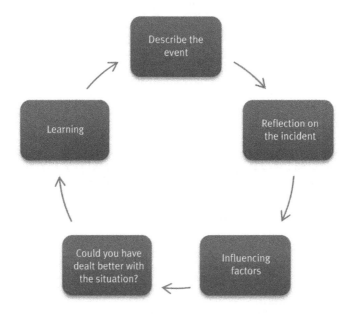

Gibbs' model was developed from an earlier theoretical model of David Kolb's four-stage experiential learning cycle (1984). Whereas Kolb's model is sometimes referred to as an experiential learning model (which simply means learning through experience), Gibbs' model is sometimes referred to as an iterative model (which simply means learning through repetition).

Whichever model of CPD you select, this first stage of your CPD activity requires you to understand yourself and what type of learner you are as this will give you additional insights into how you reflect on your learning. The importance of this exercise is not just the recording of experiences, but the thinking time you give yourself to understand the reasoning behind the situation. It is important that you consider what was successful and why that was. What did you change about yourself to make this successful? Was it a new skill that you had learnedt or did you change your behaviour to allow the outcome to be delivered successfully? Understanding yourself will allow you to clarify your internal conversations which in turn drive your behaviour. You will be able to see the linkages between what you do and how you see yourself. In time, you will be able to use this understanding to manage yourself and others better. The process of reflective writing allows for deeper reflection rather than just thinking alone. Thoughts and ideas are ephemeral and are difficult to revisit when you wish to plan your development.

STAGES OF THE CPD CYCLE

I now wish to introduce a four-stage cycle.

STAGE 1: SELF-ASSESSMENT

Figure 4.5 CPD Cycle

Following your time spent on reflective practice of your previous practice and development, you can then start the self-assess stage. Here you will conduct an assessment of yourself at this point in time about your current skills, knowledge, behaviours, experience and performance.

This self-assessment stage requires you to:

- understand and appreciate what self-assessment is and why it is important for your CPD
- appreciate the value of self-assessment
- use a particular set of skills and behaviours in the acquisition of knowledge on self-assessment
- understand how you can gain an honest view of your development needs and perceived performance.

We will now look at each of these areas in detail and see how they all contribute to creating a valuable CPD plan for you.

Understand and appreciate what self-assessment is and why it is important for your CPD

The first step in your preparation of an effective professional development plan is not action but making time and space for yourself to really understand yourself at this point in time. You need to establish your current skills, knowledge experience and behaviours. This analysis will allow you to understand how your attributes affect your delivery of an L&D service and the impact on you personally for wider self-fulfilment. This is your opportunity to spend time and think about the 'best you' you could ever be. What would that person look like? What knowledge, skills and experience would that person have? How would that person behave?

There are two different models that can help you make this self-assessment. There is a deficit model where you focus on looking at the skills, experience and behaviours you do not currently have and therefore identify a training gap. Alternatively, there is a capability approach where you ask yourself what new steps you want to take; what new areas do you want to get into and apply the skills that you already have (Megginson and Whitaker 2011). Both these approaches are a valid way in which to examine the 'current you' and to start to compose the development you will look to develop in order to create the 'future you'. The aim of this 'future you' is to achieve the best you can be. Aim high and build for your dreams, goals and plans for the future. As Henry David Thoreau (1817–1862) said: '*Go confidently in the direction of your dreams. Live the life you have imagined.*'

Whichever approach to CPD you select, you could seek the views of those around you. This may be team colleagues, your line manager, clients, customers, those who you line manage. All these are stakeholders in the 'future you' and can help you understand the development you will need to achieve this.

The process of assessment is not at all straightforward as it is a personal and can, at times, be an emotional process. It requires you to use the skills and behaviours you already have to be open and honest in your approach. Table 4.2 summarises four important behaviours from the CIPD Profession Map in comparison with L&D skills that you will need to use during your self-assessment. It will be your use of a combination of these skills and behaviours together that will ensure an effective self-assessment.

Table 4.2 Learning and Development skills comparison to CIPD behaviours

CIPD Behaviours	L&D Skills
Role model	Building rapport with stakeholders
Personally credible	Establish credibility in L&D role
Curious	Business awareness New methods in L&D
Courage to challenge	Questioning Listening Negotiating

 REFLECTIVE ACTIVITY 4.2

Consider the list of skills and behaviours required for effective self-assessment. Which skills do you already have and which will you need to improve in order to conduct your CPD plan?

Discuss with colleagues.

There are a range of sources of information that you could use to reveal aspects of your personal effectiveness:

- from others
- one-to-one session with your manager – appraisal
- 360° questionnaires
- individual psychometric testing
- demands of your current role
- organisational goals.

You could also use the spiderweb diagram shown in Figure 4.6 to assist you in documenting your own view of yourself currently. This will allow you to review what your areas of good performance are. Devise your own chart and rate your current abilities from 0 (low skill) to 10 (high skill). You could then ask your stakeholders if this is how they see your skills and behaviours.

Figure 4.6 Understanding yourself

 REFLECTIVE ACTIVITY 4.3

From your reflection, identify areas of your knowledge, skills and behaviour that you wish to develop.

Rate your ability from 0 to 10.

What do you conclude form this?

STAGE 2: PLAN AND ORGANISE

In this second stage you will need to design a meaningful personal development plan using the SMART criteria. Then you can consider your options for professional development that suit your learning style preferences. We will consider each of these steps in turn.

How to design a meaningful personal development plan

During this stage you will build on the data you have collected from your assessment of the 'current you'. You now move forward in a planning and organising phase and need to prioritise how you will develop your professional practice for the future. By summarising and prioritising your learning and development needs and selecting the appropriate activities, you will be able to achieve your aim.

At this stage you will have a range of information so you will need to select criteria to begin to summarise and to be able to give some order to your information. There are three ways in which you can summarise your development needs:

- date order – by selecting the most urgent first
- group by stakeholder
- group into skills, experience, knowledge or behaviours.

Whichever way you select to summarise your information, for your plan to be meaningful, you need to ensure that when you start to write your plan you use criteria that ensure you will achieve your aims. The use of the SMART criteria in Table 4.3 will guide you as you transfer your thoughts into a plan of action.

Table 4.3 SMART criteria

Specific	Be clear about what you want to achieve; what is the actual result or outcome that you want?
Measurable	How will you know what you have achieved? What will you see, hear and feel that will tell you that you have achieved?
Achievable	The objectives in your plan should be realistic and achievable steps to take you closer to your overall ambitions.
Relevant	Your objectives should be steps to larger career and personal aspirations, not just random pieces of learning.
Time	Each outcome should have an achievable end date – ideally within the timescale of your CPD planning period.

There are different layouts that can be used in writing your personal development plan. The CIPD suggests that you include the following,

What do I want/need to learn?

Be specific – clearly describe what you are planning to learn.

What will I do to achieve this?

Take account of your preferred learning style. Spend time to detail the specific actions you are planning. Ensure that you consider the widest types of development; do not get stuck in a rut and use the same each year. Use your imagination and be creative in the ways that you access your development opportunities.

What resources or support will I need?

This will cover the costs in terms of time and money. Be realistic. You will need the assistance of others to make this plan turn into a reality. You may need your manager, colleagues, mentor or employer.

What will my success criteria be?

You need to think to yourself: why are you doing this? What will you learn? This development should get you closer to the 'future you'. What will you be able to do after this development that you cannot do now?

Target date for review and completion

This is when you need to be at your most realistic. The date by which you plan to review or completely achieve your aim.

The example in Table 4.4 shows the types of headings you can use to assist you in your planning. The headings may stay the same regardless of the type of organisation in which you work. However, the opportunities for your development will depend on available resources. There are samples of different sector plans on the CPD section of the CIPD website (http://www.cipd.co.uk/cpd/examples-templates.aspx).

Table 4.4 Example of a development plan

Development plan				
Name		Membership number		
Covering the period from:	April this year	To:	April next year	
What do I want/need to learn?	What will I do to achieve this?	What resources or support will I need?	What will my success criteria be?	Target date for review and completion
To be more assertive when dealing with more experienced colleagues	Read texts on assertiveness skills and identify specific skills that I need to improve	Ask both my manager and a trusted friend to give me feedback about how I behave when I need to be assertive	When I do not feel guilty when I say 'no' to requests for additional work; when the ideas I express in team meetings are picked up by those more experienced	Six months

Options for your professional development

There is a wide range of development opportunities available to us all on a regular basis. We will look at development activities first and then consider the impact of our learning style and how this can impact on our success in personal development.

Types of development activity for personal development can be both formal and informal, work based, social self-directed learning outside of work or delivered by your professional body association. These can include:

- job shadowing
- joining networking groups
- attending a professional body evening meeting
- being coached
- having a mentor
- taking part in a project
- reading books, articles
- joining an action learning set
- work-based sessions
- secondment.

There will also be times during your development year when learning activities and learning experiences present themselves that you have not planned. Make the most of all these occasions and record what is relevant on your CPD record.

 REFLECTIVE ACTIVITY 4.4

Reflect on recent development you have undertaken that you both enjoyed and gained valuable outcomes from. Consider the setting, type of delivery, environment and who else was with you. What made it effective?

STAGE 3: UNDERTAKE DEVELOPMENT

During this stage, you will identify the activities that you may undertake and how you gain the most learning from them. You will have to take into account practical issues when making your selection such as resources, cost and timescales. Spending time on selecting the right development and not just doing the familiar types is important. You need to use all the effort and patience for yourself that you would afford to a valued member of staff who came to you wanting assistance in selecting the right sort of development. You are just as valuable to yourself and deserve equal treatment. Using the same approach, you also need to be the best learner while undertaking your CPD. You need to exhibit the characteristics of a skilled learner suggested by Megginson and Whitaker (2011):

- anticipate learning opportunities
- recognise developmental solutions
- seek out new learning
- take risks and innovate
- seek and accept help and feedback
- use interpersonal skills
- be constructively self-analytical
- make connections between different ideas and different people.

Anticipate learning opportunities

Learning opportunities can be viewed in three forms: one-dimensional, two-dimensional and three-dimensional (Honey 1998). One-dimensional learning opportunities are focused on individual study that could include reading and writing. Two-dimensional opportunities are where there is interaction either through talking or other forms of communication. The key is to decide if the opportunities that come along fit with your current CPD plan. Three-dimensional learning is when you use the learning you have gained and apply and use this learning in another context.

Recognising developmental solutions

As an experienced professional who is interested in managing their career, a practitioner should always be mindful of including development that will be required for their next career progression. As a skilled learner, you need to practice your ability to be able to recognise these opportunities and therefore be creative in finding the solutions to your development needs.

Seek out new learning

We all need to remember that we can accelerate our development by learning in different and new ways. We should look at new ways to learn which use the right side of our brain, the creative side that focuses on holistic, spatial thinking. Our work is often connected with the formal logical use of the left side of our brain (Rose 2000). To develop we should look to use both.

Take risks and innovate

You do not need to wait for the ideal learning opportunity to present itself. Sometimes you need to take a risk and move out of your comfort zone. The feel-good factor as well as the learning outcome can be most unexpected when we try something we have never tried before.

Seek and accept help and feedback

If you are trying to be the best learner you can be then accepting help and seeking feedback are actions that should be key behaviours to the success of your plans.

Use interpersonal skills

As an L&D practitioner you will use your interpersonal skills every day. As the learner working on your own personal development, you need to use these skills for your own benefit. Goleman's (1996) work on emotional intelligence assists professionals in understanding their interpersonal skills better and can improve your self-awareness. This may be an area for your improvement.

Be constructively self-analytical

Being self-analytical and undertaking self-analysis was discussed earlier in this chapter in relation to understanding your own performance and your current development needs. To be the 'best learner' you can be requires you to continue the analysis of yourself on a regular basis. You need to be as honest as possible for this to be valuable.

Make connections between different ideas and different people

You may already have well-established networks in your place of work. However, you need to make sure that these are wider than just the workplace. Use your professional networks outside of work to widen the number of people you will mix with and keep an open mind during all conversations so that you never miss a learning opportunity.

Jack Mezirow (2000) helpfully suggests that 'Transformational learning theory posits that adults' commitment to learning is greater when they feel that the goals of training are important and when they have control over the learning method.' The selection of your learning method has wide implications for your learning, therefore do not restrict yourself. CIPD considers that anything that helps you to meet your development objectives could count as CPD. The important part is that you can demonstrate real value to you in your work. If you read something that changes your perspective on teamwork or teaches you something about interpersonal communication, you can use it in your CPD record. You decide what goes in and what stays out.

STAGE 4: REVIEW

On a regular basis throughout the year and summarised annually, you need to review your learning over the previous year and set your development objectives for the coming year. As discussed earlier in this chapter, reflecting on the experience is a key element of the development and your ability to transfer this learning into the 'professional practitioner you'. Being able to reflect on the past and planning for the future in this way also makes your development more methodical and easier to measure. This process is also great preparation and a useful exercise prior to your annual appraisal.

The review of your personal development is of course not only an annual event. It is good practice to reflect and review each activity as you go. Again, we are all individuals, so some people find it helpful to write things down in detail, while others record 'insights and learning points' in their diaries as they go along and will then complete their review at a future point that is convenient. The importance is to assess your learning continuously. The timely way in which you review will also allow you to take remedial action if it is required. If there is knowledge or a skill that you consider is really important to the 'future you' and the activity you selected for this did not give the outcome you expected, you need to do something about this soon. You should not wait and only think about this when you complete your plan for next year.

CPD LEARNING LOGS

CPD Learning Logs will look very different depending on the type of person you are. They are individual records of personal development. I have known people who buy a special notebook every year to use as their CPD Log as, for them, the new development year is a special occasion and they enjoy the ceremony almost as a ritual of the event. Others will record this electronically alongside the plans they have written. Select whichever methods suit you. The value is in the thinking and recording you do. An example is shown in Table 4.5.

Table 4.5 CPD Learning Log example

CPD Learning Log		
Date	Event/experience/activity	Reflection on learning and how I will use it
This month	The opportunity to shadow my line manager during the start-up phase of a new project	I will use this learning when planning and setting up the next project I am responsible for. I haven't had the lead role in a project before. The opportunity to shadow someone with experience in this area gave me the confidence and skills so that I felt able to take the lead in the future.

SUSTAINING THE MOTIVATION FOR CPD

The value of CPD is the time spent on reflection, self-assessment, planning, recording and reviewing on the experiences you have had and the learning that has taken place. However, it is an ongoing process and requires you to retain motivational momentum and drive for your own development. To keep your motivation high, you need to keep reminding yourself of why you are spending your time completing it. List your drivers somewhere you can see them on a regular basis. You also need to be conscious of other elements that may impact on your completion of your CPD. There are known barriers or deterrents 4 to our completion of CPD that we need to be aware of (Friedman 2012), as seen in Table 4.6. By being informed of these deterrents you will be able to take action to overcome them.

Table 4.6 Deterrents to completing CPD

Situational	External barriers, such as the cost of activities as well as work and family issues
Dispositional	Based on personal attitudes such as you having doubts about the likely benefits of learning
Institutional	Perceived poor quality of activities on offer, inconvenient locations or timing
Informational	Lack of information about availability and suitability of activities

A record of CPD can provide evidence of competence to draw upon for performance reviews, promotions and interviews. CPD also allows CIPD L&D practitioners to demonstrate that all members (at each level – Associate, Member and Fellow) are competent, keeping their knowledge and skills up-to-date.

CPD should provide practitioners with the knowledge, skills, attitudes and values they need to perform effectively and competently in their role and to meet the expectations placed on them by their employers, colleagues and the members of professional bodies.

CPD can add to the knowledge, skills, attitudes and values that a professional already has. There is always a need to learn and develop.

SUMMARY

This chapter has explored:

The importance of CPD for professionals in a changing environment

- Self-development is an aspect of 'being a professional practitioner'.
- Knowledge is our product; we need to be up-to-date with our subject areas and our knowledge of how to help other people learn so that we can contribute to our organisations.
- The commitment to self-development is a prerequisite for membership of our professional institute.

Using reflective practice to enrich your CPD process

- The process of reflective writing allows for deeper reflection than either just thinking or writing alone would achieve
- Reflective practice gives the opportunity for considering the transfer of your learning into the work place.

Stages of CPD for Learning and Development Practitioners. CPD has four main stages:

- Stage 1: Self-assessment
- Stage 2: Plan and organise
- Stage 3: Undertake development
- Stage 4: Review.
- CPD is the action we take to maintain, update and grow the knowledge and skills required for our professional role.
- CPD is about planning our development, reflecting on our learning and recording it.
- CPD plans allow us to undertake a self-assessment of L&D capabilities to identify development needs.
- Our CPD records should detail the learning we have undertaken, what we have learned and how we will use our learning.
- The use of learning logs will assist in the reflection of our personal development

Factors which affect the selection of activities for our own development:

- Choosing development activities depends on some practical factors, like cost, time and availability, but also on what we specifically want from our learning.
- We need to maintain our specialist subject knowledge, our training skills and our understanding of the business.
- We should consider maintenance and development needs, performance requirements and personal aspirations, different learning methods and some new learning content.

REFERENCES

BOUD, D., KEOGH, R. and WALKER, D. (1985) *Reflection: Turning Experience into Learning*. London: Kogan Page.

CIPD (2015a) *Continuing Professional Development Policy*. London: CIPD. Available at: https://www.cipd.co.uk/cpd/policy.aspx.

CIPD (2015b) *L&D Evolving roles, enhancing skills*. Research Report. London: CIPD. Available at: https://www.cipd.co.uk/binaries/l-d-evolving-roles-enhancing-skills_2015.pdf.

CIPD (2015c) *Learning and Development. Annual Survey Report 2015.* London: CIPD. Available at: http://www.cipd.co.uk/hr-resources/survey-reports/learning-development-2015.aspx.

CIPD (2015d) *Fresh thinking on CPD: The value of what you do.* Report. London: CIPD. Available at: http://www.cipd.co.uk/NR/rdonlyres/A8614FFF-2FCA-4708–9DBC-C15A5C1A8743/0/5741_CPD_brochure.pdf.

DRISCOLL, J. (1994) Reflective practice for practise. *Senior Nurse.* Vol 14, No 1, pp47–50.

FRIEDMAN, A. L. (2012) *Continuing Professional Development – Lifelong Learning of millions.* London: Routledge.

GIBBS, G (1988) *Learning by doing: a guide to teaching and learning methods.* Oxford: Further Education Unit, Oxford Polytechnic.

GOLEMAN, D. (1996) *Emotional intelligence: why it can matter more than IQ.* London: Bloomsbury.

JOHNS, C. (1994) A philosophical basis for Nursing Practice. In JOHNS, C. *The Burford NDU Model: Caring in Practice.* 2nd ed. Oxford: Blackwell Scientific Publications.

KIPLING, R. (1902) *Just So Stories.* London: Macmillan.

MARCHINGTON, M. and WILKINSON, A. (2012) *Human resource management at work.* 5th ed. London: CIPD.

MEGGINSON, D. and WHITAKER, V. (2011) *Continuing Professional Development.* 2nd ed. London: CIPD

MEZIROW, J. (2000) *Learning as transformation.* San Francisco, CA: Jossey-Bass.

ROSE, C. (2000) *Master it faster: how to learn faster, make good decisions and think creatively.* London: Industrial Society.

UNDERSTANDING THE CONTEXT OF LEARNING AND DEVELOPMENT

CHAPTER 5

The Key Factors Influencing Achievement of Strategic Objectives in Varying Organisation Contexts and their Impact on Learning and Development Policies and Practice

PATRICIA ROGERS, DALBIR JOHAL AND RAYMOND ROGERS

CHAPTER OVERVIEW

- Introduction
- Historical development of strategic management
- How to carry out a strategic analysis
- Summary

LEARNING OUTCOMES

By the end of this chapter, you will be able to:

- summarise the historical development of strategic management
- explain the vocabulary of strategy
- identify the different stages of strategic analysis and the range of tools available to organisations.

INTRODUCTION

The learning and development (L&D) landscape has changed over the last 20 years from a focus on the delivery of training to a key strategic function that supports the delivery of the organisation's mission and corporate objectives. This chapter provides the foundations to strategic management and the tools and processes individuals within organisations can use to determine its strategy.

Establishing the organisation's objectives does not guarantee organisation success. Organisations must establish a structure, culture and have mechanisms in place to ensure objectives can be achieved. The way people are developed has been linked to the failure or success of organisations.

Strategic management has become the guiding force for organisations in today's commercial world. The ever-changing external environment requires organisations to respond rapidly to those changes in order to survive and thrive in the face of global competition. This chapter will cover the historical development of strategic management, the range of tools available to organisations to carry out an analysis, and concludes with examples of key external environment incidences and training implications for organisations.

Chapter 6 builds on the development of an organisation's mission and provides some foundation to the historical development of managing and organising people to new developments and the implications for L&D strategies.

HISTORICAL DEVELOPMENT OF STRATEGIC MANAGEMENT

The history of strategic management can be traced back to *The Art of War*, written by Sun Tzu in the fifth century BC (Tzu 1910). The book covered aspects of waging war and provided much strategic and philosophical advice still being used by politicians and business leaders today. The book *On War* by Carl von Clausewitz, a general in the German Prussian army influenced the US nuclear deterrence strategy and is still being referred to today. Warmongers have enjoyed over time the strategic and tactical richness of how not to go to war which created interest from business leaders who were predominantly looking at how to remain competitive and make profits.

Strategic management can be described as the art and science of devising, executing, and assessing cross-functional decisions that help an organisation to achieve its objectives. This definition suggests that strategic management focuses on integrating all management functions, to achieve organisational success. The term 'strategic planning' attracted interest from business leaders in the 1950s and became fashionable between the mid-1960s and the mid-1970s (Mintzberg 1994). Some of the writers, researchers and consultants who promoted the use of strategic management and planning were Alfred Chandler (1963). Enterprise realised the significance of co-ordinating the different features of management under one all-inclusive strategy. Before this time the different functions of management were unconnected with little if any overall co-ordination or strategy. Communications between the various departments were typically handled by a territorial boundary position that generally involved one or two managers relaying information back and forth between two departments. Chandler also stressed the importance of taking a long-term perspective when looking to the future. In his 1962 ground-breaking work *Strategy and structure*, Chandler showed that a long-term co-ordinated strategy was necessary to give a company structure, direction and focus, and stated 'structure follows strategy'.

Philip Selznick (1957) presented the idea of matching the organisation's internal factors with external environmental situations. This primary idea was later developed into the SWOT analysis still used by many today and will be discussed later in this section. Selznick (1960), Ansoff (1965), and Drucker (1954).

Throughout this period, strategic planning was generally believed to be the solution for all problems. However, in the 1980s, strategic planning became less fashionable because the various planning models did not provide greater financial returns as business leaders had expected and in the 1990s, strategic planning came back into fashion and is now practised worldwide due to the recognition of strategic planning as a powerful tool enabling organisations to compete more effectively. Strategic management and strategic planning are considered essential for organisations if they are to have a chance of competing successfully, with organisation survival and profitability being the primary objectives. A strategic plan is the result of selecting courses of action from numerous alternatives.

Drucker (1954) was a creative strategy theorist and stressed the importance of objectives: 'an organisation without clear objectives is like a ship without a rudder'. As early as 1954 he was developing a theory of management based on objectives. This developed into his theory of management by objectives (MBO). He stated that the procedure of setting objectives and monitoring progress towards them should filter through the entire organisation, from top to bottom. In 1985, Ellen Earle Chaffee summarised what she thought were the main elements of strategic management theory and stated that strategic management:

- involves adapting the organisation to its business environment
- is fluid and complex
- creates novel combinations of circumstances requiring unstructured non-repetitive responses
- affects the entire organisation by providing direction
- involves both strategy formation (she called it content) and also strategy implementation (she called it process)
- is partially planned and partially unplanned
- is done at several levels: overall corporate strategy, and individual business strategies.

HOW TO CARRY OUT A STRATEGIC ANALYSIS

The strategic management process involves the following: developing a mission and vision statement for the organisation; carrying out an analysis of the external and internal environment; selecting and implementing your chosen strategy and carrying out a review of the process and decisions before starting the process again. Figure 5.1 outlines the process and each section of the process will be discussed.

Before going through the key stages of the strategic management process, it is important to understand the vocabulary of strategy which is outlined in Table 5.1.

STEP 1: MISSION AND VISION STATEMENT

The mission statement communicates the fundamental purpose and focus of the organisation to its employees and stakeholders and unites employees in a common purpose. Mission statements can and do vary in length, content, format and specificity. Most practitioners and academics of strategic management consider an effectively written mission statement to exhibit nine characteristics or *mission statement components*. Since a mission statement is often the most visible and public part of the strategic management process, it is important that it includes most, if not all, of these essential components and organisations need to answer the questions below in constructing one:

1   Customers: Who are the enterprise's customers?

2   Products or services: What are the firm's major products or services?

3   Markets: Where does the firm compete?

4   Technology: What is the firm's basic technology?

5   Concern for survival, growth, and profitability: What is the firm's commitment towards economic objectives?

6   Philosophy: What are the basic beliefs, core values, aspirations and philosophical priorities of the firm?

7   Self-concept: What are the firm's major strengths and competitive advantages?

8   Concern for public image: What is the firm's public image?

9   Concern for employees: What is the firm's attitude/orientation towards employees?

Figure 5.1 The strategic management process

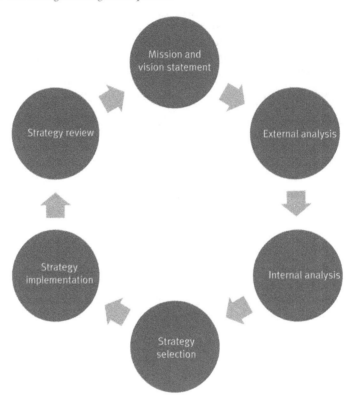

Table 5.1 The vocabulary of strategy

Term	Definition	A personal example	A business example	An L&D example
Mission	Overriding purpose in line with the values or expectations	Be healthy and fit	To create value and make a difference	Develop a digital learning culture
Vision or strategic intent	Desired future state; the aspiration of the organisation	To run the London marathon	To provide a great place to work where people are inspired to be the best they can be	To develop a learning culture
Goal	General statement of aim or purpose	Lose weight and strengthen muscles	To run a profitable business	All members of staff will be IT competent by 2018

Term	Definition	A personal example	A business example	An L&D example
Objective	Quantification (if possible) or more precise statement of the goal	Lose five kilos by 1 September and run the marathon next year	Increase market share	Be able use competently the in-house IT systems
Strategic capability	Resource, activities and processes. Some will be unique and provide a competitive advantage'	Proximity to a fitness centre, a successful diet	The ability to get your products or services to the market in a timely manner	Have the capacity to deliver L&D programs as required
Strategies	Long-term direction	Exercise regularly, compete in marathons	To introduce new products or adopt new technology	50 members of staff must complete a training program every six months
Business model	How product, service and information 'flow' between participating parties	Associate with a collaborative network (e.g. join a running club)		Introduce discussion forums and webinars
Control	The monitoring of action steps to: assess effectiveness of strategies and actions; modify as necessary strategies and/or actions	Monitor weight, kilometres run and measure; if progress satisfactory, do nothing; consider other strategies and actions		Use performance management systems to monitor progress of training on an individual basis

Adapted from Johnson *et al* (2014)

Businesses use the mission statement to remind their teams why their organisation exists. The statement helps all employees develop a clear understanding of the organisation's direction, however some people refer to this as the 'vision' which is different from the mission. The vision statement is about a favoured future, where the organisation would like to be in a year's time or even in three years. The mission tells everyone what we are doing today that will then take the organisation to where it wants to go in the future and sets important boundaries which enable business owners to delegate both responsibility and authority, and guardrails to keep the organisation on the path to the preferred future. When a new employee is hired, it is essential that the new employee knows what the organisation does and where the company is going. The statement forms the basis for alignment not only with the senior management, but the whole organisation. In general, many employees are resistant to change because it causes them to feel insecure and sometimes out of control. However, if there is a clear direction, employees are more likely to see the need for change and how it will help the organisation achieve its objectives. This creates a culture that welcomes change when it is necessary.

REFLECTIVE ACTIVITY 5.1

Below are examples of mission statements.

- How many of them address the nine mission statement questions in the section above?

IKEA's mission and vision are the same statements:

'At IKEA our vision is to create a better everyday life for the many people. Our business idea supports this vision by offering a wide range of well-designed, functional home furnishing products at prices so low that as many people as possible will be able to afford them.'

Apple's current mission statement:

'Apple designs Macs, the best personal computers in the world, along with OS X, iLife, iWork and professional software. Apple leads the digital music revolution with its iPods and iTunes online store. Apple has reinvented the mobile phone with its revolutionary iPhone and App store, and is defining the future of mobile media and computing devices with iPad.'

REFLECTIVE ACTIVITY 5.2

Review and rewrite the mission statement for your organisations or an organisation you know so that it is clear to any reader what the purpose and reason for this organisations existence is and why it is different when compared to its competitors.

Vision statement

The vision statement is the desired future state of the organisation. It is an ambitious description of what an organisation would like to accomplish in the mid- to long-term future. It serves as a clear guide for choosing current and future courses of action and is future orientated and sets out where an organisation wants to be in several years' time. The vision statement for Specsavers can be seen below:

SPECSAVERS VISION STATEMENT

Our vision: To passionately provide best-value eyecare and hearing care to everyone, simply, clearly and consistently, exceeding customer expectations every time.

Our values: Treat people as we would like to be treated ourselves.

Passionate about:

Our customers – the lifeblood

Our people – supporting our staff to be the best they can be

Partnership – at the heart of everything we do

Communities – giving back to and working with our local communities

Results – keep it simple, get it done, deliver on our promises

Source: www.specsavers.co.uk

STEP 2: EXTERNAL ANALYSIS

Developing strategies is a way to focus the organisation's efforts on achieving what it wants to achieve. Strategic planning necessitates the consideration of both the external forces outside the organisation and the internal resources within the organisation. In this section we will consider the external forces and the analytical tools available to assist in carrying out analysis in this area. A number of tools have been developed and include: SWOT (strengths, weaknesses, opportunities and threats), PEST (political, economic, social and technological), PESTLE (political, economic, social, technological, legal and environmental), stakeholder analysis and Porter's five forces. These tools enable the organisation to evaluate their situation within the context of an ever-changing external environment. The main factor that affects most business is the degree of competition. However, these tools include other factors – for example the political, economic, social and technological issues that could influence the direction an organisation might choose and needs to be taken into consideration. The SWOT analysis, while used to identify the opportunities and threats in the external environment, also focuses on the strengths and weaknesses within the organisation. An example of an independent bookshop SWOT can be seen in Figure 5.2.

Figure 5.2 Example of a SWOT analysis for a university independent bookshop

SWOT		Helpful	Harmful
Internal		**Strength** • Our workers are well-educated students who love books • The space is attractive and inviting • Long-term lease is at low rate • Customers are supportive of small bookstores • Popular café makes it easy for customers to linger and find something to buy	**Weaknesses** • Space is light • Bank gave us a limited line of credit • Health insurance costs are rising • Business is slower during summer vacation • Inventory system needs to be upgraded • High staff turnover due to students graduating
External		**Opportunities** • We can have local authors give lectures and book signings • We can make personalized recommendations to long-term customers • We can deliver the sameday to mobility-impaired customers • We can feature things that appeal to summer tourists • We can start a frequent buyer program	**Threats** • Large chains have more buying power • E-books and e-book readers eliminate need for physical books • Younger generations don't read as much • Nearby public library reopened after two-year remodel

The external factors that can affect the business are:

- Political – how changes in government policy might affect the business e.g. a decision to subsidise building new houses in an area could be good for a local brickworks.
- Economic – how the economy affects a business in terms of taxation, government spending, general demand, interest rates, exchange rates and European and global economic factors.
- Social – how consumers, households and communities behave and their beliefs. For instance, changes in attitude towards health, or a greater number of pensioners in a population.
- Technological – how the rapid pace of change in production processes and product innovation affect a business.
- Legal – the way in which legislation in society affects the business. For example, changes in employment laws on working hours.
- Ethical – what is regarded as morally right or wrong for a business to do. For example, should the organisation trade with countries which have a poor record on human rights?

 REFLECTIVE ACTIVITY 5.3

Carry out a pestle analysis of the organisation that you work for or an organisation that you are familiar with.

Other models that have been used by organisations to analyse the environment they are operating in to provide them with the options to select the most appropriate strategy for the organisation are: Porter's Five Forces, McKinsey 7S Framework and the stakeholder analysis.

Porter's Five Forces

Michael Porter developed the Five Forces analytical tool in 1979. It is considered a straightforward tool for appreciating where power sits in any business situation. It enables the organisation to recognise the strength of its current position and identify the strength of the position the business would like to move into. Knowing where the power lies means the company can take advantage of a strength situation and at the same time help to reduce a weakness situation. To get the most out of this tool the current business situation must be recognised. This means that each of the forces must be reviewed one at a time. Porter's Five Forces analysis is a structure that attempts to analyse the degree of competition within an industry. It looks to commercial organisation economics to identify five forces that determine the competitive intensity and therefore attractiveness of an industry. These forces are: threat of new entry, competitive rivalry, buyer power, threat of substitution and supplier power, as seen in Figure 5.3.

Figure 5.3 Porter's Five Forces

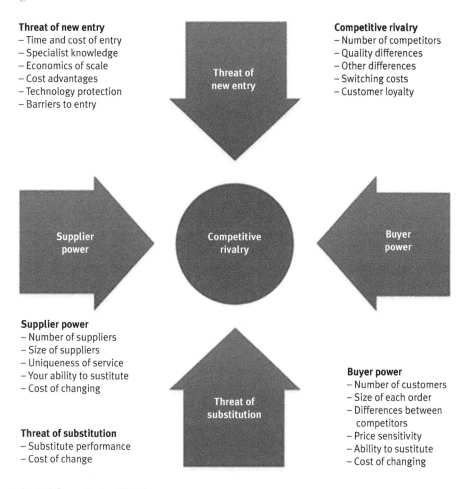

Threat of new entry
– Time and cost of entry
– Specialist knowledge
– Economics of scale
– Cost advantages
– Technology protection
– Barriers to entry

Competitive rivalry
– Number of competitors
– Quality differences
– Other differences
– Switching costs
– Customer loyalty

Supplier power
– Number of suppliers
– Size of suppliers
– Uniqueness of service
– Your ability to sustitute
– Cost of changing

Threat of substitution
– Substitute performance
– Cost of change

Buyer power
– Number of customers
– Size of each order
– Differences between
  competitors
– Price sensitivity
– Ability to sustitute
– Cost of changing

Adapted from Porter (1979)

Stakeholders and stakeholder analysis

Before an organisation undertakes a stakeholder analysis, another tool that will complement other models and help the organisation determine its future strategies, the organisation's stakeholders must be identified. Freeman (2010) defines a stakeholder as: 'any group or individual who can affect or is affected by the achievement of the organisation's objectives'.

Stakeholder analysis identifies each stakeholder, describes their desires with regard to the business and classifies them as a key or secondary stakeholder, and analyses how much influence over the organisation's outcomes they have. Once you understand the needs and concerns of the stakeholders you can manage their expectations, ensure that they are all constructively involved in contributing to the business outcome, and you can plan how to deal with stakeholders who do not share the corporate ambitions.

The common tool for stakeholder analysis is to create alignment matrix, which compares interest and influence. Ideally all stakeholders would be aligned with the company aims and very interested in the outcomes. Once you have placed each stakeholder on the matrix according to their current alignment and level of interest, you can plan how to move them to a position where they are both highly aligned and highly interested in making your outcomes happen. Figure 5.4 shows the stakeholders of British Airways. The stakeholders would be placed on the matrix illustrating their relevant power and importance either in general terms or a diagram can be drawn to illustrate the various stakeholders' power and importance for a specific issue.

Figure 5.4 The stakeholders of British Airways

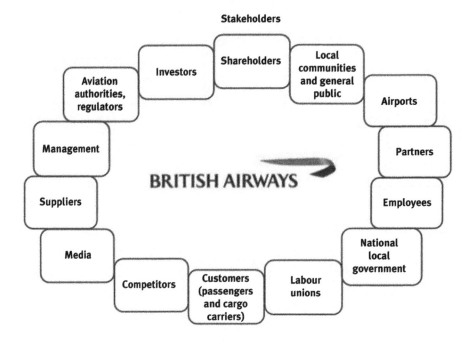

Stakeholder analysis

This tool is used to:

- identify the organisation's key stakeholders
- assess their interests, needs and expectations
- assess the ways these interests impact on the organisation
- establish prioritisation of key stakeholders and strategies to govern the relationship.

External changes that impact on L&D within organisations

The information below is not intended to cover all the external environment issues that could impact on L&D within an organisation. External factors affect organisations differently – for example, an external issue identified could be received and acted upon differently by a public or private sector organisation. For global organisations, an external issue could affect a part of the company operating in one country, but not the same organisation operating in another country. Also, some of the issues mentioned below might be part of an individual's belief and could form part of their selection criteria when choosing an organisation to work for or to do business with, therefore could be useful to be part of the organisation strategy.

Table 5.2 External environment issues that could have L&D implications

External environment issues	Possible L&D implications
Political/ Environmental/ Legal	
Government legislation and pressure groups lobbying to reduce CO_2 emissions and create a better environment by promoting recycling and reducing harmful emissions	Culture development about waste and recycling. Staff might need to be educated on how to separate rubbish and use the appropriate bins, which the company needs to supply. The use of paper: the amount used; the amount disposed of; reading documents online rather than printing them out. Looking at how the organisation can use alternative materials that are less damaging to the environment, for example biodegradable or recyclable materials. Looking at how organisations can reduce their carbon footprint by assessing the amount of travel that really needs to be done. Or looking at using electrical powered or hybrid cars for company cars. Some companies might encourage employees to work from home instead of travelling to the organisation building each day. The psychological and technological aspects of working from home will become a development issue for the organisation.
Government cuts in public funding or developing new funding to improve particular aspects of society. e.g. UK legislation: Human Rights 1998 e.g. UK legislation: The Equality Act 2010 The influx of labour through immigration both migrants fleeing persecution and also economic migrants Also changes to the retirement age of employees	Organisations that rely on funding might need to change direction to survive if funding is reduced. Individuals within the organisation might need development in new ways of working with other funders or in developing new products for the business. Some organisations where staff work or regularly travel to countries where there are conditions surrounding the treatment of people might need training especially if the country is unstable politically and economically. Ongoing training is required in managing a diverse workforce. People from different cultures entering the UK because of living in unstable environments and countries at war will need to feel part of the organisation if they choose to remain in the country and look for work. Organisations will need to develop inter- and cross-cultural development to manage the future diverse workforce. Organisations will need to consider how to develop an older workforce based on changes to the retirement age of employees. This might need to form part of a development programme that could include: managing the generation gap, fear of employment stability amongst older workers. Also the organisation might need to ensure that it provides development opportunities for older workers.
Economic/social	
Economic upturn and downturn	As the environment changes, skills can become important or less important. It is important for organisations to have an effective L&D strategy that will identify the needs of the organisation and regularly assess the skills available to meet these needs. Organisations might consider looking at offering development opportunities through offering apprenticeships to young people giving them a chance to work with and grow with the organisation and achieve a nationally

External environment issues	Possible L&D implications
	recognised qualification. Specsavers (see Case Study 5.1) has 200 apprentices in their stores. They have also engaged with universities to support the development of future employees while they are studying at university.
Brazil, Russia, India and China (BRIC) – the BRIC effect on globalisation. In the past, globalisation really was about Americanisation. This is no longer the case as organisations from the developing countries are actively expanding the operations into the developed economies. In a number of cases this is being achieved through acquisition of established businesses and known brands, an example of this is the brewer, Budweiser. This company was acquired by a Brazilian-Belgian conglomerate. The result of this change is that all companies, no matter which country they originate from, are all competing with each other. In addition to this, cheaper imports from less developed economies – for example, India and China, have impacted on the attitudes, working methods and remuneration of employees in the UK.	These impacts can force organisations to look at cost reductions and could involve developing staff to undertake new or different roles or to be more multi-skilled. In some situations where individuals might lose their jobs the organisation might provide development programmes aimed at getting individuals to think about new areas of work and how to find a job. L&D plays a significant role in ensuring that the organisation's employees have the relevant skills, knowledge and abilities that the organisation requires. By being business aware, L&D will be in a very strong position to influence and shape the organisation's direction. Once a new strategic direction has been established, L&D must be in line with the business needs, the organisational culture and in turn the employees as learners. It is vital that L&D is adaptable in playing different roles within the organisation, so they can forecast and react to changes in the external environment. In performing each of these roles L&D must be able to build flexibility and agility into every part of the organisation.
Technological	
The Internet, mobile phones, tablets and laptops Skype	These have enabled employees to work almost from any location including the following: on trains while traveling, in airports and at home. Employees need to be developed in how to work from the organisation safely and securely especially in the management of data. Companies might need to develop a range of policies surrounding the use of company technologies and ensure that they are fully understood by all staff in the organisation.

The global environment that most organisations operate in can give the appearance that change is continuous and some organisations might agree that it is. However, it is important that organisations, along with developing strategies and analysing the environment that they are operating in, develop good mechanisms for dealing with and managing change. Change can have substantial impact on organisations in terms of skills required and employment opportunities for staff. Organisational strategies developed now need to be more flexible in outlook in some cases. This is demonstrated by co-operation between organisations rather than through competition. To survive, organisations need to be swift in their response to change to be able to change strategic focus and organisational capabilities quickly. L&D plays a vital role here and must be in tune with and anticipate organisational need if they are to play a pivotal role in supporting organisational future needs, however an effectual working environment needs a degree of stability, which is a challenge and involves the organisation maximising its current capabilities while ensuring it develops the capabilities required to take advantage of new opportunities as and when they present themselves.

Managers' perception of the external environment

The perception of the external environment by managers and organisations can influence the decision-making process with regard to strategy, processes and structure. Table 5.3, adapted from Ansoff (2007), considers five perceived environment types. For each perceived environment type, read from left to right to see the organisation strategy type and management attitude that is most probable for each perceived environment.

Table 5.3: Ansoff's typology of environments

Level	Environmental change	Organisation strategy	Management attitude
1	**Repetitive** Little or no change	**Stable** Based on precedent	**Stability-seeking** Rejects change
2	**Expanding** Slow incremental change	**Reactive** Incremental change based on expense	**Efficiency-driven** Adapts to change
3	**Changing** Fast incremental change	**Anticipatory** Incremental change based on extrapolation	**Market-driven** Seeks familiar change
4	**Discontinuous** Discontinuous and unpredictable change	**Entrepreneurial** Discontinuous new strategies based on observed opportunities	**Environment-driven** Seeks new but related change
5	**Surprising** Discontinuous and unpredictable change	**Creative** Discontinuous new creative strategies	**Environment-creating** Seeks novel change

Source: Ansoff (2007)

STEP 3: INTERNAL ANALYSIS

An organisation has control over its internal resources and needs to consider its strategic capability to achieve its strategic objectives. The SWOT analysis mentioned in Step 2 and the 7S Framework is used to focus analysts on the strength and weaknesses of the internal resources. A regular review of internal strengths within an organisation helps to ensure that it is on track to achieve its strategic objectives and it helps the organisation understand and change its internal environment should the market the organisation is operating in change.

McKinsey 7S Framework

This tool does not look at or focus on the analysis of organisational structure; its focus is on the critical question of co-ordination. The 7S Framework is presented in the book *In*

Search of Excellence (1982) by the former McKinsey consultants Thomas J. Peters and Robert H. Waterman. The framework charts a collection of interconnected elements that influence an organisation's ability to change. The main assumption of the model is that there are seven internal features of an organisation that need to be aligned in order to facilitate business success. The model can be used with the SWOT analysis, as the internal aspect of this model looks at the strengths and weaknesses of the organisation. While the emphasis is different more than one model can provide an in-depth analysis of the organisation's situation. Also, the tools mentioned above can add additional features to strengthen the analysis, for example: rating and ranking can be put against each feature identified to the priorities most and least important – for example, threat to the organisation.

The McKinsey 7S model is a framework for reviewing an organisation's capabilities from different viewpoints and covers the key organisation capabilities needed to implement strategy successfully. Each of the 7S can be reviewed to evaluate how the capabilities of an organisation can be developed as the starting point of generating an action plan and developing strategies. The McKinsey 7S model contains seven co-dependent features which are characterised as either 'hard' or 'soft' elements, as seen in Table 5.4:

Table 5.4 Adapted McKinsey 7S model

Soft elements	Hard elements
Shared values: the core values of the organisation that are demonstrated in the company culture and overall work ethic.	
Skills: the actual skills and capabilities of the workers employed by the organisation.	**Strategy:** the plan developed to create a competitive advantage over the competition.
Staff: the workers and their broad competencies.	**Systems:** the daily activities and processes that employees participate in to get the work completed.
Style: the method of leadership embraced.	**Structure:** the way the organisation is organised and who reports to whom.

The 'Soft' features are not as easy to recognise and are challenging to describe, less tangible and are more influenced by culture. 'Hard' features are simpler to describe or recognise and management is able to influence them, examples of these features are: organisational charts, Information Technology (IT), official processes and strategy statements.

Ramsay *et al* (2000) state that in high-performing organisations employees who have talent work together better and departments and employees co-operate on the generation of ideas and solutions to problems. The strategic capabilities of employees are an essential business factor. If employees are motivated, talented and hardworking the outcome will be better results when compared to a less talented and less motivated workforce. The processes and relationship between and within departments can also result in improved effectiveness and efficiency. Employees are considered intangible resources along with patents, trademarks, copyrights, goodwill and brand recognition. Tangible resources include both fixed assets, such as machinery, buildings, land, and current assets such as inventory.

Figure 5.5 McKinsey 7S model

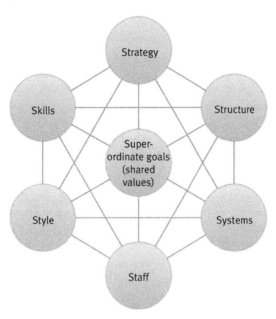

Organisations should also concentrate on having effective operational and administrative systems that are flexible and can cope with change. Poor or inaccurate record keeping, outdated or defective IT systems are factors that need evaluation against strategic objectives. If these potential problems are not monitored and resolved when they occur, customers may see the organisations as unreliable and the organisation may find that it cannot react or satisfy opportunities when they arise.

An organisation's greatest asset is its people's knowledge, creativity and passion; these are the key differentiators for industries requiring advanced skills and expertise. This makes employees a commodity that you cannot easily attach a value to. While skills and knowledge are replaceable in the mid- to long-term, there is a huge cost in terms of replacing staff and providing the necessary development needed. Investing in staff on a regular basis is paramount to maintaining or obtaining a low staff turnover rate and motivating employees to invest more of themselves into their work achievements that will contribute to the success of the firm. It is also important to capture staff knowledge before it leaves the organisation. Everyone would like to receive a little extra at the end of each month as recognition for the work they do. However, enhanced remuneration packages offer a positive effect in the short- to mid-term, even sometimes causing productivity levels to rise, but they never truly satisfy a person's longer-term aspirations and provide little long-term benefit to the organisation.

As mentioned above, L&D implications for organisations and their staff are important, however, diagnosing strategic capabilities is not an easy task. Some organisations use 'benchmarking' which is used to understand how organisations compare with others. There are two broad approaches to benchmarking:

- Industry/sector benchmarking – which is about comparing performance against other organisations in the same industry sector or between similar service providers against a set of performance indicators. Benchmarking is used by organisations in all sectors and in some cases, is a result of league-table exercise which could be carried out nationally or locally, for example with hospitals, councils, schools and universities.

- Best in class benchmarking – this compares an organisation's performance or capabilities against 'best in class' performance, for example Southwest Airlines improved refuelling times by studying Formula One Grand Prix motor racing pit stops (Camp 2006).

Johnson *et al* (2014) noted that developing strategies that provide strategic competitive advantage can be challenging. Managers need to consider addressing the following to create, extend or upgrade an organisation's strategic capabilities:

- Internal capability development – could capabilities be added or upgraded to be able to deliver against critical success indicators?
- External capability development – looking externally and developing new capabilities by acquisition or entering into alliances and joint ventures.
- Ceasing activities – the activities could be outsourced or closed down especially if the activities are not central to the delivery of value to customers.
- Awareness development – the basis of competitive advantage often is in the day-to-day activities people undertake in organisations. It is important to develop the ability of employees to recognise the relevance of what they do and how it is linked and contributes to the strategy of the organisation.

Evaluating the impact of learning

It is essential that organisations value employees as people and ensure that plans are in place to improve the performance of employees in their present role. The impact of any development should be measurable and reported to ensure that L&D carried out is in-line with the organisation's core vision and values. It is also essential that all employees are aware of the opportunities available to them. Some on-the-job training and development opportunities exist, providing an opportunity for an organisation to make use of internal resources and expertise where possible. It is important that L&D is seen as a shared responsibility between the organisation, the managers, and its employees and in some instances organisations need to be more creative in how they develop their staff, especially with regard to developing broader knowledge and understanding. Organisations might engage in partnerships to develop staff which could benefit some organisations, particularly small- to medium-size organisations or some public-sector organisations.

Individuals and line managers should engage in a review system which provides an opportunity to assess current employee skills and knowledge, identify and discuss future developments that will be beneficial to the individual and the organisation and, where appropriate, look at further development activities that are required to help the individual in their job role. This could be part of the performance management process in the organisation, where objectives should be set for employees based on the wider organisation strategic objectives and reviewed to make adjustments if possible where performance might impact on the achievement of the organisation goals. In today's dynamic and rapidly changing workplace and globalised economy, development of organisational performance is associated with the development of personal performance, skills, knowledge and experience (Covey 1989, Covey 2004).

The ability to attain and sustain high performance levels of productivity in an organisation is a significant challenge confronting management today. Management should devote significant consideration towards understanding and appreciating an individual's differences, their needs and behaviours, as well as to enable them to understand and manage organisational complexity. This degree of understanding is considered important in helping individuals develop an effective learning style that is associated with organisational objectives.

Performance measurement is an essential organisational activity. Generally, organisations have always measured performance in some way. Organisation performance can be measured in many ways; examples are profitability, market share and entry into new markets. In addition, the improvements seen by the customer can be measured as well, as by the results delivered to other stakeholders, such as the shareholders. Actual performance can be compared with targeted performance. The comparison of actual compared to target performance is important because it highlights areas that need improvement. This process to indicate activities and highlight organisational problems. Why measure performance? If the organisation can measure its performance, it will be able to manage it. Conversely the organisation cannot manage what it cannot measure. Setting timescales is important if performance measurement is to be meaningful. Measuring performance has to be done over varying time periods depending on the type of programmes that have been delivered. With the drive for continual improvement, performance measurement plays a vital role in:

- identifying and tracking progress against organisational goals
- identifying opportunities for improvement
- comparing performance against both internal and external standards.

Reviewing the performance of an organisation is also an important step when formulating the direction of the strategic activities.

The main reasons it is needed are:

- to ensure customer requirements have been met
- to be able to set sensible objectives and comply with them
- to provide standards for establishing comparisons
- to provide visibility and a 'scoreboard' for people to monitor their own performance level
- to highlight quality problems and determine areas for priority attention
- to provide feedback for driving the improvement effort.

STEP 4: STRATEGY SELECTION

All organisations need a strategy. However, strategies must not be generated before considering the external environment and all its pressures. The organisation should not be looking to copy what its competitors are doing; rather, it is prudent for the senior management team to create the most effective strategies possible to accomplish the objectives the company is setting out to accomplish. After establishing a mission statement and the company goals followed by an analysis of the external and internal analyses, the key is to use the information gathered to develop an innovative business strategy that will allow the company to achieve its goals. The aim is to adopt a strategy that, according to the analysis you have performed, will give the company a sustainable competitive advantage and allow it to grow and prosper. Table 5.5 gives a selection of the strategies that organisations might choose.

Table 5.5 Strategy selection

Strategy	Definition
Forward integration	Obtaining ownership or increased control over distributors or retailers. Forward integration is a method of vertical integration in which a company takes ownership of its distributors.
Backward integration	Looking for ownership or increased control of an organisation suppliers.

Strategy	Definition
Horizontal integration	Looking for ownership or greater control over competitors. Horizontal integration strategy is the acquisition of similar firms to increase their market share and profits. Organisations usually acquire other firms in one of three ways: 1. acquisition, 2. merger, 3. hostile takeover.
Market penetration	Introducing existing products or services into new geographical areas. This involves increasing market share within existing market segments. This can be achieved by selling more products/services to established customers or by finding new customers within existing markets.
Market development	This strategy entails finding new markets for existing products. Market research and further segmentation of markets helps to identify new groups of customers.
Product development	Looking for increased sales by improving current products or services or developing new ones. This involves developing new products for existing markets.
Retrenchment	Reorganising through cost and asset reduction to reverse declining sales and profit.
Divestiture	Selling a division or part of an organisation.
Related diversification	Adding new but related products or services. This involves moving new products into new markets at the same time. It is the most risky strategy. The more an organisation moves away from what it has done in the past, the more uncertainties are created. However, if existing activities are threatened, diversification helps to spread risk.
Unrelated diversification	Adding new, unrelated products or services.
Liquidation	Selling all of a company's assets, in parts, for their tangible worth.

STEP 5: STRATEGY IMPLEMENTATION

Once the strategy is selected the organisation must engage in a number of the internal considerations mentioned above. It must also consider developing a robust implementation plan that will take into consideration realistic timescales, costs and the appropriate communication mechanisms to use. The following must also be taken into consideration:

- Apportionment and management of adequate resources (personnel, financial, technology support, and time). Determining a sequence of command and identifying any relevant cross-functional teams that may have to be established and managed. Allocating responsibility of specific jobs or procedures to specific individuals or teams.
- It also involves planning and managing the process. This includes monitoring outcomes, comparing actual results to planned results, controlling and rectifying any variances, and subsequently making adjustments to the process that might be required.
- When implementing a strategic plan/s, this involves acquiring the relevant resources, in particular developing the organisation's people, but could include some of the organisation's stakeholders.

STEP 6: REVIEW AND EVALUATION

Periodic revision of the vision, mission and strategic plan is essential. This should be done so that organisational performance can be monitored against the strategic objectives that have been set. Organisations need to develop key evaluation matrices that measure all the areas that will identify organisation effectiveness and should include in the development of key matrices representation from across the organisation, which will give the organisation the opportunity to identify if one area in the organisation is not performing and affecting the performance in other areas. Data collected and used should be communicated to all relevant parties and used to make comparisons year on year. Good management information systems in organisations are vital in monitoring organisation performance. It is also important that the matrices used are reviewed along with the data collection mechanism. The outcome of the reviews will indicate whether organisations' systems and structures are fit for purpose.

The execution of strategy is about actually making things happen throughout the organisation. It is only after action takes place that the effects of the strategic plan will become apparent.

SUMMARY

The information in this chapter indicates the importance of strategic planning to ensure that organisations survive and the importance of L&D for the organisation and its employees. All organisations operate in environments that change. Being able to respond quickly to the changes in the external environment by making changes inside the organisation gives the organisation a better chance of survival. The L&D function has a major part to play in ensuring the organisation's staff are able to respond to change as and when it occurs. A range of tools are available for organisations to use in carrying out a strategic analysis, however, organisations need to ensure that the information they use is realistic and that they are honest with the situation that is affecting the organisation outside and inside. The strategic management process is not static and needs to be evaluated and monitored for it to be effective.

CASE STUDY 5.1

SPECSAVERS: PASSIONATE ABOUT OUR PEOPLE

Supporting our staff to be the best they can be

We firmly believe in supporting and developing our staff so they can shine in their roles. Whether working with customers or supporting partners, our people are our ambassadors. It is, therefore, crucial that they are engaged and motivated in their work, skilled and competent in their field and supported to deliver their best to customers every time.

Developing talent in our stores

We want Specsavers to be a career choice, not just a place to work. To help store staff make their way up the ladder, we offer a vast range of learning and development at all stages, with the potential to take them on a full career journey from entry level to partner. Our learning and development portfolio covers all aspects of the Specsavers business, whether staff want to improve their customer service skills, brush upon their product knowledge or study for an accredited, professional qualification.

Our optical apprenticeship scheme in the UK has placed around 200 apprentices across our stores, from a standing start in 2013. The scheme – which involves the completion of the Level 2 Diploma in Optics, monthly assessor visits, and online and on-the-job learning – has had fantastic feedback, with many partners saying their apprentices have become their star optical assistants.

Across our markets, recruitment fairs, school talks and university visits all ensure that Specsavers remains at the front of their mind when students are considering their next steps. In Australia, we have forged links with Deakin University, holding lectures for optometry students and arranging visits to the Melbourne office to give them an insight into our business. Last year, in the UK and the Republic of Ireland, we welcomed hundreds of second-year optometry students on summer placements within our stores, with a view to their returning in the following academic year as pre-registration students.

Career Ladder, an interactive tool that gives store staff a clear understanding of their development opportunities at Specsavers, is now live in all our markets. Offering a clear line of sight from current to next role and beyond, the tool provides a description of each position in store and offers advice on relevant training and development, to help staff progress through the ranks.

Alongside the Level 3 Certificate in Optical Dispensing for ophthalmic dispensing assistants, we have just launched a Level 3 Certificate for Optometric Clinical Assistants in the UK and the Republic of Ireland, aimed at non-dispensing store staff. And we offer a Level 4 (or equivalent) Certificate in Optical Dispensing across all our markets, having launched the programme in the Netherlands and all Nordic countries last year. The certificate, generally referred to as a 'Cert IV',

provides a solid foundation in optical theory, as well as practical guidance on dispensing. Several hundred people are currently on the course worldwide and it has delivered all-important dispensing expertise to stores across our network.

In the Netherlands, following the success of our Superclass Optics course, we have now introduced Superclass Hearing, a fast-track, one-year route to qualifying as an audiologist. Last September saw the first intake of students begin the intermediate vocational course, which is run in association with the Dutch HealthTec Academy (DHTA). The course involves working in store, studying at college and training within Specsavers and, once qualified, students work under a mentor for six months before taking on a full audiologist role.

We developed a new programme for supervisors in Australia and New Zealand last year, which received an overwhelming level of interest when it was made available to stores. The six-month, self-paced course is designed for store team members who are ready to move into a supervisor role and is a great opportunity for career progression at Specsavers. Managers with ambitions of becoming a store partner can complete Institute of Leadership & Management (ILM) 3 and 5 programmes, which combine classroom training, written assignments and application on the job. These accredited programmes are now run across all our markets and are a fantastic foundation in leadership and motivation.

Source: Specsavers.co.uk

REFLECTIVE ACTIVITY 5.4

Select an organisation that you are familiar with. Examples of organisations you might use are a hospital, the university or college where you are studying, a retail organisation, or any other organisation you have worked for on a full-time or part-time basis. You do not have to have been in paid employment; it could be an organisation that you did voluntary work for, such as a charity.

- Create a list of the political, economic, social, technological, legislative and environmental factors that impact that organisation and therefore L&D.
- What practical guidance would you offer to the organisation's management and L&D team?
- How would you evaluate the practical value of this exercise from an L&D perspective to the organisation?

CASE STUDY 5.2

DR JOHNSON'S

Read the following case study and answer the questions at the end.

Dr Johnson inherited his father's chemistry lab in Birmingham in 2002. Until 2009, he owned four labs in the Midlands. His ambition was to turn it into a national chain. The number of labs increased to seven across the country in 2010, including the acquisition of OXON lab in London. The number is likely to go up to 50 within two to three years from 21 at present. Injection of £9m for a 26% stake by Prima Scope has been its growth strategy.

The lab, with a revenue of £13m, is among the top three pathology labs in the UK along with Capital (£26m) and European (£17m). Yet its market share is only 2%. The top three firms command only 6% of the market, as against 40–45% by their counterparts in the Europe. There are about 20,000 stand-alone labs engaged in routine pathological business in Europe, with no system of mandatory licensing and registration. That is why Dr Johnson has not gone for acquisition or joint ventures. He does not find many existing laboratories meeting quality standards.

Dr Johnson's six labs have been accredited nationally whereas many large hospitals have not thought of accreditation. The College of European Pathologists' accreditation of the lab would help it to reach clients outside the UK and Europe. The biochemistry and blood testing equipment are sanitised every day. The bar coding and automated registration of patients do not allow any identity mix-ups. Even routine tests are conducted with highly sophisticated systems. Technical expertise enables them to carry out 1650 different tests. Same-day reports are available for samples reaching the lab by 3 p.m. and next-day reports are available for samples from 500 collection centres located across Europe. Technicians work round the clock, unlike competitors. Home services for collection and reporting are also available. There is a huge unutilised capacity. Now it is trying to top other segments. Twenty per cent of its total business comes through its main laboratory which acts as a reference lab for many leading hospitals. New mega labs are being built to Fund pre-clinical and multi-centre clinical trials within Europe and provide postgraduate training to the pathologists.

Questions

1   How can L&D assist in the successful expansion of the organisation?

2   What is the difference between 'Vision' and 'Mission' from an L&D perspective?

3   How can L&D support the business strategy that has been adopted by Dr Johnson?

4   In your opinion, from an L&D point of view what could be the biggest weakness in Dr Johnson's business strategy?

REFERENCES

ANSOFF, H. I. (1965) *Corporate strategy*. New York: McGraw Hill.

ANSOFF, H. I. (2007) *Strategic management*. London: Palgrave, Macmillan

CAMP, R. (2006) *Benchmarking: search for industry best practice that lead to superior performance*. Australia: Quality Press.

CHANDLER, A.D. (1963) *Strategy and Structure: chapters in the history of the american industrial enterprise*, Cambridge, Massachusetts: MIT Press.

COVEY, S. R. (1989) *The seven habits of highly effective people*, Simon & Schuster. UK

COVEY, S. R. (2004) *The 8th habit: from effectiveness to greatness*, Simon & Schuster. UK

DRUCKER, P. (1954) *The practice of management*, London: Heinemann.

FREEMAN R. E. (2010) *Strategic management*, Cambridge: Cambridge University Press

JOHNSON, G., WHITTINGTON, R., SCHOLES, K., *et al.* (2014) *Exploring corporate strategy*. London: Pearson.

MINTZBERG, H. (1994) *Tracking strategies: towards a general theory*, Oxford: Oxford University Press.

PETERS, T., and WATERMAN, R. (1982) *In search of excellence: lesson from america's best run companies*, New York: Harper & Row.

PORTER, M.E. (1979) How competitive forces shape strategy. *Harvard Business* Review. Vol 21, No 38, pp21–38.

PORTER, M.E. (1985) *Competitive advantage: creating and sustaining superior performance*, New York: The Free Press.

RAMSEY, H., SCHOLARIOS, D. and HARLEY, B. (2000) Employees and high performance work systems: testing inside the black box. *British Journal of Industrial Relations*. Vol. 38, No 4, pp501–531.

SELZNICK, P. (1957) *Leadership in administration: a sociological interpretation*. Evanston, IL: Row, Peterson.

SELZNICK, P. (1960) *The organisational weapon: a study of bolshevik strategy and tactics*. Glencoe, IL: Free Press.

TZU, S. (1910) *The art of war*, Canada: Prohyptikon Publishing Inc.

CHAPTER 6

The Nature of Organising and Managing in a Variety of Contexts

PATRICIA ROGERS, DALBIR JOHAL AND RAYMOND ROGERS

CHAPTER OVERVIEW

- Introduction
- The organisation
- Managing and organising organisations
- Organisation structures
- Cross-cultural competence
- Summary

LEARNING OUTCOMES

By the end of this chapter, you will be able to:

- explain the similarities and differences between various types of organisations
- evaluate the implications of varying organisation types for learning and development policy and practice.

INTRODUCTION

Organisations are designed to achieve their objectives and to do this they need to employ people with the right capabilities and with the capacity to develop and adapt, if the organisation needs to adjust to survive and achieve its short- and long-term goals. To support the organisation in achieving its objectives, key individuals within the organisation needs to consider the organisation size, structure, management and culture of the organisation. Those key individuals must also analyse the environment the organisation operates in to ensure that it has people with the right knowledge, skills and ability to help the organisation achieve its strategic objectives. How an organisation determines its strategies is discussed in the next chapter of this unit. The development of the organisation's people capabilities and the strategies that can be employed to transform organisations through developing people will be addressed in Chapter 7 but is also briefly addressed in Chapter 5 and this chapter. This chapter explores traditional approaches to organising and managing organisations making references to theories, organisation type, structure and culture. This section will also suggest considerations for the future and implications for Learning and Development (L&D).

THE ORGANISATION

So many people are part of an organisation but never really consider the organisation's key characteristics. Chester Barnard (1886–1961) described organisations as a system of consciously co-ordinated activities or forces of two or more people. Other definitions have included 'it is the way people are grouped and the way they operate to carry out activities for a business or a social unit that is structured and organised for a need or collective goals' (Needle 2010). McNamara (2012) described an organisation as 'a person or group of people intentionally organised to accomplish an overall common goal or set of goals' and Huczynski and Buchanan (2007) state that it is 'a social arrangement for achieving controlled performances in pursuit of collective goals'. The definitions seem to suggest that an organisation can be one person or a group of individuals and is an arrangement that focuses on performance measures, however, what is common amongst the definitions is that there is a common purpose or goal or set of goals. The purpose and goal(s) of an organisation will depend on whether it is a business, public or not-for-profit organisation and have a management structure that defines activities, roles and responsibilities for all those that are part of it.

BUSINESS ORGANISATIONS

Business organisations are formed to make money and ultimately profits through the offering of products and services. Using its simplest form, business organisations can be a small- to medium-size enterprise (SME) employing fewer than 250 employees, (there were 5.2 million SMEs in the UK in 2014), or a large organisation employing from 250 to thousands of employees. There is no limit on the number of employees a large organisation can employ. However, the variations and complexities can be realised by whether it is a local organisation based in normally one local area; regional based, for example based across the Midlands or the north-west; national, having operating locations across, for example, the UK; multinational corporation (MNC) with its facilities and other assets in at least one country other than its home country. MNCs generally have offices and/or factories in different countries and usually have a centralised head office where they co-ordinate global activities or a global business organisations doing business across the world.

Over the years we have seen advances in technology, in particular the Internet and new communication tools, making it easy for businesses to communicate with other businesses across the world without travelling. Also international political business agreements, developments in supply chain, distribution and innovations in national and international travel can make a small local or regional organisation link and trade easily with the rest of the world. A local business organisation can sell their products or services to customers in many parts of the world without having to set up the organisation in different countries. The organisations can also grow in size throughout a country or across the world by offering 'franchises', which involves individuals or other organisations being given the right to act as an agent for another organisation. Case study 6.1 is Specsavers, which has a turnover of £2.06bn, opened its first store in the UK in 1984 and between 1990 and 2008 opened stores in the Republic of Ireland, the Netherlands, Sweden, Norway, Denmark, Spain, Finland, Australia and New Zealand through a franchise arrangement. Specsavers refer to their franchise programme as a partnership and has grown the organisation using a partnership approach.

SPECSAVERS

Specsavers is a partnership of approximately 2,000 locally run businesses that offer high-quality, affordable optical and hearing care in the communities they serve. Each store is part-owned and managed by its own directors who are shareholders and are aided by key specialists in support offices who provides helped in some of the following areas: marketing, accounting, IT and many more. By structuring the organisation in this way individual owners working in the community feel they are part of the organisation and have a stake in its growth and development but also by providing central support it ensures that the opticians and audiologist can concentrate on providing expert eye and hearing care to their customers. There are currently more than 1,700 partners in the UK and the Republic of Ireland, 548 have been partners for at least ten years. This spirit of British entrepreneurship has been encouraged by the founders of Specsavers, Doug and Dame Mary Perkins, who 30 years ago pioneered the optical joint venture partnership model. They have revolutionised the industry with their innovative concept of affordable fashionable eye care, at a time when high prices for optical care and limited choice were the norm.

Specsavers is also the largest employer of registered optometrists and dispensing opticians (around 3,500) in the UK. All Specsavers' opticians are registered with the General Optical Council so customers can rest assured that their eyes are tested and their glasses prescribed by fully qualified and registered practitioners.

Adapted from www.specsavers.co.uk

REFLECTIVE ACTIVITY 6.1

The world of work is changing fast. What changes would you recommend to the board of directors at Specsavers? Reference a new L&D strategy for 2017–2022.

PUBLIC SECTOR ORGANISATIONS

Public sector organisations are owned, funded and run by central or local government. Organisations that are typically considered to be public sector organisations are public hospitals; the armed forces; government departments; most schools, colleges and universities. The Government controls 24 ministerial departments, 22 non-ministerial departments, 372 agencies and other public bodies, 75 high-profile groups, 11 public corporations and three devolved administrations (www.gov.uk). While most government organisations exist originally to provide services, which for various reasons are considered impractical or undesirable for the commercial sector, we cannot take for granted that this is still the case. There is, however, a number of private hospitals, schools, colleges and universities in the UK that are classified as non-public sector organisations.

REFLECTIVE ACTIVITY 6.2

The growth in private hospitals has escalated since the 1970s. Prior to this, individuals could rely only on the National Health Service (NHS) hospitals established after 1948. BMI Healthcare is the acute private hospital division of the parent company General Healthcare Group and is the largest independent provider of private health care in the UK with over 60 hospitals nationwide. Many NHS hospitals operate private facilities within the same hospital.

Think about the schools, hospitals and colleges in your local area. Are they public or private sector organisations or a combination of the two? Discuss with your peers how private or public organisations potentially view L&D differently.

Adapted from: www.bmihealthcare.co.uk

Public sector organisations are characteristically associated with limited resources, based on government policies to reduce expenditure, but improve efficiencies in a variety of government funded areas. Consequently, there has been a growth in public sector and business organisation partnerships, referred to in some instances as public/private partnerships (PPP). PPP is the general term for partnerships which involve everything from operating facilities and providing services on behalf of the public, to flexible methods of financing these services and PFI (Private Finance Initiative) which is a particular method of financing capital investment which requires that the private sector design, build, finance and operate specific facilities.

PPP and PFI have been and are still at the heart of the government's attempts to revive Britain's public services. Under Tony Blair's Government (1997–2007), PPPs developed because he believed that private companies were more efficient and better run than bureaucratic public bodies. In trying to bring the public and private sector together, the government hoped that the management skills and financial acumen of the business community would create better value for money for taxpayers (BBC 2003). This view encouraged leaders in public sector organisations to develop employees in more commercial practices and models normally used and associated with business organisations to improve performance, efficiencies, customer service and to reduce costs. Successive UK Governments have implemented a range of PPP programmes and in 2013 there were more than 130 healthcare PPPs, worth £12bn in capital value for acute, primary, community and mental health services with a high degree of engagement with clinicians and the public.

CASE STUDY 6.2

EXAMPLE OF PUBLIC PRIVATE PARTNERSHIP IN THE HEALTH SECTOR

HCP Social Infrastructure (UK) Ltd and Barts Health NHS Trust

The £1.1bn redevelopment of St Bartholomew's and The Royal London New Hospitals PFI is the largest private finance initiative hospital scheme to be undertaken in the UK and involves the reconfiguration and re-provision of clinical accommodation across two major inner London acute hospital sites.

In this project, in addition to the design, construction and maintenance of the new facilities, the private sector provides high-tech equipment, all facilities management and Central Sterile Services Department (CSSD) services. The concession runs until 2048.

Source: Healthcare: Public Private Partnership (2013) (www.gov.uk).

NOT-FOR-PROFIT ORGANISATIONS

These types of organisations do not exist to make a profit for their owners. All the money earned or donated to this type of organisation must be used by the organisation to pursue its objectives. It is not that these types of organisations cannot make a profit but as mentioned above the profits must be used by the organisation to achieve its objectives. Organisations that would be considered in this category are: all registered charities, some schools, Students' Union, housing associations, professional bodies and religious organisations. Table 6.1 lists *The UK's Best 100 Companies, 2015* (top ten, not-for-profit organisations). Factors used to assess organisations in this category are: leadership, employee engagement, management communication, training and future prospects, team working, well-being, pay, benefits and positive impact on society. These types of organisations will need to ensure that they employ and retain a good balance of employees with the knowledge, skills and abilities of both public and private sector workers. It is important for charities to have a good grasp of how to lobby for external funds and manage limited resources which could fluctuate from one year to the next, a common feature of working in a public sector organisation. Not-for-profit organisations also need to have the creativity, innovation and business acumen associated with some private organisations.

Table 6.1 Top ten of the UK's Best 100 Companies 2015, not-for-profit organisation category

Rank	Company
1	SLH Group
2	Christians Against Poverty
3	Wales & West Housing
4	Community Gateway Association
5	Bromsgrove District Housing Trust
6	Dale and Valley Home
7	B3Living
8	New Charter Group
9	BHA Homes
10	Stafford and Rural Homes

Source: www.b.co.uk

REFLECTIVE ACTIVITY 6.3

Is there any difference in the skills required to manage a public, private and not-for-profit organisation?

How should each organisation develop the skills to cope with the challenges that are facing these types of organisations?

MANAGING AND ORGANISING ORGANISATIONS

The study of managing and organising organisations is still a developing field and has been a major source of interest for classical and modern-day theorists. The purpose of this section is to establish a historical and evolutionary perspective to the development of managing and organising organisations. Many of the perspectives have been with us for many years and there is early evidence of people developing collectively, which is still evident today in small family businesses (Ward 2012). There are early forms of non-family organisations as far back as 3500 BC from the Sumerian people who settled by the Euphrates river (McKelvey 1982). The study of early management was different and not as developed as the management work published after the twentieth century and materialised in a few known documents that have survived – for example archaeologists' and historians' reports in the form of writings about events, societies or trade practices (Martin 2005). Many of the management practices we associate with organisations today can be traced back to ancient times, as indicated in Table 6.2.

Table 6.2: Management concepts in ancient times

Approximate period	Groups	Management/organisation contributions
5000 BC	Sumerians	Taxation, records and written documents
4000 BC	Egyptians	Planning, organising and controlling
2600 BC	Egyptians	Decentralisation
1800 BC	Babylonians	Business, law, minimum wage, responsibility
1600 BC	Egyptians	Decentralisation
1500 BC	Hebrews	Management by exception, chain of command
1100 BC	Chinese	Planning, organising, directing and controlling
1100 BC	Ghazali	Traits of managers
900 BC	Alfarabi	Traits of leaders
600 BC	Nebuchadnezzar	Wage incentives and production control systems
500 BC	Chinese	Job specialisation
400 BC	Xenophon	Identification of management as a separate activity
175 BC	Cato	Job descriptions

Adapted from George (1972)

Following from this period was the Dark Ages. Little documentation is available but some information emerged during the period from 900 to 1100 AD on the characteristics of leaders and managers. This period was characterised by a feudal system and with people being forced to work on land that was owned by other people. The Middle Ages saw the growth of craftsmen from a variety of trades clustering together in guilds; this started the development of regulations surrounding the entry into different trades for example the number of people allowed to practise the craft and some control over pricing, which included what individuals could charge for their skills. This era saw the early developments of trade unions and trade associations (Martin 2005).

The Industrial Revolution period was noted for its use of forced labour and the development of the early factory system. It was also the development of writers interested in the management of resources, growth of organisations and wealth. The notable writer Adam Smith published *Wealth of Nations* in 1776, where he argued that the market in which most organisations operate dictated the most efficient use of resources. While Smith recognised the benefits of the 'free market' in governing business activities, he also recognised that this approach could see the development of specialisation in the workplace and a long-term damaging work environment for workers. Along with Adam Smith, some of the writers and their interests in the managing and organising of people at work can be seen in Table 6.3.

Table 6.3 Management concepts

Year	Individual	Interest
1767	Sir James Stewart	Authority and automation
1776	Adam Smith	Specialisation and control
1799	Eli Witney	Scientific methods, quality control and span of management
1800	James Watt	Operating procedures
1800	Matthew Boulton	Planning, work methods, incentive wages
1810	Robert Owen	Personnel Management, training and housing for workers
1820	James Mill	Human movement at work
1832	Charles Babbage	Scientific organisation of work
1835	Marshall Laughin	Management aspects of work

Adapted from George (1972)

Robert Owen's work identified the importance of training and developing people at work. Employers during the period of Owen's study started to increase the number of people working in their organisations but soon became concerned that a high proportion of their employees were not able to do the activities of the job correctly and not necessarily to the right standard. Training needs of employees were taken into consideration especially as the education levels of most of the employees were poor. Engineering skills in particular were scarce and the consistency of quality and performance was concerning amongst employers who were left with little choice but to train and educate their employees initially in mathematical and reading skills (Martin 2005). In addition to this a number of problems were identified with the early factory system which included discipline and motivation issues, as workers tried to adapt to the regular attendance and controlled work activities. The scale of the factory operation made it difficult for owners to manage all aspects of the business so individuals were employed to assist the owner to manage the organisation. They were generally illiterate but were considered loyal and good workers (Wren 1994).

In more recent times, employers have raised concerns about the skills young people have prior to employment with their organisation. Major concerns have been around the lack of mathematical and communication skills that are fundamental to some organisations. This has raised some concerns at all education levels: schools, colleges and universities. The term 'employability' has been echoed for a number of years by governments and employers. This has seen a number of courses including employable skills increased. Detailed breakdowns and taxonomies of particular skills and attributes are now required to promote graduate employability and they include: core skills, key skills, common skills, transferable skills, essential skills, functional skills, skills for life, generic skills and enterprise skills. Lowden *et al* (2011) in their research commissioned by the Edge Foundation found that most employers are looking for:

> graduates who are proactive, can use higher-level skills including analysis, critique, synthesis and multi-layered communication to facilitate innovative teamwork in catalysing the transformation of their organization.

Successive governments concerned with Britain's competitiveness with the rest of the world have developed education policies focusing on STEM subjects which are science, technology, engineering and mathematics which the Government considers are the foundations of the industrial and corporate world and have offered bursaries to potential students looking to undertake teacher training in these areas at universities. There have also been a number of initiatives to promote reading and maths in primary schools and in 2014 the Department for Education (DFE) and the Office of Qualifications and

Examination Regulation (Ofqual) proposed changes to the structure and content of GCSEs taken by students in England to include a much larger, more 'challenging' GCSE in Maths with more emphasis on solving problems that require multi-step solutions.

We have seen a growth of corporate universities particularly in the US. A corporate university is an 'educational entity that is a strategic tool designed to assist its parent organization in achieving its goals by conducting activities that foster individual and organizational learning and knowledge' (Allen 2002). The concept could open up an interesting debate on the lack of confidence in education establishments preparing potential employees, but equally could been seen as forward-thinking – organisations continually developing the knowledge, skills and ability of its workforce to remain competitive. In 1993 there were only 400 corporate universities and by 2001 this number had increased to 2,000 and included: Walt Disney, Boeing, Unilever and Motorola. They are set up for a variety of reasons, but most organisations have the same basic needs, these are:

- bring a common culture, loyalty and belonging to a company
- get the most out of the investment in education
- organise training
- remain competitive in today's economy
- retain employees
- start and support change in the organisation.

MANAGEMENT PERSPECTIVES

It was not until the beginning of the twentieth century that the study of management started to feature as an activity in its own right. A number of management perspectives emerged at that time, leading to a number of writers contributing to and developing the written work in this field. While there is no accepted definition of management, the general and common understanding is that management involves planning, organising, leading and controlling resources to assist in achieving organisational goals. This definition reflects the work of Henri Fayol (1841–1925), a French industrialist and theorist who spent his entire life working in the same company and became the Managing Director at the age of 47. Under his leadership the company grew and prospered and in 1916 he published his work on management. His definition of management is still acceptable many years after it was written, he stated: 'To manage is to forecast and plan, to organise, to command, to co-ordinate and to control.'

Fayol went on to develop his 'principles of management', which included 14 key principles all managers should observe. These are listed in Table 6.4.

Table 6.4 Fayol's principles of management

1	Division of work	Reduces the span of attention or effort for any one person or group. Develops practice and familiarity.
2	Authority	The right to give orders. Should not be considered without reference to responsibility.
3	Discipline	Respect for others in accordance with formal or informal agreements.
4	Unity of command	One man, one superior
5	Unity of direction	One head and one plan for a group of activities with the same objective.
6	Subordination of individual interest to the general interest	The interest of one individual or one group should not prevail over the general good.

7	Remuneration	Pay should be fair for employees and employers.
8	Centralisation	Should be always present, depending on the size of the company and quality of its managers.
9	Scalar chain	The line of authority from top to bottom of the organisation.
10	Order	A place of for everything and everything in its place.
11	Equity	A combination of kindliness and justice towards employees.
12	Stability of tenure of personnel	Employees need to be given time to settle into their jobs.
13	Initiative	Within the limits of authority and discipline, staff should be encouraged to show initiative.
14	Esprit de corps	Harmony is a great strength to an organisation and teamwork should be encouraged.

Later followers of Fayol's work such as Urwick and Brech (1994) adopted his principles. The foundations of Fayol's principles are stability, order, respect for individuals in authority, discipline and centralisation which is typical of a formal, tall structured, bureaucratic organisation which can appear at first to see employees as not so important as management and the orderly running of the organisation. However, the inclusion in his principles of equity, esprit de corps, initiative and stability of tenure gives the impression of a paternalistic perspective (the principle or practice of managing individuals in the manner of a father dealing benevolently and often intrusively with his children) which can appear to be contradictory. Mintzberg (1973) reported from his major study of managerial work that the key management roles that were prevalent in his study were: interpersonal roles, (figurehead, leader and liaison), informational roles (monitor, disseminator and spokesman) and decisional roles (entrepreneur, disturbance handler, resource allocator and negotiator). These roles are very generic and some can be applied to non-managerial roles (Cole 2004).

Other writers have contributed to Fayol's original definition, for example Brech (1994) and Koontz and O'Donnell (1984). Rather than use the word 'command' Brech replaces it with 'motivation' and Koontz and O'Donnell use 'directing and leading'. Peters (1988) moves the definition on from what is management to what management needs to do. He emphasises the chaotic world that managers operate in and states that:

> an obsession with responsiveness to customers, constant innovation in all areas of the firm, partnership – the wholesale participation of and gain sharing with all people connected with the organisation, leadership that love change, instils and shares an inspiring vision and controls by means of simple support systems aimed at measuring the 'right stuff' for today's environment.

Peters' definition of management includes: responsiveness, innovation, leadership, change, vision, control and measuring which are key words that feature in management literature today and each have been the topic of research and wider discussions. It is also important to note that responsiveness, change and vision are also associated with the strategic planning process which involves setting corporate objectives and (goals this will be discussed later in this chapter). We also need to consider that Peters wrote his definition approximately 72 years after Fayol had published his definition of management and the environment that most businesses operated in 72 years ago would be different to the environment most businesses operate in today.

The notion of goals and results are central to our understanding of management and without goals there is no purpose that guides decision about planning, organising, leading and directing. There is also in Peters' definition a wider responsibility view of management that seems to include looking beyond the organisation into the wider environment which some of the early definitions seem to exclude. Although subject to debate mainstream management can be divided into five general perspectives: classical, behavioural, quantitative, integrating and contemporary.

The classical perspectives

Under the classical perspectives, two well-documented management theories can be found: scientific management which was concerned with work specialisation, working methods and improving productivity; and administrative management, focused on different ways to manage the whole organisation.

One of the leaders in scientific management was FW Taylor (1911), who was most famous for his work at Midvale Steel and the Bethlehem Steel Company in the US. After the industrial revolution in the eighteenth and nineteenth centuries many organisations in different countries made attempts to introduce highly structured and deliberate activities to improve work and management practices, some with the main intention to improve productivity. Taylor brought together many of the different strands of thinking into one methodology. He spent some time trying to determine how much work could be expected from a worker each day. The general assumption was that workers tried to keep their output low to reduce the demands on them from management. His preoccupations with design of appropriate tools and equipment, the selection and training of appropriate employees who should be capable of doing the job, the development of incentive-based wage structures to encourage high productivity and the appropriate management to support these changes formed the basis of scientific management. The elements used by Taylor in the development of scientific management can be recognised in organisations today in recruitment and selection, training and development and performance management techniques (particularly where the scheme is linked to pay).

Taylor focused his ideas on work that was repetitive. One example documented in his work was the study of men loading pig iron into railway wagons. The average production for this work was 12.5 tonnes per day but Taylor calculated that if the person doing the task worked 42% of the time it would not be unreasonable for the person to produce 47 tonnes. To demonstrate this Taylor selected a man called 'Schmidt', supervised him closely and gave him clear instructions how to do the job and scheduled substantial breaks throughout the day for the worker. The result was Schmidt's productivity was 47.5 tonnes for the day and Taylor trained more men doing the same work and over a short period of time they produced the same tonnes per day as Schmidt. After a number of similar experiments with different production tasks within the organisation, Taylor's experiments proved successful in improving productivity for the organisation and increased wages for the labourers, based on the pricing of each job. The higher the output achieved, the higher the wage earned. This became known as 'piecework'.

Henry Ford supported Taylor's work and further developed Taylor's methods in the production of motor cars between 1903 and 1926, which was later referred to as 'Fordism'. Motor cars were seen as luxury items built by craftsmen and only affordable to people who were more prosperous. Ford wanted to sell more cars and make his product affordable to the masses so he focused on a number of things to reduce costs. Standardisation, interchangeability, precision, simplicity, specialisation, synchronisation and conveyor belt production were all introduced at Ford's Model T plant, Highland Park, Michigan in 1914.

Taylor's and Ford's developments and results were seen as impressive and adopted by organisations in the US and other parts of the world but the scientific methods adopted produced some negative impact for the employee and the employer. For example, more control over the production process by management demotivated workers who, when worked faster, increased their outputs and expected a higher wage. These workers found that some managers would reduce the unit value for a job which in some instances would reduce the wage for workers producing high outputs. The new processes also generated a 'carrot and stick' approach by enabling pay to be geared closely to output (Cole 2004). At Ford, repetitive work resulted in boredom amongst workers who would try to organise in unions to fight for their rights. Well supported, highly organised unions could disrupt production and this was not always received well by some employers. While new production methods resulted in high quantities and cheaper goods being produced this met with higher demand from customers. When demand slowed down but high quantities were still being produced but not sold, employment was uncertain leaving employees looking for methods to remain in employment, even if it involved slowing down production (Smith 2011). Globalisation with the import of cheaper products being produced in countries like India and China has contributed today to the slowing down or closing down of production of some goods in the UK. New technology has seen production workers having to retrain in how to produce items using fewer skills or learn new skills making them multi-skilled consequently reducing the number of production workers required.

Administration management included writers like Fayol and Max Weber (1864–1920). Weber, unlike Fayol and Taylor, was an academic sociologist and not a practising manager. He was particularly interested in organisations especially the authority structures that he found in organisations. He wanted to find out why people in organisations obeyed individuals in authority over them and tried to provide guidelines for a rational organisation which had rules enabling the organisation to perform predictably and consistently. The findings from his observations were published in 1947 and it is in his work that the word 'bureaucracy' was used to describe a rational form of organisation, and this term is still being used in organisations today. Weber noted the key features of bureaucracy as:

- a continuous organisation of functions bound by rules
- specified scope of competence – the specialisation of work, the degree and rules governing authority
- a hierarchical arrangement of jobs
- appointment to jobs based on technical competence
- the separation of officials from the ownership of the organisation
- rules, decisions and actions formulated and recorded in writing (Cole 2004).

Weber attempted to improve office operations in a similar way to how Taylor tried to improve factory production. Researchers since Weber have noted weaknesses in the bureaucratic model and these can be summarised as:

- Relationships can be depersonalised and lead to rigid behaviour (predictability).
- Decision making can be categorised; that is, choices are previously programmed and can discourage the search for further alternatives.
- The effects of rigid behaviour can be very damaging for client or customer relations and also for the management–worker relationship. It is unlikely that customers can obtain tailor-made services but have to accept standardisation.
- Standardisation and routine procedures make change difficult when circumstances change.
- The exercise of 'control based on knowledge' has led to a growth of experts whose opinions and attitudes may clash with those of the generalist managers and supervisors.

The behavioural perspectives

This perspective includes the human relations school, based on the importance of groups and the social context, and Organisational Behaviour, an approach to managing organisations that incorporate individuals, groups and organisational processes.

Elton Mayo's (1880–1949) work on the Hawthorne experiments made significant contributions to the human relations school. Mayo was an Australian who taught logic, psychology and ethics at the University of Queensland. In 1922 he moved to Harvard Business School to become Professor of Industrial Research. His experiments at Hawthorne (an electrical plant near Chicago) began in 1924 with the objective of gauging the effects of illumination on workers' productivity. A series of experiments were carried out which involved two groups of workers working under different conditions. One group was the control group and continued their work in the existing conditions while the other group worked under varied levels of illumination. In the experimental group, as the illumination rose so did productivity but, interestingly, the productivity also rose when illumination was reduced. It was concluded that the increase or decrease in illumination was not the key factor but the attention they were receiving as being part of the experiment.

Further studies in other parts of the factory showed how groups working in the bank wiring room controlled the amount that was produced by each worker by establishing an agreed amount that can be produced even if it was lower than what could realistically be produced. If a worker produced above or below the expected amount they would be the subject of sarcastic comments from their fellow workers. Mayo concluded that it was important for managers to take account of social and psychological factors, for example social norms and group dynamics. Research, publications and courses at colleges and universities were inspired by the work of Mayo and the many that developed his work, for example Mary Parker Follet (1941), McGregor (1960), Maslow (1970) and Alderfer (1972) helped to establish the growth in the field of organisational behaviour.

The quantitative perspectives

This perspective concerns the growth in management science and the use of mathematical models for decision making and problem solving. This was developed during the Second World War, when mathematical and statistical techniques were used to solve large-scale military, production and logistical problems. Models were used to allow variables to be quantified and the relationship between them identified. Techniques developed under this area paved the way for the establishment of systematic methods for measuring product quality and contributed to the developments in Operations Management research. Courses, production planning, forecasting and scenario-planning techniques developed around this era. With the development of technology and technological support for data collection, analysis, modelling and computation, management science soon adopted it in industry (Martin and Fellenz 2010). Scenario planning allowed the development of 'what if' options so that different options can be evaluated before execution.

Integrating perspectives

This includes the systems theory which is a range of approaches that uses a set of interrelated elements to emphasise how the study of organisation and management function as a whole. The contingency theory looks at the behaviour in any given context as a function of a wide set of contingent factors.

Boulding (1956) and von Bertalanffy (1968) developed the phrase 'general systems theory' after it was suggested that a proliferation of management theories was causing confusion and did not offer a comprehensive explanation of management and organisational phenomena. Advocates of system theory set out to rectify the confusion by considering organisations as a whole made up of a set of interrelated parts that need to function as a whole to a common purpose in the same way doctors need to consider the human body as a whole. The general assumption is that each part of the organisation impacts on other parts and that for the organisation to work, all parts need to work together in a co-ordinated way (Smith 2011). Systems can be closed or open. Closed systems are systems that are self-supporting and do not need to interact with their environment. They are referred to as 'linear' systems and it is normally clear what actions must be taken to achieve a given goal. An open system, on the other hand, needs to interact with its environment, which it relies on to obtain essential inputs and the discharge of outputs. Organisations, biological and information systems are open systems. Figure 6.1 shows a basic model of a closed and open system. The key feature of an open system is the interdependency on the environment, which may be stable or relatively uncertain at different points in time. This is an important feature for most organisations that need to adapt to the changes in the market they choose to operate in.

Most systems are made up of subsystems; Martin (2005) uses the example below to demonstrate subsystems and larger systems:

> Consider, for example, a school class. It is probably made up of family and friendship groups, teacher and pupil groups and ability groups. However, it is also part of a school, which in turn is part of education system and a town and a country and so on. Therefore, a network of systems exists in an exceedingly complex interactive and mutually dependent set of relationships.

The environment that an organisation operates in can be difficult to define. Using the above example of a school the environment can consist of: family members, friends, other classes, teachers, local education authorities, employers, government officials at local, national and even international level and the list could go on. Stakeholders are any individuals or groups that are affected by an organisation and would also be added to an extended open-system diagram. An open system is complex as it can have more than one system or environment and this can change over time which can imply a considerable degree of uncertainty and ambiguity with the system approach.

Figure 6.1 Example of a closed and open system

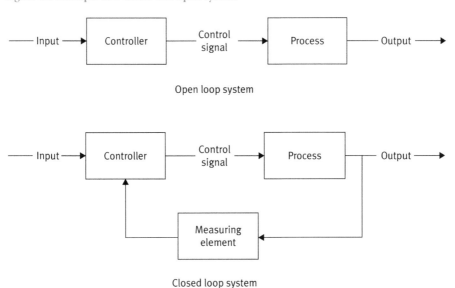

Open loop system

Closed loop system

Contingency theory builds on the systems approach and suggests the most appropriate organisational style and management style for a given set of circumstances taking into consideration the following variables: the external environment, technological factors, human skills and motivation. Lawrence and Lorsch (1967), two Harvard researchers, suggested the label 'contingency approach' and took the view that there was no one best way to manage and organise. They hoped their studies in the approach would provide a systematic understanding of what conditions of differentiation and integration are related to effective performance under different environment conditions. Others who have continued the approach have included Joan Woodward, who carried out studies between 1953 and 1958 and Burns and Stalker (1961). The Aston Group, all originally from the University of Aston in Birmingham, began a major study in various aspects in the late 1960s.

ORGANISATION STRUCTURES

Fayol's theory of authority structures mentioned above gives the first sense of how an organisation could be structured and organised to provide order, recognition, control, formality, development, specialisation and equity. This section considers how managers divide, supervise and co-ordinate work and how this is linked closely to organisation dynamics and culture.

The characteristics of an organisation chart generally include the following: departments, levels, job titles, lines linking senior staff/managers to people they are responsible for, who people report to, the major activities of the organisation and subdivisions, as seen in Figure 6.2 (Boddy 2014). While this is what we would find in a formal structure, informal structures (the many patterns of work and communication that are part of organisational life) exist but are not normally made explicit on formal organisation charts. The informal organisation can take on a life of its own and work towards goals that are different from the formal organisation goals – for example, through 'grapevine' information communicated or decisions made through this method may be inaccurate or distorted; information organisation can also exclude certain people and their ideas. It is important in understanding the formal structure that we consider the elements of job design.

JOB DESIGN

Job design is organising what people need to do as part of their job and how this links into the organisation structure. Aspects of job design can include: specialisation, authority and span of control. Within a formal structure, work can be divided into smaller specialised tasks for individuals or departments. Specialisation can be vertical, where people at different levels have distinct responsibilities or it could be horizontal specialisation, where tasks are divided amongst separate people or departments. In both vertical and horizontal examples the lines of authority are used to signal who people should report to or who they are responsible for. It gives people across the organisation or sometimes individuals outside the organisation a sense of who is responsible and who they can ask to do various activities. Authority is the formal power to make decisions, employ and deploy resources and give instructions to others. It is part of the job characteristics of an individual and remains the same if the job is held by a different person. It does not, however, mean that if someone is in a position of authority that subordinates will obey their authority, which can make the study of authority complicated. Also someone in authority might be a senior manager, and may follow the judgement of a HR manager when selecting new staff because of the HR manager's expertise. The modern trend is to delegate authority where possible and push authority as far down the organisation as possible.

SPAN OF CONTROL

The number of employees any one manager has to supervise is referred to as the 'span of control'. Traditionally it was suggested that six subordinates was the optimum span of control and that responsibility for more than six subordinates could result in 'communication overload' for the manager. However, the span of control can vary depending on environmental factors – for example, stability. The increased use of technology may also be one of the reasons why spans of managerial control have increased over the years.

CENTRALISATION AND DECENTRALISATION

Authority, span of control and specialisation are all key characteristics of developing organisation structures. As an organisation grows, however, other considerations may include how we divide it into functions, divisions and matrices and whether particular functions should be centralised (when a relatively large number of decisions are taken by management at the top of the organisation) or decentralised (when a relatively large number of decisions are taken lower down the organisation in the operating units) (Boddy 2014). Some of the disadvantages to centralisation include: slower response rate to local conditions, local suppliers to the organisation may be better value than corporate ones, staff motivation because of more responsibility. However, some centralised staff pay little attention to ideas and suggestions at local level. Centralisation can benefit some organisations as costs can be reduced if central common systems are employed. A centralised system can also help to promote consistency across an organisation.

Some organisations choose to centralise some functions and decentralise others and over the years there have been developments in outsourcing, a growth of organisations through franchising, and increased market capabilities through partnerships with other organisations and sharing activities.

DIVIDING WORK INTERNALLY

Work can be divided into the following: a functional, divisional, matrix or network structure. A functional structure is where staff are divided according to profession or functions. This is generally a popular way to structure an organisation and is easy in that grouping individuals together who understand each other might best serve organisations as it is simple and might be more effective, as seen in Figure 6.2. A divisional structure is normally structured around products, services or customers. The functions within the division would co-operate because they all depend on the same set of customers; the focus enables good internal relations. However, divisional structures can create isolation from the wider professional and technical developments and the structure can potentially have conflict with other divisions over priorities.

Some structures, which do not fit exactly into one of the structures mentioned above, are referred to as 'hybrid structures'; one of the best known of these structures is the matrix structure. Responsiveness to customer demand and the need to reduce costs has forced some companies to integrating competitive features of small companies with the resources of large corporations. Some large organisations have abandoned rigid structures around functional responsibilities and the strict obedience to rules and efficiencies which had sometimes kept them out of touch with their customers and the market (Drucker 1991).

Small businesses that were seen as more customer-focused, seemed to perform better in the marketplace, because they had the speed and flexibility to respond to customer needs and changes in the market. They also had decentralised structures which pushed staff responsibilities towards the business unit allowing maximum agility (Lentz 1996). Robertson (2015), explores the concept of 'Holacracy' which is a practice for organisations that individuals engage in and involves working together and moving the organisation and cultures along its natural evolutionary journey. This concept advocates a flexible way to organising people and developing organisational cultures and avoids the use of organisational structures as outlined in this chapter. Some individuals could find this concept frustrating especially if they have experience of working in a more structured organisation; also, it could be a difficult organisation to manage. Some companies, however, could thrive in that type of environment.

Figure 6.2 Example of a simple structure and a matrix structure

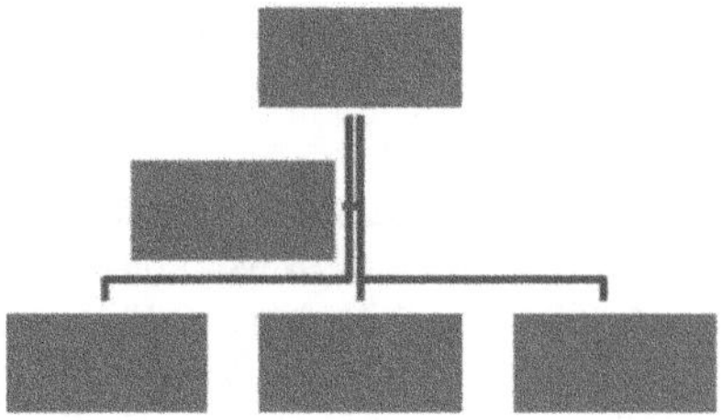

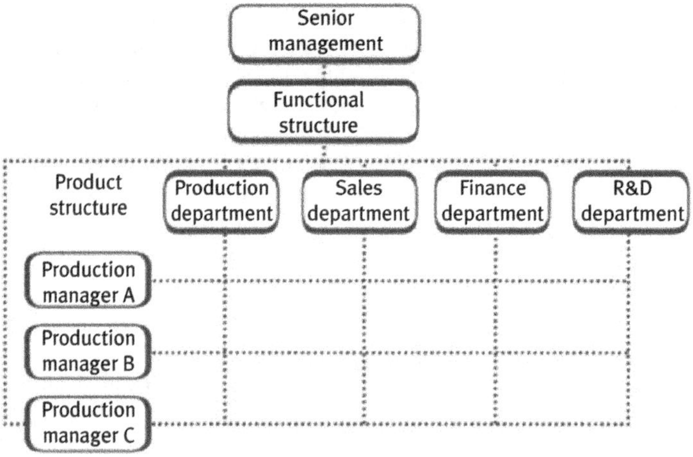

Larger organisations trying to replicate this model struggled with resource duplications and high cost. Some organisations have managed to mix the competitive features of customer focus and flexibility with the use of economies of scale. For example, a consulting company might decide to use a 'project structure,' which is centred on project needs with internal resources, with a functional structure for its support functions. The matrix structure allows for the sharing of key people and expertise across products and projects. Where it is structured according to projects, individuals can move from one project to another and stay with each project for a period of time. This type of structure can be stimulating, rewarding and a development opportunity for individuals that are part of it. Hybrid structures such as the matrix structure can bring challenges and difficulties – for example, their complex arrangements are characterised by multiple reporting relationships. For individual employees, they often create conflict because of competing and incompatible expectations, demands and objectives (Martin and Fellenz 2011). Atkinson (2003) stated that a matrix structure should be regarded as a process and not a structure, which should evolve and self-renew based on feedback and reflection from members and the environment. He also suggested that for matrix structures to be successful a supportive culture needs to be in existence.

ORGANISATIONAL CULTURE

Schein's (1992) definition of organisational culture is culture is: 'deep basic, assumptions and beliefs that are shared by organisational members.' Managing the culture of an organisation is sometimes presented as an easy task, however, it is complex, difficult to really define, comprises habits and values, referred to as norms by which people identify themselves and others. Schein differentiates between three levels of culture outlined in Table 6.5, starting with aspects that define an organisational culture that is visible to aspects that are hidden and almost invisible. Handy (1993) from a management consultant view, points out that:

> ...anyone who has spent time with any variety organisations... will have been struck by the differing atmospheres, the differing way of doing things, the differing levels of energy, of individual freedom, of kinds of personality.

He observed four main types of culture: power, role, task and person culture, although his general view was that culture cannot be precisely defined as it is perceived by individuals and observers or something that is felt. The power culture symbolised by 'a web' was characterised by the power base within the organisation emanating from the centre of the organisation, the figurehead and the leader. Role culture is symbolised by a Greek temple and is a classical structure characterised by its bureaucratic nature where the role is more important than the people who fill them and position power predominates while expert power is tolerated. Task culture symbolised by a net focuses on completing the job, individuals' expertise and contributions are valued highly. Expert power is important along with personal and position power. This type of culture encourages and supports collaboration. Finally the person culture which is symbolised by a cluster or galaxy and is characterised by a loose collection of individuals, usually professionals, sharing common facilities but pursuing their own goals separately, therefore power is not really an issue since individuals are professionals and experts in their own right. This type of culture serves the individual.

Cole (2004) notes that culture may be different between organisations but there is normally a shared understanding within them. Also, the culture of an organisation is not established until there is a shared understanding that is collectively accepted by members. He also noted that within any single culture there are usually subcultures which operate at a lower level of influence within the organisation and Morgan's (1998) example of this is 'just as individuals in a (national) culture can have different personalities while sharing much in common, so too with groups and organisations.'

The dominant culture in organisations is primarily the product of the aims and methods of its founders or their successors in senior management and combined with aspects of their integration with external and internal forces. Some of the interrelationship between culture and other aspects of an organisation includes: purpose and goals, external customers and competitors, rules and procedures, communication channels, decision-making mechanisms, the use of technology, employee skills and attitudes, organisational structures and organisation policies (Cole 2004).

Table 6.5 Schein's three levels of culture

Schein's three levels of culture
Level One – consists of visible organisational features, e.g. physical structure of buildings, uniforms and interior design. This level is visible but does not reveal everything about the organisation culture. Some rich and powerful organisations use architecture to impress the less fortunate with the grandeur of their wealth.
Level Two – comprises espoused values. Values are a non-visible aspect of culture that includes the norms and beliefs that employees express when they discuss organisational issues, e.g. the company mission statement or commitment to diversity.
Level Three – includes the basic assumptions that shape organisational members' world views, beliefs and norms which guide behaviour without being explicitly expressed. This is the most influential level because it works surreptitiously and shapes decision-making processes. This level is said to be hard to observe and hard to change, but the level that carries the most potential for transformation.

Hofstede (1997) referred to culture as a form of mental programming – patterns of thinking, feeling and doing learned from childhood. He states that culture is derived from shared experiences in the same social environment, which distinguishes one group of people, or organisation from another and also that a group's culture reveals itself in a variety of ways through symbols, heroes, rituals and values. He describes symbols as external signs that mean something to those who share the culture, this could be pictures, objects, styles of dress, particular words or even gestures, he considered symbols to be the outer layer of culture and used the analogy of an onion. Heroes was referred to as the next layer of the onion and are people living or dead who are looked up to in the culture and serves as a model for acceptable behaviour. Rituals he noted as collective activities that are considered as socially essential and included ways of greeting strangers, public and religious ceremonies and business meetings.

Table 6.6 New developments and implications for L&D

Leverage learning optimism	It is important that the L&D function continues to influence changes in the organisation and push to maximise resources to achieve the L&D strategies.
Integrate learning and work	85% of L&D leaders want to improve business performance. 61% say L&D activity is aligned to the strategic goals of the business. 54% consider their role is shifting towards performance consultancy. 48% still believe the course is the only option for building performance. 36% L&D have a plan for how they will meet agreed business metrics.
Actively seek to understand 'internal customers'	It is important that L&D professionals understand their learners, the environment they operate in and the different ways people learn to ensure success.
Put technology on the learning agenda	Technology is important to create flexibility and agility in the learning environment. It is important that L&D professionals keep abreast of innovations in technology to support the L&D strategies in organisations. However, the report notes the following: 23% of L&D leaders think their L&D teams have the right skills to exploit technology for business advantage. 50% still say that L&D staff lack knowledge about the potential use and implementation of technology.
Think digital	L&D functions need to invest in social learning technologies as a future key development for the whole organisation. However: 34% have the skills in-house for live online learning delivery. 37% plan to increase this in the next two years. 20% have the skills in-house for facilitating social and collaborative learning; 46% plan to increase. 32% have the skills in-house for supporting ongoing workplace performance; 46% plan to increase.
Proactively invest in new L&D skills	L&D professionals need to ensure that they continue to develop themselves and have the right skills to devise the appropriate strategies to ensure organisational success

Source: Preparing for the future of Learning, CIPD (2016)

Clegg (1990) described a new type of organisation, the 'post-modern organisation', which is less rigid and predictable than those outlined above in the early management and organisational perspectives characterised by highly differentiated, demarcated and de-skilled. Post modern organisations and jobs are highly de-differentiated, de-demarcated and multi-skilled. Clegg also noted that bureaucracy, macho managers and boring jobs have been replaced in the post modern world with flexible organisations, with employees participating in decision making, supportive managers and interested multi-skilled jobs. Clegg's description supports Tom Peters' view of the chaotic world that managers operate in and the open system mentioned above could help complement their thinking by considering the organisation as a whole and interacting with the environment to support the organisation in coping with changes outside the organisation and achieving its objectives with the changed environment inside the organisation. Organisations need employees that can embrace the challenges that Clegg and Peters describe above and still perform at high levels to help the organisation achieve its objectives. Organisations need to support employees to develop knowledge, skills and ability in a wide range of areas to cope with complex and changing organisations. Some of the key area organisations should focus on are: creativity, innovation, intrapreneurship and cross-cultural awareness.

The term intrapreneur stems from the rise of enterprising employees who are inspired to make a difference and introduce dynamics that support cost saving and increased revenues. The only difference between an intrapreneur and an entrepreneur is that an intrapreneur usually operates within an existing business. Entrepreneurs are normally associated with small organisations noted for their creativity, innovation and flexibility but large commercial organisations and even public sector organisations can foster an intrapreneurial culture.

Organisations need to provide, where possible, time within an employee schedule to focus on wider organisational problems. This could be a development opportunity for staff particularly if the experience is cross-disciplinary. The CIPD research series on Entrepreneurs (2013) stated that to create an intrapreneurial culture employees need to be in a supportive organisation that is willing to work with and provide space to incubate new ideas, creating the right culture to develop creativity and innovation amongst employees. Amabile *et al* (1996) suggested that organisations need a culture that: encourages creativity through fair, constructive judgement of ideas, rewards and recognition; provides supervisors and managers who can set appropriate goals and are a good work model; has a diverse skilled group in which people communicate well, are open to new ideas and constructively challenge each other's work; has access to appropriate resources; gives challenging work to employees; provides the freedom to decide what work to do and when to do it.

CROSS-CULTURAL COMPETENCE

Bennett and Bennett (2004) describe cross-cultural competences as the ability to communicate effectively in cross-cultural situations and to relate appropriately in a variety of cultural contexts. With some organisations operating in a number of countries and a number of workers from the European Union and countries outside this area, organisations need to prepare their internal infrastructure, management and communication systems to support a diverse workforce. In addition, many countries across the world will experience the arrival of individuals and families from unstable countries where there is war, political unrest and economic hardship. Some will stay in the countries where they feel safe and seek employment in these countries. The workforce in some organisations could include people from cultures that were absent in that organisation or in the minority. It is important that organisations build a programme of ongoing cross-cultural development in the future which could include the following:

- being able to understand and engage with people from different cultures

- managing attitudes towards cultures
- creative learning opportunities to understand cultures
- ongoing research into cultures
- developing cross-cultural organisational communication.

Marks & Spencer's management development team selected Communicaid Consultancy as its training partner for the design and delivery of a suite of intercultural programmes for the General Merchandising and Food divisions. Communicaid was commissioned to develop the intercultural competence of Marks & Spencer employees and equip them with the strategies and techniques required to work more effectively in the expanding international environment in which the company now operates, see Case Study 6.3.

CASE STUDY 6.3

MARKS & SPENCER

Marks & Spencer is one of the world's leading retail organisations, employing over 80,000 people in the UK and internationally, with over 700 stores in the UK and over 400 stores in 44 territories across Europe, the Middle East and Asia. In November 2010, Marks & Spencer set out a three-year plan with the aim of becoming a truly international, multi-channel retailer. As part of this strategy, an increasing number of UK-based employees worked with international colleagues, suppliers and customers. The degree of engagement was varied and included collaboration on projects, managing international teams and influencing key stakeholders.

M&S decided that a development programme was required to:

- raise awareness of the impact that culture and cultural differences have on business relationships and working practices
- provide employees with the knowledge and tools to work and communicate successfully with different cultures
- develop practical strategies for building more effective cross-cultural team relationships.

They commissioned an intercultural consultancy, Communicaid, to work with

their management development team, who gained a thorough understanding of the organisational culture, the strategic international vision and the types of interactions employees have with their international counterparts. A programme was designed for 600 employees with diverse roles, responsibilities and at different levels within the organisation. The programme had to be relevant to employees with varying degrees of international experience. Key to the success of the programme was the need to design a high-impact, interactive workshop for more than 600 employees with diverse roles, responsibilities and levels of experience at Marks & Spencer. Training also had to be relevant to employees with varying degrees of international experience and incorporate practical examples and exercises. Following a detailed diagnostic consultancy with key stakeholders at Marks & Spencer, Communicaid created a blended three-part training programme to meet the objectives of the target population. The resulting programme, 'Working across cultures', was a practical and highly interactive workshop suitable for employees who work or plan to work with international colleagues, suppliers and customers.

REFLECTIVE ACTIVITY 6.4

How would you design and deliver a cross-cultural development programme in your organisation?

How would you ensure cross-cultural development is embraced by senior managers and that it becomes part of a long-term programme?

Outside a learning and development programme how would you maintain a cross-cultural community in your organisation?

SUMMARY

Managing and organising people in organisations has been established for many years and an historical account of early documents point to activities that demonstrate a fascination with organising people in groups to work and produce products and services normally for a profit in business organisations. However, not all organisations are business organisations and the different types of organisations, large and small, have different objectives which are not necessarily about making a profit. In the early twentieth century, clusters of thinking about how people should be organised and managed focused on introducing structures and processes that were centred around controlling individuals at work, while other industrialists and writers focused on developing work processes that promoted increased production, specialisation and control, coupled with financial incentives. While many of the principles and practices used in early organisations still exist today, the current environment that most businesses operate in is typically characterised as chaotic, unstable and constantly changing – very different from the environment that Taylor, Fayol and Mayo were writing about.

Organisations today need to develop structures and resources internally that can cope with the chaotic environment organisations operate in and the advancements in technology and globalisation has encouraged new ways of working, flexible structures and a growth in digital/data management. Organisations need to develop their resources to embrace working in partnerships that are across functions and with other organisations and skills in intrapreneurship and cross-cultural awareness.

REFERENCES

ADLER, P. S. and BORYS, B. (1996) 'Two types of bureaucracy: enabling and coercive'. *Administrative Science Quarterly*. Vol 41, No 1, pp61–69.

ALDERFER, C. (1972) *Existence, Relatedness and Growth*, New York: Free Press.

AMABILE, T.M., CONTI, H., LAZENBY, J. *et al.* (1996) Assessing the Work Environment for Creativity. *Academy of Management Journal*. Vol. 39, No. 5, pp.1154–1184.

ATKINSON, P. (2003) Managing chaos in a matrix world. *Management Services*. November, pp8–11.

BBC (2003) BBC News UK, February 2003, www.bbc.co.uk.

BENNETT, J. M. and BENNETT, M. J. (2004) Developing intercultural sensitivity: an integrative approach to global and domestic diversity. In Landis, D., Bennett, J. and

Bennett, M (Eds.), *Handbook of intercultural training.* 3rd ed. pp.147–165. Thousand Oaks: Sage.

BODDY, D. (2014) *Management: an introduction.* 6th ed. Essex: Person.

BOULDING, K. E. (1956) General systems theory: the skeleton of science. *Management Science.* Vol 2, pp97–108.

BRECH, E.F.L. (1975) *Principles and Practice of Management.* 3rd ed. London: Longman.

BURNS, T. and STALKER, G.M. (1961) *The Management of Innovation,* London: Tavistock.

CIPD (2016) *Preparing for the future of learning.* Report. London: CIPD. Available at: http://www.cipd.co.uk/binaries/preparing-for-the-future-of-learning_2016-a-changing-perspective-for-l-and-d-leaders.pdf.

CLAUSEWITZ, C.V. (1832) *On War.* Marie von Brühl.

CLEGG, S.R. (1990) *Modern organisations: organisation studies in the postmodern world.* London: Sage.

COLE, G.A. (2004) *Management, theory and practice.* 6th ed. London: Thomson Learning.

FAYOL, H. (1947) *General and Industrial Management.* London: Pitman.

FOLLETT, M.P. (1941) *Dynamic Administration.* New York: Harper Bros.

GEORGE, C.S. (1972) *The history of management thought.* 2nd ed. Englewood Cliffs, NJ: Prentice Hall.

HANDY, C. (1993) *Understanding organisations.* 4th ed. Harmondsworth: Penguin Business.

HOFSTEDE, G. (1997) *Cultures and organisations.* McGraw-Hill Education.

HUCZYNSKI, A. A. and BUCHANAN, D. A. (2013) *Organisational behaviour.* 8th ed. Pearson Education.

JOHNSON, J., SCHOLES, J. and WHITTINGTON, R. (2005) *Exploring corporate strategy text and cases.* 7th ed. Pearson Education.

KOONTZ, H. (1980) The management theory jungle revisited. *Academy of Management Review.* Vol 5, No 2, pp175–188.

KOONTZ, H. and BRADSPIES, R.W. (1972) 'Managing through feed-forward control'. *Business Horizons.* June, pp25–36.

LAWRENCE, P.R. and LORSCH, K.W. (1967) *Organization and Environment.* Boston MA: Harvard University Press.

LENTZ, S.S. (1996) *Hybrid organisation structures: a path to cost savings and customer responsiveness.* Chichester: John Wiley & Sons.

MARTIN, J. (2005) *Organisational behaviour and management.* 3rd ed. Thomson Learning.

MARTIN, J. and FELLENZ, M. (2010) *Organisational behaviour and management*. 4th ed. Hampshire: Thomas Rennie.

MASLOW, A. (1970) *Motivation and Personality*. New York: Harper & Row.

MCGREGOR, D. (1960) *The Human Side of the Enterprise*. McGraw-Hill.

MCKELVEY, W. (1982) *The evolution of organisational forming in ancient Mesopotamia, Organizational Systematics*. Los Angeles, CA: University California Press. pp 295–335.

MCNAMARA, C. (2012) Basic definition of organisation. Available at: http://managementhelp.org/organizations/efinition.htm.

MEAD, R., and ANDREWS, T.G. (2009) *International management*. 4th ed. Chichester: John Wiley & Sons.

MINTZBERG, H. (1973) *The nature of managerial work*. New York: Harper and Row.

MORGAN, G. (1998) *Images of organization*. Thousand Oaks, CA: Sage Publications.

PETERS, T. (1988) *Thriving on chaos: handbook for a management revolution*. London: Macmillan.

RAMSAY, H., SCHOLARIOS, D., and HARLEY, B. (2000) Employees and high-performance work systems: testing inside the black box. *British Journal of Industrial Relations*. Vol: 11, No 4, pp501–31.

ROBERTSON. B. J. (2015) *Holacracy: the revolutionary management system that abolishes hierarchy*. Penguin, UK.

ROETHLISBERGER, F.J., DIXON, W. J. and WRIGHT, H.A. (1939) *Management and the Worker*. Cambridge, MA: Harvard University Press.

SMITH, M. (2011) *Fundamentals of Management*. 2nd ed. Berkshire: McGraw–Hill Education.

STUART, J. and ROGERS, P. (2012) *Developing people and organisations*. CIPD, London.

TAYLOR, F.W. (1947) *Scientific Management*. New York: Harper & Row.

WARD, J. L., (2012) *A Family Business*. New York: Palgrave Macmillan.

WEBER, M. (1947) *The theory of social and economic organisation*, New York: The Free Press.

WOODWARD, J. (1965) *Industrial organisation: theory and practice*, Oxford: Oxford University Press.

WREN, D. (1997) *The evolution of management theory*. 3rd ed. New York: John Wiley.

CHAPTER 7

Developing Learning and Development Policies and Activities to Respond to and Exploit the Limitations and Opportunities arising from Varying Contextual Factors

PATRICIA ROGERS, DALBIR JOHAL AND RAYMOND ROGERS

CHAPTER OVERVIEW

- Introduction
- Strategic alignment
- Trends in L&D delivery
- Considerations in delivering an L&D strategy
- Developing the business case for L&D
- Undertaking a learning needs analysis
- L&D planning
- Summary

LEARNING OUTCOMES

By the end of this chapter, you will be able to:

- discuss the key trends in the delivery of learning and development
- explain how to undertake a learning needs analysis
- discuss a range of learning methods, both formal and informal
- explain the main factors to consider when developing an L&D Strategy
- identify the factors which will impact the design and delivery of the learning interventions
- develop a coherent business case to promote learning and development
- make recommendations on the most effective learning methods to meeting specific learning needs.

INTRODUCTION

The learning and development (L&D) landscape has been rapidly changing and evolving over the past 20 years. Increasing organisational and global competition, constant transformational change and the realisation of the value of learning and impact upon organisational performance has considerably raised its profile to play a more strategic, business-focused role, moving away from its core delivery of training. L&D has therefore become a driver for change and a key stakeholder in the advancement for sustainable competitive advantage (CIPD 2015). This is further supported by Goldstein and Ford (2002) who argue that investing in employee development is a source of competitive advantage.

As organisations become more and more focused on results, measuring organisational capability and developing people, the nature of L&D has shifted from local training delivery to being a business partner and an internal consultant, advising and influencing the agenda for people capability and development which aligns the organisation's strategy and direction. This all forms an integral part of the L&D strategy.

In Chapter 5 and Chapter 6, the context of learning was explored, along with the key factors that influence the achievement of strategic objectives. This is imperative for any organisation to establish before they embark upon designing and delivering an L&D strategy that complements and aligns the organisational strategy and objectives. By doing this, L&D will be able to identify the core essential knowledge, skills and ability (KSA) needed by the organisation to achieve its strategic objectives. This chapter will explore the fundamentals of developing L&D strategies and policies which will include trends in delivery and the importance of developing a business case and plan for L&D.

STRATEGIC ALIGNMENT

There is much debate on 'strategic alignment' as to where L&D fundamentally fits in the organisation. Observations made by Stewart and Harris (2003) in their study of local government and in a similar scenario by Hirsh and Tamkin (2005) suggested horizontal integration posed a challenge for L&D as HR mainly focuses on HR processes rather than capability and HR's knowledge was limited on the link between L&D and HR strategy. These cases reinforce the lack of joined-up thinking and further reinforce the notion of L&D being the poor relation of HR (Harrison 2009). There needs to be some integration otherwise L&D would be seen as operating in isolation of the wider organisation, which can result in a failure to add value or a conflict in service delivery.

Therefore, alignment should be both vertical and horizontal across the organisation, to give the L&D strategy a central key focus which will impact all functions.

Stewart and Rigg (2011) suggest the alignment of L&D can happen in two ways:

Horizontal integration: where L&D interventions are integrated with other HR policies and practices and HR interventions ensuring there is consistency across the whole HR function. An example is rewarding employees for undertaking professional development.

Vertical integration: where L&D interventions are integrated and complement the overall organisational strategy. An example is L&D strengthening the KSA required to enhance the organisational values, behaviours and competencies to enhance performance and organisational effectiveness.

Furthermore, research from CIPD suggests that L&D can still operate successfully whether the function reports to the business or HR, as long as there are clear connections between the functions and the agreement on L&D's role and purpose (CIPD 2015).

The emphasis here informs that, regardless of the two approaches above, the L&D strategy must connect with the overall organisational strategy as well as HR policies and practices.

Furthermore L&D plays several roles to enhance an organisation's performance and competitive edge. These can fall into three distinct categories, as seen in Figure 7.1

Therefore the L&D strategy has a multitude of varying roles at differing levels which can be challenging to achieve, especially if the organisation is not strategically connected and there are differing priorities and requests. In such cases L&D can be torn or divided as to conflicting priorities. It is therefore important for clear direction and alignment throughout an organisation. Figure 7.1 outlines this multiple alignment.

Figure 7.1 The roles of L&D in enhancing organisational performance

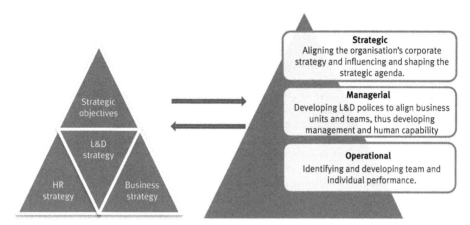

Having explored the importance of this alignment, consideration must be given to the most effective way to deliver a strategy that fits and aligns these key areas. One of the initial problems is the use of the word 'strategy' which can be over used and cause confusion. In essence a strategy is a clear plan for achieving goals which will deliver a successful business. There are many definitions of a strategy, Henry Mintzberg (1996) defined strategy as 'a pattern in a stream of decisions' to contrast with a view of strategy as planning while Max McKeown (2011) argues that 'strategy is about shaping the future' and is the human attempt to get to 'desirable ends with available means'.

Both have a consensus view of shaping the future through making decisions and planning. An L&D strategy outlines how L&D will support the organisation by developing HR capability through identifying KSA required and addressing the gaps to ensure people are performing effectively to achieve the organisational goals.

TRENDS IN L&D DELIVERY

The agenda for L&D is constantly evolving. There has been a gradual shift from the classical approach of offering a catalogue of courses to, more recently, a move to a more focused approach of tailoring and bespoke L&D solutions to meet organisational and individual needs. The latter approach promotes a pragmatic approach to learning allowing a richer learning environment where people can connect much more easily and apply the learning to their role in a clear and transparent way.

Whilst the catalogue of courses provides ample opportunity and a range of solutions, these are not always covering the specific areas of need and can been seen as a hit or miss with learners. In addition offering such catalogues of courses whereby it is open door for all employees to attend, encourages 'serial course attenders' who are the same people making their way through the catalogue of courses, without reference to a development plan or consideration of the learning that is appropriate for their role.

As mentioned earlier, another key trend is aligning learning to focus on increasing business results, whereby L&D put greater emphasis on effective and cost-efficient learning that positively impacts business results. An example of this – coaching – will be discussed later.

Secondly, a growing trend is to align the L&D strategy to talent management. According to a survey carried out by Deloitte's (2015) strategic development, attraction, incorporation and retention of an 'expertise elite' is getting more attention, with organisations investing in human capital that can increase organisational performance.

In addition, there is push towards learners becoming more self-directed and responsible for their own learning and professional development (CPD). Many organisations hold their employees accountable for their development and employability and one way this is achieved is through a personal development plan (PDP) which forms part of the performance review appraisal.

Furthermore the increase in mobile learning is evidently becoming popular, as it offers the scope for flexibility for the modern learner to access learning anywhere at any time and encourages learning to be more accepted. Given the globalisation of organisations and consistency in delivery this approach is essential.

On-the-job learning, thus creating a learning culture, has also become more prevalent, making learning become an essential part of daily work by integrating and using informal learning tools and sharing knowledge and team learning. This growing approach provides a great opportunity to coach, develop and offer practical learning methods which encourage faster transfer of knowledge and are cost effective as employees are not being asked to move away from their workplace to learn. The pragmatic approach offers ample opportunity to apply the learning directly and seek clarification instantly.

There is an increasing necessity for the role of managers to act as role models in learning and promoting and encouraging learning through self-teach and a top-down approach whereby everyone is accountable for disseminating learning in the organisation.

CONSIDERATIONS IN DELIVERING AN L&D STRATEGY

Whilst ensuring the L&D strategy incorporates the latest trends and developments in L&D, there are many other aspects and considerations in formulating an L&D strategy. The underpinning notion of an L&D strategy is not just about what employees need to learn, but also about why learning is important and how learning takes place. This latter aspect will fundamentally differ from organisation to organisation based on various contextual facets. The L&D strategy has several dimensions to consider starting from diagnosing and understanding learning needs through to evaluating their investment and return on the business.

When exploring the most effective way to deliver an L&D strategy, L&D practitioners need to explore and scan the organisational environment to determine the best approach, therefore the analytical tools discussed earlier in this chapter provide a solid framework to investigate which approach will be right for the organisation and how the L&D strategy should be delivered.

Furthermore, a strategy can have a focal point such as transformational change. There are many drivers for organisational change to which L&D needs to respond to ensure it meets the learner needs and organisational challenges. A key consideration is creating an agile L&D environment where the L&D strategy is flexible to the changing organisational agenda, especially as organisations are going through continual change.

Figure 7.2 highlights the key aspects that need to be taken into account when determining the right strategy. Whilst this is not limited, every L&D practitioner should factor this in when deciding upon the most effective L&D strategy.

The factors are:

- **Learning climate:** creating an environment where learning is encouraged, positive and self-directed. Garvin (1993) defines learning climate as the creation of conditions that support experimentation and risk that do not always fit with the originally accepted behaviours and routines. Encouraging a positive learning climate that is open and agile will enable organisations to be more adaptable to learning and therefore determine the approach, style and design of L&D interventions.

- **Culture:** the 'make up' of the organisation which tends to refer to the way things are done, the behaviours, values and beliefs are an integral part of how learning takes place and its value in the organisation. Does the culture promote and encourage learning or place little value on L&D? Cultural differences and norms and the acceptance of L&D can be a challenge in terms of delivery and style.
- **Size/structure:** the size and structure of the organisation will impact upon the L&D strategy and method chosen. Whereas global international organisations will offer a wider range of learning, smaller enterprises will offer focus on the essentials such as mandatory training. Organisational structures will influence the design of how L&D is approached overall and the pedagogy of delivery. The structural environment of an organisation closely links to the culture and the extent to which employees have autonomy such as matrix or flat structures (Beevers and Rea 2016).
- **Budget:** similar to the above point, factoring how the training budget is allocated and spent will determine how the L&D strategy is driven. Priorities and mandatory training will take precedent. Whilst the demand for L&D is on the increase, L&D budgets are continuously monitored and recent trends suggest in many sectors they are reducing year upon year (https://www.cipd.co.uk/binaries/learning-and-development_2014.pdf).
- **Location/country:** whilst technological advancement offers scope for virtual learning environments, consideration must be given to how an organisation is dispersed and how accessible and consistent L&D can be, in addition to taking account of cultural differences as mentioned earlier.
- **Industry sector:** certain industries such as retail, regulation, manufacturing and construction will have core priorities that take precedent over all other activities. L&D needs to align the 'peaks' and 'troughs' of the industry and also keep up with changing demands and expectations.
- **Organisational stability:** another consideration is analysing the growth, decline and stability of the organisation. Where turnover is high (for example, in a call centre) the strategy must take account of the loss of skills and knowledge but also how much it will invest to retrain staff. Consideration must be given to provide essential L&D whilst balancing the cost for short-term measures.
- **PEST:** the influence of external factors such as the political agenda, economic conditions and the labour market, the influence of legislative requirements such as mandatory training, the changing social structures and demographics in addition to the shift in technological advances all play an important role in the design and delivery of L&D.

 REFLECTIVE ACTIVITY 7.1

Discuss how each of the above key aspects of an L&D strategy will apply to your organisation.

What will you need to consider for each of these?

One of the first steps in developing an L&D strategy is to explore and understand its purpose and how it will add value to the organisation. There are several questions that should be explored and answered to ensure the strategy fits the agenda expected to satisfy the needs of its stakeholders. Questions to consider:

- Is the organisation clear on its strategic goals?
- Is the focus short term or long term?
- Who owns the strategy?
- Who will be involved in developing and implementing the strategy?
- What is its scope?
- Who are the key stakeholders and what role do they play?
- How will success be measured?

Whilst these questions explore the inputs and outputs of the strategy and begin to address the key focus points, the development and implementation responsibility usually falls upon L&D. However, the responsibility lies beyond L&D with a shift towards encouraging line managers to take an active role in the development of their employees. Such roles extend to the offering of coaching and mentoring which will be discussed later in this chapter.

Figure 7.2 Factors in determining an effective L&D strategy

DEVELOPING THE BUSINESS CASE FOR L&D

Although learning and development has gained more prominence and appreciation from organisations, there are still myths that L&D is more a cost to organisations than an investment (Thales L&D 2014). Research from Thales L&D shows strong evidence that a robust L&D programme can improve performance and organisational effectiveness in various ways, outweighing the investment. However, convincing organisations can be a challenge and therefore a coherent business case, focusing on value adding and core business drivers, is essential.

With a more strategic focus on L&D, the business case can influence difficult decision makers by delivering focused L&D programmes that impact organisational performance and also outline the risk in the absence of L&D.

Continuously highlighting the benefits and aligning the business agenda to L&D, emphasising crucial points to engage stakeholders and influencing their agenda is a must for any business case to strengthen it and make it more visible amongst other agenda topics which can side line L&D. Whilst this can seem apparent, there is value in reiterating these points and underpinning L&D to become an integral part of everyone's agenda. Otherwise, gaining momentum and securing financial investment can be challenging, especially when stakeholders cannot clearly see the benefits.

Thales L&D (2014) have highlighted some of the accepted benefits of L&D as:

- greater employee retention rate stemming from the feeling that the organisation is taking an interest in their future and that they are highly valued within it
- less money spent on hiring new employees to replace the ones that have left
- improved employee productivity because they are more skilled and generally better at their jobs
- overall better employee engagement because they have confidence in their future and feel their desires are being considered.

To support the benefits, it is imperative to provide a clear strategy on how the benefits will be evaluated, what metrics will be produced which inevitably support the organisational strategy and the underlying issue L&D is managing. Providing coherent evidence which can be measured and where visible results can be realised will give L&D a stronger case for influence.

Thales L&D (2014) suggest that making a successful business case for L&D focuses on proving:

- high profitability
- high productivity
- high employee engagement.

If L&D can convince key business decision makers that these three aspects are attainable, the case for L&D will become more robust.

 REFLECTIVE ACTIVITY 7.2

You have been advised that the management team are not managing their teams effectively. Whilst there is some good practice, there are also many inconsistences of practice between managers. Your senior management team have asked L&D to propose how you can support this.

List all the issues arising from this scenario and write a convincing business case detailing how L&D can add value and support this training issue. Consider:

- the benefits of your chosen approaches
- how your approaches will add value
- the risks of doing nothing.

UNDERTAKING A LEARNING NEEDS ANALYSIS

Once an intelligible business case is established, and before any training takes place, a learning needs analysis should be undertaken. It is useful to explore the purpose of a learning needs analysis (LNA). Gibb (2003) defines a LNA as:

the gathering of systemic information to ascertain the skills, knowledge and abilities of employees to which will enable the organisation to identify current and future performance gaps and how to address them.

Harrison (2009: 191) defines it as:

a generic term used to cover the process of identifying what successful task, job or role performance looks like, and what is needed from individuals in order to achieve those results.

Both definitions emphasise the impact on the performance and what is required from employees – for example, skills knowledge, behaviour and abilities to ensure they can perform effectively now and in the future. Iqbal and Khan (2011) discovered the use of many different terms such as 'training performance analysis', 'assessment', and 'needs'. Although the terminology may differ the process and outputs are essentially the same.

Everyone in an organisation will have some form of learning need. Given employees are deemed the biggest asset in an organisation, maximising their potential and return on investment is a key concern (Stewart and Cureton 2014). A LNA exercise will establish the differing learning needs. For instance, the learning needs of technical experts and graduates or apprentices will all differ based on their existing knowledge, skills and ability (KSA) and all of this will need to be factored into the LNA design.

Carrying out an LNA will take time to ensure it reflects an accurate picture of the organisation and understands the KSA requirements to meet current and future organisational needs. Furthermore, the credibility of L&D will be questioned if poorly conducted, given the LNA usually takes place at the start of the learning cycle, it is the central diagnosis point of any design and delivery of future L&D interventions. (Stewart and Rigg 2011).

Failure to carry out LNA effectively will result in a misalignment of development needs, consequently wasting valuable resource and time. Hence it must be acknowledged that the LNA can deliver substantial benefits for an organisation which outweigh the investment. To increase its integrity, such an activity should be undertaken in partnership with key stakeholders with an integrated approach, so that it is owned by the organisation and not by L&D as mentioned earlier. This in turn will promote its importance and also acceptance that it is a well-formulated LNA which aligns and complements the organisation's agenda.

Given the outputs of the LNA will impact upon all employees in the organisation, their involvement and input is vital.

There are many approaches to an LNA. The gathering of both qualitative and quantitative data can be done in various ways, again determining what is most appropriate to the organisation. Methods can include:

- workplace observations
- reviewing performance appraisal documents
- interviewing employees
- focus groups with subject matter experts and managers
- key performance indicators
- 360-degree feedback
- individual assessment and testing
- questionnaires and surveys
- organisational performance metrics and management information.

Whilst the above methods provide an opportunity to engage at all levels in the LNA, further in-depth data will be required for different organisational needs. With any given approach to conducting an LNA, the ethics should reinforce the current and future learning needs of the organisation.

Figure 7.3 An approach to conducting a Learning Needs Analysis

Objectives (What KSA do we need?)

- Identify key priorities for the directorate (objectives and targets), aligned from the strategic business needs
- Identify key stakeholders

Recommendations/Develop Action Plan & Evaluate

- Develop & implement an action plan
- Evaluation of recommendations and any further L&D solutions to meet directorate needs

What KSA already exists?

- Look at L&D needs of the teams
- Review existing information: appraisals/development plans

Analyse information

- Analyse information into overall LNA
- Create learner profile
- Report or presentation on recommendations—best way to meet needs identified

How will information on KSA be collected?

- Determine design of LNA
- Collect information via appropriate method

Identify the skills gaps

- Organisational/directorate/team/ individual
- Link to overall development strategy plan & key priorities

The RAM approach (Relevance, Alignment, Measurement) developed by CIPD focused on organisational outcomes as identified below (CIPD 2012):

- Relevance: ensuring the proposed L&D solution will meet the opportunities for the organisation
- Alignment: ensuring that all learning interventions are integrated and support the overall business strategy (vertical and horizontal integrated mentioned earlier)
- Measurement: ensuring that all learning interventions can be measured, linked to success criteria with notably the expected change in behaviour and improved KPIs.

LEVELS OF LNA

The size, culture and climate of the organisation will fundamentally have an influence on the approach it considers to LNA (Connor and Clawson 2004). Whilst there are several approaches to a LNA, traditionally the most common model is the three-tiered system model developed by McGehee and Thayer (1961):

- Organisational: focusing on the strategic needs of the organisation
- Role specific: focusing on specific KSA required for roles
- Individual: focusing on personal development needs.

Although three distinct levels, all three levels interlink and support the others, aligning from strategic to individual. This alliance supports whole organisational performance – for example, the individual needs the right skills and knowledge to perform in their role effectively, which in turn will support the organisational strategic objectives.

An alternative approach is to concentrate on influencing factors; one such method is outlined in Figure 7.4.

Top-down organisational priorities focus on the strategic L&D agenda and corporate goals. Internal influences, i.e. role level, focus on the specific knowledge, skills and attributes (KSA) required to undertake roles effectively. External influences, e.g. legislation, focus on critical and legislative requirements. Individual learning needs focus on individual bespoke needs which will encompass personal development.

 REFLECTIVE ACTIVITY 7.3

Levels of Learning Needs Analysis

Reflect on your experience and identify an example for each of the levels of Learning Needs Analysis listed below:

- organisational
- role specific
- individual.

There are several influencing approaches to a LNA; L&D will determine the most appropriate approach based on the factors discussed earlier in this chapter.

CONDUCTING A LEARNING NEEDS ANALYSIS IN A LEGAL ORGANISATION

This case study refers to a legal organisation which has a number of different entities all of which have varied and differing needs. One challenge for L&D is to offer a consistent approach to the LNA across the organisation, however differentiate the approach to meet the local needs of each entity. The organisation is made up of three core areas, which all operate differently and are also different in size, culture and management style. One approach adopted in one area of the organisation will not work in another and this is greatly debated by the distinct three management teams who are the key decision makers.

L&D have therefore the added the challenge of communicating with three different senior management teams who are demanding in what they want from L&D and consistently seeking a bespoke approach and one which has not been aligned to another part of the organisation.

With this scenario in mind, L&D considered various approaches to complete a LNA.

Approach 1

In the larger part of the organisation, feedback was collected via a spreadsheet from managers asking them to identify core training needs in various categories such as technical skills, behavioural skills, management skills and IT skills. This approach was mainly considered due to the large number of employees. However, this approach became problematic due to the inconsistency in completing the spreadsheet and the varying degrees of detail provided which was difficult to comprehend by L&D. This in turn proved difficult to provide an accurate overall picture of the training needs and report back on priorities. In cases, the technical training was vague, listing legislation with little clarity on what the development actual was. In addition managers were asking for

development on communication skills when the learning need was more about assertive or presentation skills.

Furthermore training needs was used as a shadow instead of dealing with performance management where the manager clearly had a role to play, however employees were referred to L&D for development. In these instances, L&D had to spend considerable time contacting managers to gain more clarity and figure out exactly what the training needs were.

Approach 2

In the smaller part of the organisation, meetings were arranged with line managers who inevitably had already discussed the training needs with their teams. Managers were asked key questions and L&D noted down the requirement during each discussion. This approach allowed L&D to explore scenarios and probe further to understand more about that particular business case but also gave them a better understanding of the business areas in addition to building relationships. In some cases it was evident the issue was more performance management than a specific training need hence L&D could support the manager to oversee this.

The collated information was compiled and a report highlighting the outputs and core themes were presented to the senior management team.

Questions

Based on the case study, how could approach 1 and approach 2 be improved?

List all the factors that will impact on the approach you undertake to complete a Learning Needs Analysis. Consider how this would apply to your organisation:

1   Outline the challenges of your approach

Figure 7.4 Factors influencing Learning Needs Analysis

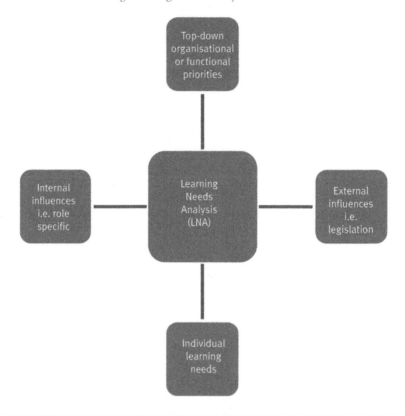

L&D PLANNING

Planning is crucial in any aspect of an organisation to support its growth, performance, financial control and forecast future trends and risks as a few examples of its importance.

In terms of L&D, planning is a crucial activity that, if carried out effectively, could have extensive benefits for the organisation. It is not a process that should be taken lightly and the investment outweighs the time and resource. Whilst initial planning also takes place before the LNA, it is essential to continue once it has been completed, which is the emphasis here.

Once a LNA has been completed the outputs should be analysed and presented to the senior management team or key stakeholders. The LNA should in theory be for the whole organisation and provide an overall representation of development needs. The next step would be to carry out an extensive planning exercise to focus on the priority of needs and establish critical timescales for immediate, short-term and long-term needs so a design and delivery plan or schedule can be carefully crafted.

There are many considerations to take into account when doing this and the most important is to ensure that the proposed solutions are feasible and closely align with the LNA results. Engagement with key stakeholders and subject matter experts is crucial to ensure a 'joined up' approach and one that is flexible and does not duplicate effort where other change programmes, for example, may also be ongoing. Therefore, it is vital that before developing and delivering a proposed learning intervention, a thorough plan outlining what it will entail and the learning outcomes are clearly identified. The content should be justified and aims and objectives given. As well as helping to address development needs on an individual and group level, the learning intervention must also help to deliver overall business and organisational objectives.

Again, engagement and the involvement of relevant stakeholders for comment and approval is key as this ensures overall buy-in and also presents an advance opportunity for the learning proposal to gain exposure prior to delivery.

Obtaining feedback from senior stakeholders and managers about any learning intervention proposed is important as they will be able to identify whether the proposed learning intervention is relevant and fits with the needs of their teams and the organisation, which in turn will provide L&D with a platform for feedback and review so any necessary adjustments can be made to ensure the best results are achieved.

Before making recommendations on the design and delivery of the learning interventions, the following interconnecting factors should be considered:

LEARNING PRINCIPLES AND METHODS

What methods will be the most effective approach for different outcomes and groups of learners?

What are formal or informal learning options?

Is the learning instructor-led or learner-led?

What is the role of learners in self-facilitated learning?

Having in place core principles and practices of learning which are 'threaded' throughout the whole organisation will support the design and method of delivery. For instance, managers and learners should have a clear understanding of their role as an employee and a line manager in relation to managing their learning and development. A partnership approach with L&D can in turn support the design and deliver a range of methods to suit learners' needs and obtain the most effective results possible.

ORGANISATIONAL ALIGNMENT, CULTURE AND CONTEXT

How will the learning intervention align the overall business strategy and HR practices?

What policies and procedures govern access to learning?

What is the possibility of trying something new? Or are traditional methods the preferred way?

Does the organisational culture and management practice encourage and promote learning?

Who is the key stakeholder that champions learning and how much influence do they have?

One of the most important aspects is getting the learning to match the organisational culture and context so learning is seen as 'business as usual' and is readily accepted. Understanding the organisational culture of what learning methods may work and what will be ineffective will support L&D to deliver the best approach. In addition the buy-in and influence of key stakeholders along with a clearly aligned strategy will all add credibility to L&D's role.

LEARNER PROFILE

Are learners motivated or compelled to learn?

What learning skills and experiences do they have?

What learning opportunities are available to suit learners that take account of their time available and their level of interest?

What are their expectations from L&D and are these realistic?

Do any learners have specific learning needs, such as dyslexia, and what additional support can be provided?

Learners are central to any approach and time should be invested in considering how the learning experience can be enhanced to suit learner preferences. Varying degrees of KSA of learners will influence the different learning styles and the design of learning. Learners will have different levels of work experience, skills and learning expectations.

ETHICS AND EQUALITY

Is the L&D budget fairly distributed amongst different groups and individuals?

Are there any unfair barriers to access learning such as equipment and location?

Is learning accessible for all groups and not differentiated on sex, race, disability, age and also employment status which could be unlawful?

Do any learners have specific learning needs, such as dyslexia, and what additional support can be provided?

Any organisation is bound by legislation to ensure it adheres to equality, however thinking beyond legislative requirements and ensuring ethical practice is fundamental. L&D's credibility is not solely built on delivery of training but by instilling a culture of professional responsibility committing to ethical standards and values which should be embedded through any training (Harrison 2009).

TRANSFER OF LEARNING

What opportunities exist for learning to be transferred to the workplace?

What role do managers have in supporting and following up the learning?

What performance indicators will enable review of the extent to which the learning has been successful?

What systems are in place to encourage learners to share knowledge?

Any form of learning will only be as successful as its transferability back into the workplace, otherwise it can be seen as no value and a cost. However, it must be remembered that responsibility does not solely fall on the individual to enable this to happen, the organisational culture and line managers must create an environment for learning and provide opportunities to share knowledge and good practice as without this, no matter how good the training is, its value will be forgotten.

STAKEHOLDER EXPECTATIONS

Who are the key stakeholders, both internal and external?

What are their varying relationships and partnerships with L&D and their expectations?

What concerns and needs do they have?

What opportunities can they provide to support L&D?

Key stakeholders, both internal and external, are the decision makers and can be catalysts of L&D driving its agenda and promoting a culture of learning. Consequently, they need to be on board from the outset of any L&D initiative to empower, influence and sign off approval for L&D. It is imperative for L&D to recognise and build strong positive relationships with stakeholders to maximise L&D's influence (Mankin 2009).

DESIGN AND DELIVERY OF METHODS

Traditional methods of learning, such as a classroom style, will always have a role to play, however it is useful to explore other options and more innovative ways to develop learning solutions (see Table 7.1 for an overview of learning methods).

One of the growing trends is the move away from focusing on a singular method of delivering training, such as purely e-learning, and more towards blended learning strategies which offer a range of learning methods and are underpinned by a range of learning theories which are combined (Mankin 2009).

Blended learning is a method of using a range of learning interventions based on different modes of delivery such as classroom-based, web-based e-learning, group learning, coaching, mentoring, case study, simulation based, (Rees *et al.* 2013). Whilst this list is not limited to all of these, including others offers a combination of learning methods and approaches which support the varying learning styles. In addition blended learning encourages a richer learning environment, continuously inspiring learners to think and behave and respond differently to the 'norm' so they are exposed to as many different learning approaches possible.

Table 7.1 Overview of learning methods

Method	Overview	Pros	Cons
Group dynamics	Learners are placed into groups to undertake exercises and scenarios and their behaviour and interactions are observed such as problem solving, conflict, decision making and communication	Useful to observe how learners interact and behave in a scenario; safe environment to test knowledge and skills	Can be seen as fake and learners can have learned behaviour for the task duration
Coaching	Coaching focuses on the learner taking ownership of their development; coaching	Develops skills and knowledge, improves behaviour, and develops confidence.	Requires good coaching skills

Method	Overview	Pros	Cons
	develops skills and knowledge so that performance improves although it focuses on a personal goal. It usually lasts for a short time and focuses on specific skills and goals (CIPD 2010)	Tailored to individual needs Encourages ownership of learning Motivating for the coachee/learner	Coaching style may not match the learner style Coachee/learner can become dependent on coaching long term
Mentoring	Focuses on identifying and nurturing of potential for an individual through a more experienced person. It can be a long-term relationship where goals can change. The learner owns both the goals and the process (Clutterbuck and Megginson 2005: 4)	Develops skills and knowledge, improves behaviour, and develops confidence. Motivates the learner Identifies talent and potential for development Exposes learner to opportunities and networks	Dependent on availability of mentor Mentoring style may not match the learner style Learner may find they are not getting the time and guidance they need from their mentor Learner can have unrealistic expectations
Simulations	Based on virtual reality scenarios which usually focus on managerial skills or specific skills in strategy, decision making, process flow or management (Stewart and Rigg 2011: 209)	Useful to observe how learners interact and behave in a scenario simulation scenario. Safe environment to test knowledge and skills	Can be expensive to set up in equipment is required Can be seen as fake as learners can exhibit learned behaviour for the task duration
Projects	Undertaking a specific project with clear objectives, usually work based which can be individual or group based such as developing new decision making process or developing a new product or service	Learners learn new skills and knowledge through taking part Builds network opportunities when working as part of a team Project is completed alongside individual development Can be motivating to see end results so learners engross themselves in the project	May have to cover roles if learners are purely focused on the project Learners can feel they cannot cover both their day role in addition to the project role, hence quality may suffer
On-the-job training	Learning is undertaken in the workplace through real activities, usually involves a 'show and tell' scenario and demonstration of the task	Cost effective as no major reduction in work time Timely to provide training when required Learner learns the realities of the job	The right expertise may not be available Can learn bad habits if trainer is not an expert Learner may lose out on the bigger picture

Method	Overview	Pros	Cons
		Training is carried out by an expert who knows the practical elements of the job Can be tailored to specific needs	Learners may find it difficult to 'switch off' from work demands Learners can be easily interrupted in the same work environment
Job rotation	Learning is undertaken by moving around different roles to build experience and knowledge. Often used for graduate and apprenticeships	Widens experience and understanding of other roles and how they impact each other Similar to on-the-job training, can be cost effective as learning takes place in the work place Helps to multiskill people and use them to cover roles when people are absent	Requires a great deal of planning to organise and set up. Lack of commitment from line managers to support employees whilst in their team Can cause a lot of disruption when employee moves to new role
Secondment	Learner moves to another role on a temporary basis usually 3–12 months but could be longer. The new role usually is a development opportunity, different to their substantive role	Widen experience and understanding of other roles Offers potential for career development Cost effective as saves external advert for roles Can test individual capability during secondment in readiness for a permanent position	Difficult to get cover for learner's substantive role Secondment can be extended continuously whereby the learner may no longer be able to return to their substantive role
Action learning	Learning takes place via groups of people meeting on a regular basis to support each other on work projects or issues through questioning each other with the aim to provide potential solutions (Stewart and Rigg 2011, p192)	Learning from others' experiences and perspectives Cost effective as relies on internal resource for learning Encourages ownership of learning and actions Encourages consistency in practices with sharing knowledge, experience and ideas	Takes time away from the workplace Require as discipline and commitment from the group Dependent on everyone wanting the same format Group can become 'stale' if attendees remain the same
e-learning	Learning is delivered using electronic technology for the explicit purpose of training (CIPD 2009)	Learner can work at own pace Cost effective if set up once and used for learner numbers Flexible access to use as and when required	Learner has no opportunity to ask questions Requires self-discipline to sustain Learner misses the interaction and

Method	Overview	Pros	Cons
		Access to use globally which ensures consistency in learning	stimulation of learning with others Can be expensive to set up if bespoke for the business
Shadowing	Practical learning where the learner observes a more skilled/ experienced person at work with the aim to learn new skills and knowledge	Learner can observe what is involved before undertaking the role Good opportunity to ask questions Chance to learn the reality of a job from an experienced employee	Can learn bad habits if the person demonstrating the role is not the right person Learners may find it difficult to 'switch off' from usual work demands Can be tedious if done for long periods
Case study	Based on a scenario (real or fictitious) which simulates organisational issues or practices. Learners are asked to analyse the scenario and reflect on practise of how they may respond, behave in the described circumstances, i.e. dealing with a customer complaint or a financial issue	Flexible as can work individually or in a group Exposes learners to real-life situations which otherwise could be difficult. Ability to test a number of skills such as analytical, problem solving, time management and understanding of context	May be difficult to find an appropriate case study scenario that reflects work practices There is not usually one right answer which can cause problems to validate responses.
Role play	Learners enact a role they may have to undertake in the workplace such as customer service or interviewing. Actors can also be employed to undertake specific roles to enhance quality	Exposes learners to real-life situations which otherwise could be difficult Ability to test skills such as decision making and behaviour in a lifelike situation	Scenarios can be seen as unrealistic and not tackle real work challenges Poor acting can lead to poor results and outcomes Can be expensive to employ actors
Lecture	A structured presentation to provide knowledge on specific topics such as new products/polices procedures	Useful for providing detailed complex information to larger groups of people Learners can make their own notes to clarify understanding	Can become tedious if continues for too long All knowledge may not be retained

Method	Overview	Pros	Cons
Discussion/ debate	An exchange of information, ideas and perspectives between individuals or groups on various topics led by a trained facilitator		Can become an unhealthy discussion or debate if not managed by a trained facilitator Learners my find it uncomfortable to share thoughts
Mobile learning	Learning delivered via mobile technologies such as Smartphones, and tablets	Useful for 'just in time' training Cost effective once equipment is in place Can be used for interactive voting in training sessions i.e. reaction feeds quizzes	Remaining up to date with new technology Security and pirating issues Requires an Internet connection
Peer to peer	Learning through discussions and observations with peers. This can now involve online social communities of practice and forum activities	Learning can be enriched by focusing on real-life situations Good opportunity to ask questions Chance to learn the reality of a job from an experienced employee	Risks to work-life balance if continuously using Can learn bad habits if the person learning from and observing is not the right person
Trial and error	Learning through trying various methods/ approaches and outcomes which are tentatively tried and some discarded until a viable solution is attained.	Exposes learners to different perspectives and solutions to try and test Broadens the knowledge and understanding of the learning topic	Can be time-consuming and expensive if continuously used

Adapted from: Glaister *et al* (2013, pp166–169), and Beevers and Rea (2013, pp94–98)

 REFLECTIVE ACTIVITY 7.4

Selecting the most effective learning methods

Think of your own organisation, which learning methods are the preference for your organisation's workplace learning?

Consider your learners needs, their time available, their knowledge, skills and ability and provide examples of methods used and the justification for choosing them.

Whilst exploring the various learning in the table earlier, two of the more prevalent methods which are discussed in more detail are coaching and mentoring. Organisations have increased their perception and value in both methods and use both coaching and mentoring more regularly in the workplace than previously especially for specific development programmes such as graduate schemes and for senior and executive management teams.

CIPD suggests that coaching and mentoring have different development techniques based on the use of one-to-one discussions to enhance an individual's skills, knowledge or work performance. It can be argued that mentoring is a developmental partnership through which one person shares their knowledge, skills, information and perspective to foster the personal and professional growth of someone else. Everyone has a need for insight that is outside of their normal life and educational experience. The power of mentoring is that it creates a one-of-a-kind opportunity for collaboration, goal achievement and problem solving. Crosby (2003) defines mentoring as 'a brain to pick, an ear to listen and a push in the right direction.'

Whilst a mentoring relationship is usually where one wiser and more experienced person assists another person to grow and learn and can be seen in the role of a 'teacher', coaching is more of an equal relationship, facilitating someone else's thinking and helping them to learn by working on live work issues and can also be integrated into everyday workplace in conversations (Garvey 2009).

One key distinction is that mentoring relationships tend to be longer term than coaching arrangements (CIPD 2015). In mentoring the learning is a lifelong process and focuses more on career and knowledge development rather than a short-term intervention. Mentoring happens in all organisations whether it is fostered as a development strategy; allowed or encouraged as an informal process; or is an activity that occurs below the consciousness of individuals. People are learning from others, adopting modelled behaviours and attitudes and absorbing the culture and perceived values of the organisation through their personal interactions with their peers and all the stakeholders they interact with.

Coaching adopts a similar principle to mentoring. It focuses on developing the individual, however, there is a distinct difference in the approach undertaken (Garvey *et al* 2009). Coaching supports the notion of enabling others to achieve their own goals by helping them to unfold their thinking and is done in the belief that the answer is within them. The coach has a specific role to seek out responses through asking questions, constructively challenging thinking and empowering the individual to seek out their own answers. Whitmore (2002) defines coaching as 'unlocking a person's potential to maximize their own performance.'

Unlike mentoring, coaching does not rely upon the coach to be experienced or knowledgeable in order to coach, whereas mentoring usually is reliant upon the mentor's expertise, knowledge and experience which is drawn upon (Stewart and Rogers 2012).

To differentiate between coaching and mentoring, Clutterbuck (2005:67) defines them as follows:

> Coaching primarily is a short-term intervention aimed at performance improvement or developing a particular competence whereas mentoring is a mixture of parent and peer, the primary function is to be a transformational figure in an individual's development.

This definition supports the view that whilst coaching and mentoring offer a similar outcome (to support individuals), coaching is focused more heavily on improving performance or a situation as such, whereas mentoring is focused on general development and not always a particular issue or performance area. Mentoring can be viewed as broader learning scope and one which relies on the experience and wisdom of the mentor.

Adams (2010) distinguishes the process and role of the two disciplines. He states that mentoring implies a longer, less formal and structured relationship which can be extremely powerful and beneficial over the medium to long term, whereas coaching extracts all the various options available to the coachee through the art of questioning and encouraging them to select the options they feel best fit the issue. Whilst both coaching and mentoring are valuable learning interventions, identifying the outcome intended for the individual and the rationale for development will determine whether it is coaching or mentoring that will be the most effective intervention. This therefore needs to be carefully planned and built into an L&D strategy with clear outcomes.

REFLECTIVE ACTIVITY 7.5

Coaching or mentoring?

Consider and discuss the brief scenarios below and discuss whether coaching and/or mentoring would be the most appropriate intervention.

Justify your choice.

1   A graduate scheme has been running in an organisation for several years. Each year six university graduates are recruited on a two-year programme. They undertake a work placement for six months in four departments for the duration of the programme. In addition to the placement, they are encouraged to broaden their experience by meeting with senior managers.

2   Each member of the graduate programme has been instructed to create a personal development plan and set goals they would like to achieve during the course of the programme.

3   A previous team member has been promoted to the role of a manager and will be managing a team of four people. She has no previous managerial experience and is concerned she will not be accepted in the team as the new manager, given she was previously a team member in the same team.

4   A member of the team has come to see you as they are keen to develop and take on more responsibility with the ambition of becoming a team leader in the next 18 months.

5   You are keen to broaden your experience in the finance team and your manager has suggested you meet with the new Finance Director.

SUMMARY

The learning and development agenda is rapidly changing, bringing with it challenges, opportunities and a new way of working for L&D practitioners. The shift from offering a list of courses to bespoke learning interventions which strategically align the organisation vertically and horizontally and add value to the strategic objectives is an ongoing trend. L&D therefore requires a more proactive, engaged and strategic approach in its operation and delivery. To support this, careful planning is required in the formulation of an L&D strategy to ensure it fulfils the current performance capability and future needs of the organisation. Whilst there are many facets to an L&D strategy, there are key elements which must be considered, including:

• the role of learning and development in the organisation
• understanding the organisation's L&D needs through undertaking a Learning Needs Analysis
• the culture, size, budget, location and nature of learners as a few factors to shape the strategy
• developing a coherent business case to promote and market L&D

- engagement of key stakeholders with a primary role for managers to facilitate learning opportunities
- examining the most effective methods of delivering learning and how these methods will complement the organisation culture
- exploring the role of learners, expectations, both from them and L&D and discovering their learning styles.

Organisations nowadays need to have in place a planned approach to L&D and an L&D strategy which integrates with the organisation's strategic objectives.

FURTHER READING

Websites

CIPD (2014) Learning and development report. Available at: www.cipd.co.uk/binaries/learning-and-development_2014.pdf.

BPI Network. How to make a business case for learning and development. Available at: http://www.bpinetwork.org/thought-leadership/views-commentary/397/how_to_make_a_business_case_for_learning_and_development.

CIPD (2005) Producing and implementing L&D strategy. Free sample chapter from *Learning and Development*. Available at: http://www.cipd.co.uk/NR/rdonlyres/0BBFAB21–8A39–4B49-A82D-6D7DC0C0C4EF/0/1843980509SC.pdf.

CIPD (2015) Coaching and mentoring factsheet. Available at: https://www.cipd.co.uk/knowledge/fundamentals/people/development/coaching-mentoring-factsheet#6995.

Identifying learning and development needs factsheet. Available at: https://www.cipd.co.uk/knowledge/fundamentals/people/development/learning-needs-factsheet#6601Personnel Today (2010) A four-step guide to planning your training, learning and development. Available at: http://www.personneltoday.com/hr/a-four-step-guide-to-planning-your-training-learning-and-development/.

REFERENCES

ADAMS J. (2010) Coaching v mentoring. *Training Journal*, 68–70.

BEEVERS, K. and REA, A. (2013) *Learning and development practice.* 2nd ed. London: CIPD.

BEEVERS, K. and REA, A. (2016) *Learning and development practice in the work place.* 3rd ed. London: CIPD.

CIPD (2009) *Innovative Learning and Talent Development: Positioning practice for recession and recovery.* London: CIPD.

CIPD (2010) *Real-world coaching evaluation: A guide for practitioners,* London: CIPD. Available at: https://www.cipd.co.uk/Images/real-world-coaching-evaluation_2010-practitioners-guide_tcm18-10982.pdf

CIPD (2014) *Learning and development annual survey report.* Available at: https://www.cipd.co.uk/Images/learning-and-development_2014_tcm18–11296.pdf.

CIPD (2014) *Modernising learning: delivering results 2014–2015; Towards Maturity.* Benchmark report. London: CIPD.

CIPD (2015) Learning and Development – Annual Survey Report, London: CIPD.

CLUTTERBUCK, D. and MEGGINSON, D. (2005) *Making coaching work: creating a culture*. London: CIPD.

CONNOR, M.L. and CLAWSON, J.G. (eds.) (2004) *Creating a learning Culture: Strategy, Practice and Technology*. Cambridge University Press.

CROSBY (2003) *Transforming teaching-learning process: mentoring and coaching*. Available at: http://www.open.edu/openlearnworks/mod/oucontent/view.php?id=57506&section=7.1

DELOITTE (2015) *Deloitte: 8 key trends in learning and development*. Available at: http://www.consultancy.uk/news/2428/deloitte-8-key-trends-in-learning-and-development.

GARVEY, R., STOKES, P. and MEGGINSON, D. (2009) *Coaching and mentoring, theory and practice*. Sage Publications.

GARVIN, D.A (1993) Building a learning organisation. *Harvard Business Review*. Vol 71, No 4, pp78–91.

GIBB, S. (2003) 'Line manager involvement in learning and development: Small beer or big deal?', *Employee Relations*, Vol. 25 No 3, pp281–293.

GILBERT, A. and WHITTLEWORTH, K. (2009) *The OSCAR coaching model: simplifying workplace coaching*.

GLAISTER, C. HOLDEN, R., GRIGGS, V. *et al.* (2013) The practice of training: the design and delivery of training. In: GOLD, J., HOLDEN, R., ILES, P., *et al.* (eds) *Human resource development; theory and practice*. 2nd ed. Basingstoke: Palgrave Macmillan.

GOLDSTEIN, I. L. and FORD, K. (2002) *Training in organizations: needs assessment, development and evaluation*. 4th ed. Belmont: Wadsworth.

HARRISON, R. (2009) *Learning and Development*. 5th Ed. London: CIPD

HIRSH, W. and TAMKIN, P. (2005) *Planning training for your business*: Institute for Employment Studies Report 422, London: IES.

IQBAL, M.Z. and KHAN, R.A. (2011) The growing concept of training needs assessment: a review with proposed model. *Journal of European Industrial Training*. Vol 35, No 5, pp439–466.

KVINT, V. (2009). *The global emerging market: strategic management and economics*. Routledge.

LOWDEN, K., HALL, S., ELLIOT, D. *et al.* (2011) *Employers' perceptions of the employability skills of new graduates*. The Edge Foundation.

MANKIN, D. (2009) *Human Resource Development*. Oxford: Oxford University Press.

MCGEHEE, W. and THAYER, P. (1961) *Training in business and industry*. New York: Wiley.

MCKEOWN, M. (2011) *The Strategy Book*. Financial Times/Prentice Hall.

MINTZBERG, H. and QUINN, J. B. (1996) *The strategy process: concepts, contexts, cases*. Prentice Hall.

REES, G. and FRENCH, R. (2014) *Leading, managing and developing people.* 4th ed. London: CIPD.

ROGERS, J. GILBERT, A. and WHITTLEWORTH, K. (2012) *The manager as coach: the new way to get results.* McGraw Hill University Press.

STARR, J. (2008) *The Coaching Manual.* 2nd ed. Pearson Education.

STEWART, J. and CURETON, P. (2014) *Designing, delivering and evaluating L&D: essentials for practice.* London: CIPD.

STEWART, J. and HARRIS, L. (2003) HRD and HRM: an uneasy relationship. *People Management,* Vol 9, No.19, 25 September: 58.

STEWART, J. and RIGG, C. (2011) *Learning and talent development.* London: CIPD.

STEWART, J. and ROGERS, P. (2012) *Developing people and organisations.* London: CIPD.

WHITMORE, J. (2002) *Coaching for performance: the new edition of the practical guide.* London: Nicholas Brealey.

ZEUS, P. and SKIFFINGTON, S. (2007) *The complete guide to coaching at work.* Australia: The McGraw-Hill Companies.

USING INFORMATION METRICS AND DEVELOPING BUSINESS CASES FOR LEARNING AND DEVELOPMENT

CHAPTER 8

Using Learning and Development Data

JIM STEWART

CHAPTER OVERVIEW

- Introduction
- Key terms and concepts
- HR analytics
- L&D data, metrics and analytics
- Summary

LEARNING OUTCOMES

By the end of this chapter, you will be able to:

- analyse the place of learning and development data in the wider context of Human Capital Measurement
- identify, evaluate and access relevant sources of learning and development data
- assess the relevance and quality of learning and development data
- evaluate the validity and utility of learning and development metrics
- apply learning and development analytics in decision making and in supporting a business case.

INTRODUCTION

This chapter provides guidance on accessing and utilising data relevant to learning and development (L&D). Accessing such data requires knowledge of the main *sources* of data and ability in searching available datasets. Sources of data include both those internal and external to a specific organisation. Internal sources will normally be freely available although some external sources may require payment for access. Data of itself has little if any value or utility. Therefore, a second and important part of the content of the chapter is the notion of *metrics*. This notion refers to the measurable aspects of the practice of organising and managing which can be useful and important in decision making. The best illustration of this is the financial metrics which are commonly used in investment decisions and in resource allocation decisions in organisations. You are probably familiar with some of these; for example, dividend yield informing investors in firms of part of the likely return for their investment or Net Present Value (NPV), used to judge whether resources are better allocated to investment in project X or project Y; for example, developing a new market for an existing product or developing a new product for an existing market. It is a matter of debate whether metrics for L&D should utilise and be expressed in similar terms and language. For example, the perennial debate on whether measuring return on investment (ROI) is either possible or desirable as a metric to evaluate the value of allocating resources to L&D continues (see Devins and Smith 2013). What is less debatable is that L&D metrics are closely associated with more general attempts to develop HR metrics and so the chapter will locate the examination of L&D measures in the wider context of Human Capital Measurement (HCM).

The main aim of the chapter is to provide sufficient guidance to enable you to judge when and what L&D data will be of value in support of decision making and in making a business case for allocation of resources. This is a large, emerging and developing topic. So, some detail on the content here can be usefully followed up and expanded on by accessing the recommended texts at the end of the chapter. The chapter itself is intended to meet the learning outcomes detailed above.

KEY TERMS AND CONCEPTS

It will be useful to start the chapter with a brief examination of some of the key terms and concepts. This will enable and support later discussion of their use and application. We will begin with basic building block of *data*.

Data can refer to information in various forms. Commonly the term in this context is used to denote information available and expressed in numerical form. The associated terminology is quantitative data. A simple example is the number of employees working in a particular organisation. So, organisation X employs 1000 people. That piece of data can be usefully analysed further to inform us that of the 1000, 50 (5%) are senior managers, a further 200 (20%) are middle managers/supervisors, 100 (10%) are professional staff and the rest are technical and operative level staff (650, or 65%). Data can also be in the form of text, or words, for example, the written comments a set of participants provide on an evaluation sheet at the end of a learning event. There is an important and related point to make here. That is the written comments can be and often are translated into positive or negative assessments of the event, and then presented in numerical form; e.g. 75% of participants rated the event a positive overall experience and 25% a negative overall experience. More will be explained about this point in the next chapter but it is necessary here to state that saying 5% of employees are senior managers is a fact while saying the learning event was a positive experience is not. The only fact in the latter case is that 75% of participants made comments that could be inferred to mean they judged the event a positive experience overall. What both sets of numbers have in common is that they remain at the level of data. They have no or limited value in and of themselves.

Data can become useful and so valuable when it is used in the form of *metrics*. This term refers to a set of numbers that give information about a particular process or activity. The key distinction therefore is that a metric is data turned into information that can be used. To take our previous examples of data, turning the raw data of numbers of employees in various categories into percentages is a measurement of the relative proportions of employees of different types. This might be useful by itself. But, some comparative standard will improve the usefulness and so the value of the metric. For example, are the proportions changing over time? And is that a signal of beneficial or detrimental change in how the organisation is structured? Perhaps increases over a period of say three years in the proportion of senior managers would signal an organisation becoming 'top heavy' with employees who are not directly productive. Similar increases in the proportion of professional employees may reinforce this signal. Very many contextual factors would have to be taken into account, and probably examining additional metrics as well, before firm conclusions could be drawn on whether the organisation is indeed becoming unnecessarily top heavy. But, the example illustrates the key distinction between data and metrics. A metric is data used to measure something in a way which provides potential value. The potential value can lie in a number of purposes; for example, signalling emerging problems, formulating solutions, making judgements on the value of activities and processes and in decision making. We will examine some of these uses when exploring specific examples of HR and L&D metrics later in the chapter.

REFLECTIVE ACTIVITY 8.1

Search for and access three definitions of 'data' from any academic and/or professional sources; for example, academic journals or professional publications. Analyse these definitions to identify similarities and differences. Use your analysis to produce your own definition of 'data'.

The penultimate term to consider is that of *analytics*. This term is similar in meaning to metrics and they can be and often are used as synonyms. However, there is also a commonly used distinction between the two concepts. A metric is a particular measure. Analytics analyse performance against a chosen metric in more detail. Statistical techniques often enable and support this more detailed analysis, and applying analytics also often utilises more than one metric to compare and assess performance. The previous example of analysing changes in proportions of employee in different categories over a given time period is an example of applying analytics. In the other example of positive and negative statements on the value of a learning event, more detailed analysis of additional variables (for example, differences in responses from different gender or different work functions or different lengths of service of participants, or all of these) is an additional example of applying analytics. These two examples illustrate a key point about the difference between data and analytics, and between metrics and analytics, and that is that analytics is about looking for and identifying *patterns* in sets of data. So, in the first example, patterns of changing proportions over time are looked for and in the second example, patterns according to participant characteristics are looked for and identified. In each of these cases, the results may be useful in decisions about future action.

Looking for patterns is one use and outcome of applying analytics. This requires some basis for comparison. Our first example most clearly illustrates the use of an additional basis of comparison through our final key concept of *benchmarking*. This term refers to using known and accessible internal or external metrics to assess comparative performance. The relevance of external data is most often seen to be determined by the similarity or otherwise of the comparator. Using our first example as an illustration, this means that data on proportions of employees in different categories will be most relevant if the comparative, or benchmark, data is drawn from organisations of a similar size and/ or organisations in the same industry. Ideally, organisations of a similar size in the same industry will be used as comparators. So, as well as analysing changes over time, those changes identified can be compared through benchmarking with changes being experienced by organisations in the same industry over the same period. This will provide a firmer foundation for judging whether the changes being experienced by the organisation are a cause for concern or not. If the changes are common across the industry, there may well be good reasons for that to do with other factors in the industry. If they are not common and the target organisation is shown to be 'top heavy' compared with other organisations, then there may be cause for concern and action. Our second example of participant responses to a learning event illustrates the use of internal benchmarking. The responses to the particular learning event can be compared with, and benchmarked against, other and similar internal learning events. This process of internal benchmarking has many other possible applications, especially in large organisations and/ or those with many operating units. In retail for example, performance of branches in similar-size towns and similar-size geographic markets can be benchmarked against each other.

CASE STUDY 8.1

Dr Bina Gupta feels overwhelmed. Her line manager in the newly formed Talent Pipeline Department, part of the Group HR Division of the construction and civil engineering multinational Bina has just joined as a Talent Assessment Manager, has tasked her with producing a status report on potential talent across the MNC's twelve operating companies. Bina has quickly established that the company employs around 120,000 people in twenty different countries and in over 50 different roles. These roles are also not standard across all operating companies, even though some have similar job titles – Chief Engineer, for example. The main problem though is that the Group human resource information system seems to Bina to be antiquated and 'clunky'. The accuracy of the data in the system, according to some of Bina's longer-serving colleagues, also cannot be relied on for any but the most basic purpose. Even if accuracy could be guaranteed, Bina is certain that the system as currently constructed would be of little help. It provides lots and lots of data on, for example, numbers employed, in what job families, in what operating companies, in what geographic locations, and similar information. Bina considers this to be simply raw data with little if any value. That is certainly the case in relation to Bina's current task. The

system has very little functionality to produce useful analyses of the raw data. And being human and not a computer, Bina does not have the personal capacity to crunch the data so that it provides useful and useable metrics, let alone HR analytics of any value.

Bina is familiar with the information system from one of her previous jobs. That experience tells Bina that the system has optional modules which can be added to improve the functionality of the system, and in particular producing reports which analyse the available data in many different ways to identify patterns, trends and full pictures of the current situation against a wide range of variables. Bina is also aware that the system can be set up to export data into other software packages which have the capability of carrying out more detailed and specific analyses than even a fully functioning version of the system is capable of providing. One such piece of software is Statistical Package for the Social Sciences (SPSS). Bina is very familiar with and skilled in using that tool from her research for her doctoral degree. If her line manager wants the task set for Bina done well, and in the timeframe set for completion, then Bina will have to be given the tools for the job and so money will have to be spent for a SPSS licence.

In summary: *data*, sometimes referred to as raw data, is a set of numbers or set of text; *metrics* are measures of performance which draw on and use data; *analytics* are detailed analyses of actual performance against one or more metric and *benchmarking* is a process of comparing metrics to inform analytics by providing a relevant comparator. We will now turn our attention to how these concepts are applied to the function and processes of HR.

REFLECTIVE ACTIVITY 8.2

Search for and access three definitions of 'metrics' from any academic and/or professional sources; for example, academic journals or professional publications. Produce a short statement which identifies the key differences in these definitions with those of the definition you produced of the term 'data'.

HR ANALYTICS

There are three important introductory points to make about HR analytics. The first point is that, despite a relatively recent surge in interest, the use of these is in fact long established (Carlson and Kavanagh 2014). Secondly and despite this long interest and recent surge of interest, application and use of HR analytics is still in its infancy in relation to both quantity as measured by the number of organisations utilising HR analytics and the quality of that use as measured by the sophistication of the techniques used and results produced (Rasmussen and Ulrich 2015, CIPD 2016). Third and finally, there is some confusion about terms. Two related terms are Human Capital Management and Human Capital Measurement, both often and unhelpfully shortened to HCM. The two terms do have similar meanings and refer to accounting for the value of human resources in an organisation and assessing the value of investment in those resources. In partnership with a number of other organisations, the CIPD has led a major project on HCM termed 'Managing the value of your talent' (CIPD 2014). The resulting framework from this project is shown in Figure 8.1.

Figure 8.1 The valuing your talent framework

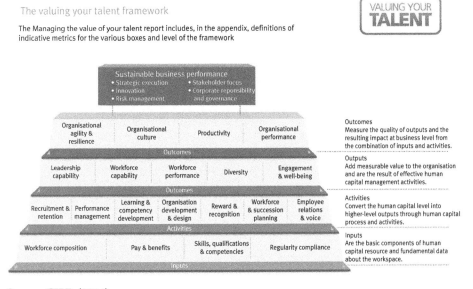

Source: CIPD (2014)

While the framework is suggestive and not intended to be prescriptive, it does provide a comprehensive catalogue of possible metrics for use in HR analytics. More importantly, the framework distinguishes and categorises different aspects, and their relationships, of HR measures. This is clearly illustrated by use of the terms 'inputs', 'activities', 'outputs' and 'outcomes'. Inputs describe the basic 'raw material' and focus of HR management, as well as a source of raw data. These provide the basis of HR activities such as performance management and L&D. In turn, the HR activities achieve HR-related outputs such as workforce capability and performance. These are capable of measurement and form some of the key HR metrics. The outputs have consequences in the form of organisational outcomes such as productivity and organisational performance, the latter usually measured in financial terms. They represent the impact on organisations of the combination of inputs and activities. The overall strategic aim of HCM is represented by the term 'sustainable business performance' which, using the word 'business' in an inclusive sense, is the ultimate purpose of the strategies adopted by all organisations in all sectors of the economy; public and voluntary as well as the private sector.

A major focus of the CIPD Valuing Your Talent project is to facilitate progress on yet another term, which is human capital accounting. This refers to long-standing efforts to enable organisations to account for and report on the contribution of, value of, and investment in their human resources. Currently, such accounting and reporting is limited to the more tangible resources of physical and financial capital. An additional result of the CIPD project is a recommended set of indicators for use in human capital accounting and reporting in organisations' annual reports. Four specific indicators, or measures, are suggested as shown in Table 8.1.

Table 8.1 Four levels of investment into human capital

Metric	Level	Business model value driver
Return on people employed	Outcomes	Outcomes measure the quality of outputs and the resulting impact at business level from the combination of inputs and activities
1 Employee engagement survey score	Outputs	Outputs add measurable value to the organisation and are the result of effective human capital management activities
2 Recruitment costs	Activities	Activities convert the human capital input level into higher-level outputs through human capital processes and activities
3 Training and development costs	Activities	Activities convert the human capital input level into higher-level outputs through human capital processes and activities
4 Staff compensation and benefits costs	Inputs	Inputs are the basic components of human capital resources and fundamental data about the workforce (e.g. financial, human or manufactured capitals)

Source: CIPD (2014)

As well as providing relevant and valuable information to organisation stakeholders, including investors in the case of private sector organisations, such reporting would provide data on HR metrics for benchmarking purposes and so support the use of HR analytics in all organisations. Of those suggested in Table 8.1, training and development costs would be of particular interest here. In addition, applying statistical analyses to a combination of metrics would provide even more valuable analytics. For example, correlations over time in changes in training and development costs and changes in scores on employee engagement surveys may reveal an interesting relationship. Extending such analyses outside a single organisation through benchmarking similar changes across a range of organisations would be even more revealing and valuable. The former is possible if an organisation adopted and applied the recommended metrics. The latter would be facilitated if all, or at least many, organisations followed suit.

REFLECTIVE ACTIVITY 8.3

Assess how easy or otherwise it will be to apply the measures given in Table 8.1 to an organisation you know well, and how relevant and valuable to the organisation applying the measures will be.

THE SARATOGA INSTITUTE

As mentioned previously, interest in HR analytics is not new. Influential work was done on the topic in the 1990s by the US-based Saratoga Institute in partnership with what is now the Society for Human Resource Management; the latter is the US equivalent of the CIPD. Table 8.2 provides a list of metrics that came out of that work.

Table 8.2 Measures in the Saratoga Institute/SHRM Human Resources Effectiveness Report

Revenue per Employee	Time to Start Jobs
Expense per Employee	HR Department Expense as a Percentage of
Compensation as a Percentage of	Company Expense
Revenue	HR Headcount Ratio–HR Employees: Company
Compensation as a Percentage of	Employees
Expense	HR Department Expense per Company Employee
Benefit Cost as a Percentage of Revenue	Supervisory Compensation Percentage
Benefit Cost as a Percentage of Expense	Workers' Compensation Cost as a Percentage of
Benefit Cost as a Percentage of	Expense
Compensation	Workers' Compensation Cost per Employee
Retiree Benefit Cost per Retiree	Workers' Compensation Cost per Claim
Retiree Benefit Cost as a Percentage of	Absence Rate
Expense	Involuntary Separation
Hires as a Percentage of Total	Voluntary Separation
Employees	Voluntary Separation by Length of Service
Cost of Hires	Ratio of Offers Made to Acceptances
Time to Fill Jobs	

Source: Carlson and Kavanagh (2014)

What is interesting from Table 8.2 is that there are no obvious or clear measures related to L&D. As we will see shortly, that situation has changed in recent years with L&D metrics now being more likely to be included in HR analytics. The CIPD project is one example of that. Also of interest from Table 8.2, and more clearly shown in the CIPD work, is a distinction to be drawn between metrics which measure the functioning of the HR department and HR professionals (what we might call efficiency metrics) and the value to the organisation of what the HR department and HR professionals do (what we might call effectiveness metrics). For example, time to fill jobs and costs of hires measure how efficiently HR activities are carried out. Revenue per employee and absence rate on the other hand are metrics of the contribution and value of HR activities to the organisation and so indicators of HR effectiveness. This is not a hard and fast distinction and some metrics are relevant measures of both efficiency and effectiveness. It is, however, a useful device to use when thinking about HR analytics and when considering L&D metrics in particular. So, it will be useful to bear in mind as we now consider those particular metrics.

CASE STUDY 8.2

Jill Beadle is a Talent Development Advisor with a medium-sized local authority in the rural west of England. Her role encompasses all departments in the council but has a particular focus on professional and managerial staff. This covers approximately 40% of the 550 total employees. Jill is aware that this is a relatively high proportion of such staff compared to many organisations in the private sector, and even compared to some similarly sized organisations in her own sector of local government. The disparity is mainly due to her authority's policy of outsourcing many of its services such as leisure services and refuse collection and disposal. This policy has resulted in a significant decline in technical and operative level staff, both in absolute and proportional terms. It has also resulted in an increase in the number of professional and managerial employees necessary to manage the outsourcing process and functions. These two changes in absolute numbers result in the high proportion of professional and managerial employees.

The demands on Jill's time and services have seen an increase in the previous two years to the extent that, in her assessment, additional professional resources are now needed to maintain the same level of L&D activity and support for her client group. Current levels of demand are unsustainable in Jill's judgement and failure to meet them is already having negative consequences on satisfaction levels expressed in employee and line manager evaluations of Jill's services through the council's annual engagement survey. Her own analysis of changes in proportions of employee categories in the council, and her benchmarking exercise, has shown Jill that the level of specialist L&D expertise relative to the proportions of employees in her client group is much lower than national and sector averages. This, together with declining satisfaction levels, makes Jill confident that a persuasive business case can be made to the HR Director for recruiting an additional Talent Development Adviser.

L&D DATA, METRICS AND ANALYTICS

Analytics cannot work without data. Data can be generated, for example through a research project. Designing a research project is explored in the next chapter. However, existing data can also be very valuable. We will begin this section by examining sources of useful existing data for use with L&D metrics and analytics.

SOURCES OF L&D DATA

A useful starting point is to identify sources according to whether they are internal or external to a particular organisation. We will begin with *internal sources*. It is important to recognise and acknowledge that not all organisations will have the same sources, or have the data in the same form and format. Organisation size will be a consideration. The larger the organisation, the more likely will be the existence of all sources. Larger organisations are also more likely to have data in easily accessed and useable forms and formats. For example, human resource information systems (HRIS) are now very common (see Carlson and Kavanagh 2014). These enable easier access to and analysis/

manipulation of HR data. However, small and medium enterprises (SMEs) and small charities in the voluntary sector for example are less likely to have such systems and so data may be available only in the form of paper records. In addition, most if not all HRIS products have optional modules, or functionalities. So, even if a particular organisation has an HRIS, and even if it is the same commercial product as other organisations, it doesn't follow that all will have the same datasets. A final consideration that applies in sources of data is that access to and/or use of data may be restricted by the terms of the 1998 Data Protection Act in the UK and similar legislation in other countries. While there is not space in this chapter to discuss the UK Act, or that of any other country, it is important to highlight the possible impact of such legislation on access to data sources.

As will be clear from the above, the most common internal source of L&D data will be personnel records, in whatever form and format. Such records commonly include data relevant to L&D; for example, educational qualifications held by each individual employee. Depending on varying policies and practices, they may also hold data on previous L&D experienced by employees. Again depending on varying policies and practices, individual personnel records may also include details of performance management outcomes – completed appraisal forms, for example. The latter may be kept separately as well as in the form of a complete record of performance management outcomes in each period. Aggregated data may also be available, or calculable, in an HRIS: labour turnover amongst varying categories of employees and over varying time periods, and numbers of employees attending and/or completing various learning events, for example. In this case, the HRIS will be a direct source of directly relevant L&D metrics.

Another source of information relevant to L&D is financial data in management and accountancy information systems (MIS). These will provide data on expenditure, and so the costs, of L&D activities. Again, depending on the functionality and degree of sophistication of such systems, financial MISs can be a direct source of directly relevant L&D metrics. Total expenditure on L&D activities is the minimum likely to be available but other metrics such as expenditure on varying forms of such activity are also possible and commonly available.

Additional financial information may be available in organisation annual reports. This will vary from organisation to organisation as to what data is provided relevant to L&D, but even basic financial performance figures can have some potential value. Written statements in annual reports can also provide relevant and useable data. The now clichéd thanks to and statements about staff being 'our most valuable asset' in reports to stakeholders from Chief Executives are not really relevant or valuable. However, the legal requirements for annual reporting that apply to narrative content now include what is referred to as a 'strategic report'. This can include much more relevant information including use and application of Key Performance Indicators (KPIs). These can and do embrace HR and L&D indicators. KPIs also include information on the risks firms face in achieving their strategy and sustaining the business into the future, which is a mandatory reporting requirement. Companies are also required to address environmental, employee, social, community and human rights matters (EESCH) where these are material to the reporting year and/or to future risks and performance. So this requirement too might lead to information relevant to HR generally and to L&D specific metrics. There are additional specific reporting requirements on, for example, gender diversity and remuneration which can also be relevant. Finally, annual reports also have to include information to do with corporate governance on what is known as a 'comply or explain' basis. This means information can be excluded but an explanation for why that is the case is required. Most companies therefore include relevant information and this content may have some relevance to L&D metrics. Strategic and directors' reports in company annual reports may contain data in numerical form but will always contain qualitative data, which can be more difficult to analyse but which is nevertheless potentially useful and valuable (see also Chapter 9).

A final source of internal data may also provide data in both quantitative and qualitative form. This source is internal management meetings. What form and names are taken for such meetings are too variable to indicate here, and most medium- to large-sized organisations are likely to have a number of different groups of managers holding regular meetings. Depending on the degree of formality attached to these meetings, which is likely to vary according to the size of the organisation, agendas and minutes will probably be available for most, together with reports considered at the meetings. These reports are likely in many cases to draw on data produced by HRIS and MIS data, as well as additional internal and external sources. Such reports may alleviate the need for compiling separate reports from the same sources for L&D purposes. Qualitative data in the form of minutes can be a useful source of information on managerial perceptions of and attitudes towards L&D. If monitored and analysed at various time points, the data can be useful in the metric of managerial satisfaction with the L&D activities taking place in the organisation.

 REFLECTIVE ACTIVITY 8.4

Identify the main sources of L&D data in an organisation you know well. Assess the relative value and benefit to L&D professionals of each of the sources.

As suggested above, internal management meetings often consider data from *external sources.* There are a number of external sources specifically of relevance to L&D. The first of these is the CIPD which has a range of relevant publications. A few examples of regularly available and updated reports are *Labour Market Outlook, HR Outlook, Employee Outlook* and the annual *Learning and Development Survey Report.* As well as the latter, additional annual surveys such as *Absence Management, Reward Management* and *Resourcing and Talent Planning* can also be useful and relevant sources of data for L&D metrics. These reports provide a very useful basis for benchmarking. Just as important, they also provide the basis for analysing important and significant trends over time; for example, in the composition of the labour market, in attitudes of employees, in developments in HR and L&D practice and in some of the various metrics to be considered later in the chapter; for example, organisations' expenditure on L&D. In addition to these regular reports, the CIPD is also a significant source of research on current and emerging topics; for example, on use of mobile technology in L&D and, as we saw earlier, on HR analytics. Many research reports include case studies of organisation practice which again can be very useful for benchmarking purposes. Commercial sources of benchmark data are also available; for example, Towards Maturity (http://www. towardsmaturity.org/).

Many if not most of the resources mentioned so far are freely available from the CIPD website and so can be accessed and used by anyone. A related source which is only available free to members is the CIPD magazine *People Management.* This can be a useful source of organisation case studies which again provide a basis for benchmarking. There are of course other professional magazines providing a similar source/resource; for example, *Personnel Today, HR Magazine, TD Magazine, Training Journal* and *Training.* Academic journals are also relevant and should not be discounted as sources of relevant data, especially on current research into emerging professional practice and trends in, for example, changing labour markets. A list of the most relevant titles is given in Table 8.3. CIPD membership gives access to some of these relevant journals through the CIPD website. Also available there for a subscription fee is the *Learning and Development Professional Development Hub* (http://www.cipd.co.uk/future-learning/default.aspx).

Table 8.3 Main L&D academic journals

Advances in Developing Human Resources – Sage Publications
European Journal of Training and Development – Emerald Publishing
Education & Training – Emerald Publishing
Human Resource Development International – Taylor and Francis
Human Resource Development Quarterly – Wiley
Human Resource Development Review – Sage Publications
International Journal of Training and Development – Wiley

As the professional body in the UK, the CIPD is an important source of data. This also extends outside the UK, for example their reports on HR analytics in the Middle East and in Asia published in 2015 (CIPD 2015a, CIPD 2015b). Other professional and similar bodies outside the UK will also be potentially useful sources of data, especially for those working in companies with overseas markets and supply chains, in multinational corporations or in voluntary sector organisations with international reach and operations. In the US, for example, there is the Society for Human Resource Management and the Association for Talent Development. It is always worth investigating what professional bodies are operating in particular countries. An organisation with a global membership base is the International Federation of Training and Development Organisations (IFTDO) which is a useful source of information on L&D professional associations across the world. Two academic organisations are also of potential value: the UK-based University Forum for HRD and the US-based Academy of HRD. The latter is well established and active in Asia and is becoming increasingly so in the Middle East and Africa.

Many government, non-governmental and supranational organisations are also excellent sources of data for L&D metrics. In the UK, the government portal at https://www.gov.uk/ provides access to many relevant resources. The portal opening page offers a number of options and of those, 'business and self-employed', 'employing people' and 'education and learning' are likely to lead to the most relevant resources and data. For example, the site hosts the results of the Workplace Employment Relations Study (WERS) which contains data on a range of relevant topics; for example, employee engagement and diversity. The portal is also a gateway to additional sites. Two of the most relevance are first that of the UK Commission for Employment and Skills (UKCES). This site has a wealth of research reports, for example the UK Employer Skills Survey. A second site is the Skills Funding Agency which, for example, has data on the employment of apprentices. An additional government agency with its own site is the Office for National Statistics. This site hosts relevant data on population demographics and trends as well as data on employment. Depending on the nature of a particular organisation, data and information on higher education and the links with the graduate labour market may also be relevant. Three organisations with potentially relevant data are first the four HE funding agencies for the UK (HEFCE for England; SFC for Scotland; HFCW for Wales and the Department for Employment and Learning in Northern Ireland); second the Higher Education Statistics Agency (HESA) and third the Quality Assurance Agency (QAA). These sites will be sources of information on, for example, participation and achievement in UK higher education as well as some indicators of the quality of individual HE institutions and degree courses. All of the sources mentioned in this paragraph enable access to data of potential value in L&D metrics, especially for analysing trends over time.

Supranational organisations include the United Nations and the European Union. The former has a number of agencies of potential value with the most relevant here being the International Labour Organisation (ILO). This organisation provides many reports of interest and value to L&D professionals including the annual World Employment and Social Outlook. It also provides a range of statistical databases of varying interest and value. The European Union and its Commission is of course a vast organisation. The two most relevant parts are the Directorate for Employment, Social Affairs and Inclusion, and the Directorate for Education and Culture. These directorates produce publications on general EU and country-specific labour markets and educational systems. Similarly, general and country-specific reports are produced by the Organisation for Economic Cooperation and Development (OECD). Given the role and purpose of that organisation their reports often focus on labour market issues and so will be of potential interest.

REFLECTIVE ACTIVITY 8.5

Access three of the external sources of data discussed in this section. Identify and assess the value of two resources from each of the sources.

L&D METRICS

All of the sources discussed above will provide a range of quantitative and qualitative data in a variety of forms. Some will constitute raw data only and some will have been subject to varying levels of analysis. However, even when 'fully' analysed by the source (for example, an internally sourced analysis of expenditure or an externally sourced analysis of a national labour market) the accessed data may well need further analysis for the purpose of producing useful and valuable L&D analytics. This is because the data needs to be related and connected to some measure of importance and significance to a particular context. That in turn depends on what specific metrics are most relevant. So, we will identify and discuss some of the most commonly used L&D metrics in this section. To begin this, Table 8.4 below provides a list of those and the following paragraphs will elaborate on some of the most important points arising from the table.

The first general point to make is that the table is not intended to be comprehensive and so additional metrics are possible. Those included, however, do provide a useful list and indicator of the main kinds of L&D metrics. Second, the table categorises metrics into different types. Finance is the common language used in most organisations and decision makers at all levels are always interested in costs, and so the first column is allocated to those metrics. The second column is concerned with what actually happens in relation to L&D and so contains metrics which analyse activity against a range of variables of possible interest and significance. For example, any given organisation may have no choice about providing legally required L&D; referred to as 'regulatory' in the table. An example is the requirement for some employees in financial services organisations to undertake statutory training. Another example is health and safety training, as is data protection policy, which applies to most if not all organisations. It is also the case that a given organisation may decree that all or some specified employees engage in some specified learning; referred to as 'mandatory' in the table. A common example here is induction and orientation learning at the commencement of and during the early part of employment. The relative proportions of these two 'must do' learning activities against the total amount of learning activity, and against the proportion of optional/voluntary learning activities can be very revealing of a number of important features of L&D activity. At the very least, the distribution will be suggestive of managerial and employee perceptions of the value of and attitudes towards L&D. The results of this simple analysis cannot be taken as final and can and should be checked against other metrics in the table; for example, some of the outcome metrics. The point does, however, illustrate the potential value of the metrics.

The third column is concerned with the L&D function and suggests two different metrics related to size. Each of these can be further analysed into job titles, roles and specialisms. The metrics as they are allow benchmarking against other organisations of similar size and/or operations. As with many other metrics in the table, the CIPD annual Learning and Development Survey Report (CIPD 2015c) is a very useful external data source for this purpose. The fourth column is labelled 'outcome metrics'. These are a mixture and range of metrics that can be used to assess the contribution and value of L&D. The metric of qualifications can be an important indicator of successful contribution in the context of, for example, mandatory L&D and in apprenticeship schemes. Many organisations also have in-house qualification programmes ranging from low-level NVQs through undergraduate degrees up to and including MBA and other masters' degrees. Success of participants on these, and increasing proportions of employees with relevant qualifications, is a useful metric of L&D outcomes in those circumstances. Staff satisfaction/engagement surveys can and do include measures directly associated with L&D and so those specific measures can be a specific focus. Wider, or general, employee satisfaction and engagement can be associated with L&D and so is of possible use and value. Wider HR analytics such as absence and staff turnover levels can also be associated with L&D. There may well be more direct connections where L&D activity has focused on absence management learning events for managers and supervisors, for example, or where leadership development learning has been provided. As the CIPD survey (CIPD 2015c) shows, comprehensive evaluation is still absent in most organisations. Utilising the metrics in Table 8.4 will help address that situation. But, the table also includes the most commonly used approach to evaluation. This is participants' and managers' feedback/ratings of L&D activities, which is also an important and useful metric.

The final column has just one entry. This is because it is not possible to anticipate and predict performance metrics that will be relevant to all organisations in all sectors of the economy. Therefore, L&D professionals need to establish what matters in their own organisation. It is possible to say that in the majority of organisations, outputs contributing to reducing costs and/or to increasing income will be valued. Quality measures and indicators of customer or client service and satisfaction are also commonly used as metrics of added value and so these too may feature in column 5 for some organisations. It is also important to point out that final output/contribution metrics can take time to emerge and be noticeable. In some cases, this can be a matter of years and this adds to difficulties in identifying and attributing causal relationships. This is one example of the problems referred to earlier with ROI as a L&D metric.

Table 8.4 L&D Metrics: a sample

Cost metrics	Activity metrics	L&D function metrics	Outcome metrics	Output/contribution metrics
Total expenditure on L&D Expenditure on each learning activity Expenditure by type of learning activity Expenditure by organisation department/function	Average time spent on L&D per employee Average time spent on L&D by type/category of employee Number of employees engaging with learning activities Number of employees engaging with regulatory L&D	L&D function size-numbers employed L&D function size-employment costs	Qualification levels of all employees Qualification levels by type/category of employee Overall absence levels Absence levels by type/category of employees Overall turnover/churn levels Turnover/churn levels by type/	Organisational financial and non-financial performance measures

Cost metrics	Activity metrics	L&D function metrics	Outcome metrics	Output/ contribution metrics
Expenditure by type/ category of employee Expenditure on regulatory L&D Expenditure on organisational mandatory L&D Expenditure on optional/ voluntary learning	Number of employees engaging with organisational mandatory L&D Number of employees engaging with optional/voluntary learning Number of employees engaging with each learning activity Number of employees engaging with each type of learning activity Number of employees engaging with learning by organisation department/ function Number of employees engaging with learning by type/ category of employee		category of employees Disciplinary and grievance problem levels Disciplinary and grievance problem levels by type/ category of employees Overall staff satisfaction/ engagement levels Staff satisfaction/ engagement levels by type/category of employees Staff satisfaction/ engagement levels by type of learning activity Participant and manager feedback/ratings by type of learning activity	

CASE STUDY 8.3

Len Edwards considers himself fortunate to be able to combine work with his commitment to helping young people. As the newly appointed HR Manager of a small local charity providing support to unemployed teenagers in a part of a large industrial town, acknowledged by government and its agencies to be 'disadvantaged', he sees every day the benefits achieved by the work of the charity. This is not always, or even often, in the form of employment. That would be too much to hope for in a town of high and rising unemployment across the whole of the working age population; a situation in turn due to a serious decline in the industry which provided the basis of the town's former expansion and previous prosperity. But, developing the skills and confidence of the town's unemployed youth, and helping them avoid the less productive and potentially harmful uses of their time which are easily available alternatives to engaging with the charity, are all outputs of the organisation's work which are valued by all stakeholders. One of the most important of these stakeholders is the local trust set up by one of the town's previously large employers. Being a significant funder of the charity Len works for, the trust takes a keen interest in the work and achievements of the charity.

As with many charities, Len's employer depends heavily on the contributions of volunteers as well as direct employed staff. In Len's experience and judgement, the charity would fail without that contribution. He was therefore surprised to find on appointment that very little of the budget allocated for L&D was utilised to support volunteers. Len is aware from his previous experience in the voluntary sector that such a situation is not unusual, but he had assumed coming into his new role that things would be different at this charity. This was because much of the work of the charity is in providing training to its clients, and many volunteers devote their time to acting as instructors in that

training. While all involved in that role have the necessary subject expertise and experience, very few combine that with previous instructing experience and so Len had assumed the charity would provide L&D in instructional skills for the volunteers. A quick look at the metrics of expenditure by type of learning activity and by category of those working in the charity (that is, employees and volunteers) shows this is not the case. An additional analysis of qualifications and previous L&D shows that few full-time employees and even fewer volunteers hold qualifications in or are likely to be skilled in acting as instructors and tutors on the training provided to the charity's clients. Len now knows he needs to produce a business case for additional resources to provide L&D in instructional skills for volunteers as well as employees, and that the business case will have to persuade the trust's representatives on the charity's Board if additional resources are to be provided.

L&D ANALYTICS

As discussed earlier, we can draw a useful distinction between L&D metrics and L&D analytics. The former provide a measure of something but do not of themselves provide useful insight into the added value of investment in L&D, or even if the current situation is appropriate. The distinction is similar to a philosophical distinction between what is referred to as empirical and normative. In simpler terms, empirical describes *what is the case* and normative specifies *what should be the case*. So, where there is a difference between the two then corrective action is called for and can be attempted. An important point is to recognise that normative specifications are value judgements and that there can be and often are variations and significant differences between peoples' perceptions of what should be. We will illustrate this with an example from Table 8.4.

The metrics relating to the L&D function will provide an empirical description; they will say what is the current situation in relation to how many individuals are employed in the L&D function. For illustration purposes, let's say the answer is ten. That figure of itself does not tell us very much of value. So, we benchmark that against other organisations using data in the CIPD survey report (CIPD 2015c). From that report, we find that organisations with up to 5,000 total employees employ an average of 11 L&D professionals. Our organisation has 7,500 total employees. We now have a L&D analytic; we know more than the simple empirical fact that we employ ten L&D professionals because we can compare, or benchmark, that figure against other employers. And using that analytic, we can conclude that we employ less than the average number of L&D professionals for organisations of our size. That statement describes the empirical case. The next question is of course normative: is that a 'good' thing or not? It might suggest that we are more efficient in relation to providing L&D services to employees. Or, it might suggest that we are not investing enough in specialist L&D expertise. We can use additional analytics to help answer the question but, as a question, it relates to *what should be* (keep the same number or increase the number of L&D professionals) and so it is a normative question. Therefore, different people are likely to have different answers for their own individual reasons; for example, the Head of L&D may be expected to favour increasing the number while the Finance Director may be expected to favour keeping the number the same.

As the above example demonstrates, L&D analytics go beyond looking at a single metric in isolation. Again, as illustrated in the example, this can involve benchmarking against external comparators. An additional way of turning metrics into analytics is to combine metrics. For example, we can combine cost and activity metrics to analyse the relative costs of different types of learning activities. So, combining expenditure by type of learning activity with number of employees engaging with each type of learning activity, we can produce a cost per employee for each type of learning activity. This can be an important and significant analytic in informing decisions on future spending on each type of learning activity. That analytic, however tells only part of the story and that is the input part; input here is expressed as a combination of expenditure and participation. To get a fuller story and understanding of the value of different types of learning activity, we need to add in some outcome metrics to our analysis. So, we can produce a fuller and more detailed analytic on types of L&D activity by using the staff satisfaction/engagement levels by type of learning activity and/or participant and manager feedback/ratings by type of learning activity. Comparing the cost per employee of type of learning activity analytic with the metrics of employee and manager satisfaction produces a form of cost-benefit analytic of different types of L&D activity. This will be a much sounder basis for decisions on future activity. For example, it may be that the type of activity with the highest cost per employee also produces the highest satisfaction ratings by both employees and managers. Without the latter information, it might have been tempting to reduce expenditure on that type of activity, perhaps even to zero. With the outcome metrics included in the analytic, what might have been a mistake will have been avoided.

The previous paragraph provides one example of how the metrics can be used together to produce analytics which are of significance and value. The example also illustrates the use of cost and/or activity metrics and outcomes and/or outputs metrics to produce inputs-process-outputs analytics. It is these analytics which are of most value as they can indicate, or in some cases directly measure, the added value of investment in L&D. Some examples of this include the one mentioned earlier where a L&D activity on absence management for managers and supervisors could be selected as a specific activity from within the 'number of employees engaging with each type of learning activity', in this case the learning activity for managers and supervisors on managing absence. This can then be compared with changes in the outcome metric of 'overall absence levels' in relevant time periods; for example, in each of the three years following the learning activity. This will produce an analytic of the impact of the learning activity on levels of absence. Producing such an analytic can utilise statistical techniques of varying sophistication which will be able to demonstrate a direct relationship between the two variables. The resulting analytic can be used for further analysis and demonstration of added value. Assuming there is some cost of absence metric available, any reductions in levels of overall absence can then be calculated as a reduction in costs to the organisation and so demonstrate a contribution to the output metric of organisational performance. While such a process will strictly apply only to absence management, any positive results can be used as an example of and in support of a general argument supporting investment in L&D. The metrics in Table 8.4 provide many additional opportunities for constructing similar analytics depending on individual organisation circumstances.

LEARNING ANALYTICS

There is one final topic to consider before closing this chapter and that is the concept of learning analytics. The distinctions between this and L&D analytics are mainly of level and of purpose. Learning analytics focus on the learning process of participants engaged in learning activities. The purposes can be and are varied from monitoring progress through a learning activity to learning more about how participants learn in order to adjust design of the learning activity and so improve the learning of future participants (Chatti *et al* 2012). The application of these analytics is primarily associated with learning activities delivered through information and communications technology (ICT) – what is often referred to as digital learning which relies on various forms of ICT devices such as PCs, laptops, tablets and mobile phones (see Holden and Stewart 2013). One form of technology which forms the basis of much of the application of learning analytics are the various 'learning platforms' which are used to design and deliver digital learning activities. An additional form of technology are social media sites which are also capable of generating relevant data which can be used to construct learning metrics and analytics. In both cases, but especially the latter case, applications can provide a particular focus on social learning (Ferguson 2012, Sinha *et al* 2012).

Learning analytics is still in its infancy as an area of research and professional practice. The concept does offer some potential value currently as well as in the future as new and more developed approaches and techniques are developed. The main purposes of introducing the concept in this chapter is first to alert readers to the difference between L&D analytics and learning analytics when accessing other resources, and second to highlight an emerging topic for the future. Achieving these purposes brings the chapter to a close.

 REFLECTIVE ACTIVITY 8.6

Using the metrics listed in Table 8.4, produce three L&D analytics that combine one or more metrics from each of columns 1, 2 and 4.

SUMMARY

The use of data in the form of metrics and analytics will be of increasing importance in L&D. This is in part related to the growing interest in HCM which in itself demonstrates the importance of linking L&D analytics with wider HR analytics. So too does the potential connections between the two forms of analytics and their symbiotic relationship in showing added value, illustrated by some of the examples in this chapter. Another reason for this growing importance is the increasing recognition of the significance of human resources in achieving organisation strategies and objectives. Related to this is the equally growing interest in measuring, assessing and demonstrating that contribution. Finally, the growing availability of large datasets, referred to as 'big data', adds importance to the topic of using L&D metrics and analytics. We have not specifically examined that phenomenon here but some of the sources discussed contain some examples of such datasets. Using big data, plus any and all forms and sources of data, is now a necessary skill of L&D professionals. This will become even more the case in the future. This chapter has provided a basic grounding in that skill.

REFLECTIVE ACTIVITY 8.7

Reread Case Study 8.3 on Len Edwards and then consider and respond to the following questions.

Questions

1   What financial outputs will be relevant to the charity's Board?

2   What non-financial outputs will be relevant to the charity's Board?

3   Which cost, activity and outcome metrics should Len consider using in building his business case?

4   How could Len combine the metrics into relevant L&D analytics?

5   How could Len connect these L&D analytics to relevant financial and/or non-financial output metrics?

6   What arguments, supported by L&D analytics, will be persuasive to the trust in the business case for additional funding for developing instructional skills among the charity's employees and volunteers?

FURTHER READING

Baron, A. and Armstrong, M. (2007) Human Capital Management: Achieving Added Value Through People London: Kogan Page.

Bassi, L. Carpenter, R. and McMurrer, D. (2012) HR analytics handbook. McBassi & Company.

Burkholder, N.C., Golas, S. and Shapiro, J.P. (2007) Ultimate performance measuring at work. New York: Wiley.

CIPD (2014) Managing the Value of your Talent: A new framework for human capital measurement. London: CIPD.

Fitz-Enz, J. (2010) The new HR analytics: Predicting the economic value of your company's human capital investments. New York: American Management Association.

Smith, T. (2013) HR Analytics: The What, Why and How. London: CreateSpace Independent Publishing.

REFERENCES

CARLSON, K. D. and KAVANAGH, M. J. (2014) HR metrics and workforce analytics. In KAVANAGH, M. J., THITE, M. AND JOHNSON, R. (eds.) *Human Resource information systems: basics, applications, and future directions.* 3rd ed. London: Sage Publications.

CHATTI, M.A., DYCKHOFF, A. L., SCHROEDER, U. and THÜS, H. (2012) A reference model for learning analytics. *International Journal of Technology Enhanced Learning.* Vol 4, No 5–6, pp318–331.

CIPD (2014) Managing the value of your talent: a new framework for human capital measurement. London: CIPD.

CIPD (2015a) *Evolution of HR analytics: a Middle East perspective*. London: CIPD.

CIPD (2015b) *Evolution of HR analytics: Perspectives from Singapore, Hong Kong and Malaysia*. London: CIPD.

CIPD (2015c) *Learning and Development annual survey report* 2015. London: CIPD.

CIPD (2016) *HR Outlook-Winter 2015–16*. London: CIPD.

DEVINS, D. and SMITH, J. (2013) Evaluating HRD. In GOLD, J., HOLDEN, R., STEWART, J. *et al* (eds.) *Human Resource Development: Theory and Practice*. 2nd ed. Basingstoke: Palgrave Macmillan.

FERGUSON, R. (2012) Learning analytics: drivers, developments and challenges. *International Journal of Technology Enhanced Learning*. Vol 4, No 5–6, pp304–317.

HOLDEN, R. and STEWART, J. (2013) E-learning. In GOLD, J., HOLDEN, R., STEWART, J. *et al* (eds.) *Human Resource development: theory and practice*. 2nd ed. Basingstoke: Palgrave Macmillan.

RASMUSSEN, T. and ULRICH, D. (2015) Learning from practice: how HR analytics avoids being a management fad. *Organisational Dynamics*. Vol 44, pp236–242.

SINHA, V., SUBRAMANIAN, K. S., BHATTACHARYA, S. and CHAUDHURI, K. (2012) The contemporary framework on social media analytics as an emerging tool for behaviour informatics, HR analytics and business process. *Management*. Vol 17, No 2, pp65–84.

CHAPTER 9

Conducting a Research Project

Jim Stewart

CHAPTER OVERVIEW

- Introduction
- Research paradigms
- The research process
- Summary

LEARNING OUTCOMES

By the end of this chapter, you will be able to:

- articulate and justify a research paradigm
- formulate research questions
- search, select and review literature and other sources
- select, design and apply relevant methods and techniques of data collection and analysis
- design and effectively implement an appropriate research project
- report findings and results of research projects to support a business case.

INTRODUCTION

This chapter covers the main aspects of doing a small-scale research project in learning and development (L&D). There are many books on doing research in business and management and so this single chapter provides a broad overview only of the most important points. These include a brief examination of the nature of research, varying paradigms applied in research projects, the stages of a research project, methods of data collection and analysis, drawing conclusions and recommendations from research evidence and reporting the results of research projects. In presenting and reporting the results of projects it is important to recognise and acknowledge the limitations of small-scale projects since, in most cases, research projects in this context will have been undertaken to produce evidence to support the business case for investment in L&D activity in a single and specific context. It is important that the business case for such investment is not overstated and does not go beyond the available evidence. So, common limitations will also be identified and discussed.

It will be helpful to state and clarify the overall purpose and related content of the chapter. The purpose is to facilitate learning about doing research. It is not about producing or writing business reports. The content therefore focuses on technical words, terms and concepts associated with the design of research projects. Some of these concepts will be new to most readers and may also appear challenging. This is a common response and so is to be expected. However, as with any other activity, research will be undertaken more successfully from a position of understanding, leading to informed choices and decisions, rather than from a position of ignorance. Therefore, the main content of the chapter provides sufficient guidance to support design and implementation of an effective research project. Some detail on some of the steps in the process of conducting research can be followed up and expanded by accessing the recommended texts at the end of the chapter.

RESEARCH PARADIGMS

MEANING OF RESEARCH

Research is undertaken in many different contexts and for many different purposes. The word often conjures images of people in white coats working in laboratories. Perhaps images of academics or students in university libraries studying ancient texts also come to mind. The same word though also applies to projects conducted in and for organisations. A common example is market research on consumer or client preferences, which is undertaken by many organisations. The marketing example is only one of many. Additional examples include HR departments establishing levels of employee satisfaction and engagement. Methods to achieve that are research projects. L&D professionals frequently seek to find out the impact and effectiveness of learning interventions. That, too, commonly needs a research project to establish an answer and so is another example. So, these marketing, HR and L&D professionals are doing the same as the people in laboratories or libraries: they are conducting research projects. It is a basic assumption of this chapter that the same principles apply to conducting research projects in any and all contexts. Therefore, professionals undertaking research in and for organisations need the same knowledge and skills as people in laboratories if they are to produce worthwhile results from their research projects. But, what exactly do we mean by research? According to the Oxford English Reference Dictionary, research means 'the systematic investigation into and study of materials, sources etc. in order to establish facts and reach new conclusions'. The same source goes on to add an additional definition of the word as 'an endeavour to discover new or collate old facts etc. by the scientific study of a subject or by a course of critical investigation'.

There are many clear similarities in these two definitions. We might, for example, highlight that both use the words 'investigation' and 'facts'. We might also argue that the words 'systematic' and 'scientific' are used as synonyms in the context of the definitions. The first definition implies that investigations in research are not carried out in any haphazard way but must be 'systematic'. This in turn suggests application of predetermined and established steps in a recognised and accepted process. Any approach varying from this process would be considered 'unsystematic' and so would not be research. The same is true of 'scientific' in that the word implies application of what is known as the scientific method. The scientific method could thus be the approach implied by the word 'systematic' since the method consists of a series of predetermined and established steps. The precise number, names and activities attached to these steps varies in different representations and descriptions. Figure 9.1 summarises the main steps to be found in most descriptions. The two definitions and Figure 9.1 contain some concepts which we will examine in more detail later in the chapter. We will begin with examining the scientific method as a whole as that raises some fundamental questions about doing research in any context, including in L&D.

Figure 9.1 The scientific method

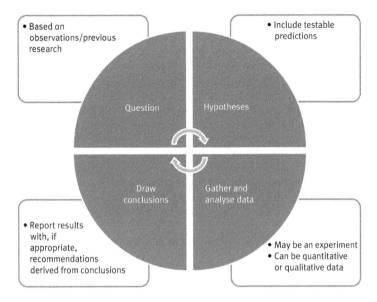

THE SCIENTIFIC METHOD

The first point to make is that the rise in use of the scientific method as a basis for systematic investigation is associated with the establishment of the disciplines we commonly associate with the term 'science'; that is, physics, chemistry and biology. We will return to that point later in the chapter. Second, and as suggested above, there are debates and disputes on what steps and activities are required for applying the process and so what does and does not count as the scientific method (see Nola and Sankey (2014) for a full account of these points and the method). This latter point is worthy of more exploration which we will achieve by examining some of the steps in Figure 9.1 in more detail.

The starting point suggested in Figure 9.1 is to have a question. That in turn suggests that the purpose of conducting a research project is to establish an answer to a question to which the answer is currently unknown. Such questions can be suggested by looking at previous research and identifying some gap or gaps in current knowledge. This can be at a very general level or related more precisely to a specific context. For example, we might want to know what employees like and dislike about using e-learning. At a general level, there are answers to that question based on previous research. However, that previous research may not have included employees in the industry of interest, and in any case is highly likely not to have included employees in every organisation. It may also be a few years old and so conducted before the most recent innovations in e-learning. So, while general answers may be available to the question, no answer will be available for the specific employees in a specific organisation at a specific time. Whether it is worth finding an answer in the specific context is a matter of judgement, which will be informed by the factors related to previous research; for example, when and where and with whom the research was conducted. The judgement will also be informed by the second source of questions in Figure 9.1; that is, observations. To continue the example, let's assume that observing existing data suggests declining numbers of employees choosing to engage in e-learning, and the most noticeable decline is in use of particular e-learning programmes considered important by the organisation. These additional factors may support the case that the question is worth investigating and so worthy of a small-scale research project.

The next step in the process focuses on formulating hypotheses. This is one area of debate and dispute. Debates include whether hypotheses are always appropriate or even necessary. They also focus on what does and what does not represent a hypothesis. These debates and disputes arise from the scientific method being associated with sciences such as physics and chemistry. Alternative conceptions of science are associated with the social sciences such as psychology and sociology. Differences in conceptions of science also apply to the next step of gathering and analysing data. This step is often restricted to design and conduct of experiments in descriptions of the scientific method. The step is also commonly restricted to the collection and analysis of quantitative data. Experiments and quantitative data are traditionally used in physics and chemistry. However, the social sciences are more relevant to research projects focused on L&D. These are more likely to use alternative methods, and to use qualitative data. We will examine these different conceptions of science in the next subsection. Finally, in Figure 9.1, results of and conclusions drawn from research need to be reported. When conducted by professional researchers, this usually means making the results and conclusions public so they are available to all other researchers. Making public by *publi*cation also enables the research to be replicated and so the conclusions can be checked and verified. However, in small-scale research done in and for an organisation, the results and conclusions are unlikely to be published. They are usually reported only internally in a specific organisational context. So, small-scale projects are not commonly subject to the same degree of scrutiny and checking as published research.

REFLECTIVE ACTIVITY 9.1

Consider the pros and cons of applying the scientific method to small-scale L&D research projects. Identify three pros and three cons.

DISPUTES ON THE SCIENTIFIC METHOD

As stated, the scientific method is an area of dispute and not all research follows that process, at least not in a formulaic manner. This is in part because of the existence and application of different research paradigms. In this context, a paradigm refers to a framework which informs, shapes and influences understanding of the world. Different frameworks mean that there are different ways of understanding the world (see Bryman and Bell 2015). There are varying numbers of paradigms that are claimed to exist which determine different approaches to conducting research. We will examine three of the most commonly discussed in research textbooks (Fisher 2010, Saunders *et al* 2015). First, however, it is important to understand a basic distinction within science itself which accounts for some difference in paradigms. This is the distinction between the material and social worlds. The sciences such as physics and chemistry are often referred to as the physical sciences. Disciplines in this category share a focus on the physical world. This is also referred to as the material world. In contrast, disciplines such as psychology and sociology are referred to as the social sciences. They have a focus on understanding the experience and behaviour of human beings. The attention of this focus is referred to as the social world.

The scientific method was developed within the physical sciences for the study of the material world. Study of the social world and the development of the social sciences occurred later in history than development of the physical sciences. The social sciences were initially influenced by the more established natural sciences and so applied the same approach to research by applying the scientific method. This was regarded as necessary to gain the same status for the then new social sciences of psychology and sociology as already enjoyed by the physical sciences. However, gradually and over time, some social scientists became dissatisfied with the relevance of the scientific method as an approach to studying the social world. As we all know, human beings behave very differently and for very different reasons to inanimate objects such as atoms, molecules and physical objects and forces. One significant example of the difficulties experienced by the social sciences in applying the scientific method is in designing and applying experiments to the study of human behaviour. There are ethical questions to do with that. In addition, the practical challenges of controlling the large number and complex nature of variables involved in human behaviour render experiments not only difficult to conduct but also very limited in generating understanding of human behaviour. So, different approaches based on different paradigms have been developed in the social sciences. Put very simply and very broadly, the paradigm informing the scientific method assumes that the material world has independent existence separate from human experience, and is knowable objectively. An alternative paradigm informing the social sciences, or more accurately some social scientists, assumes that the social world does not exist independently of human beings and can only be known subjectively. This raises questions to do with some complex concepts which we will examine next.

 REFLECTIVE ACTIVITY 9.2

Consider your responses to the previous activity and whether you now wish to reject any of the pros or cons. Produce a new list of three of each. Explain and justify your list.

ONTOLOGY AND EPISTEMOLOGY

The concepts of ontology and epistemology have a long history in the study of philosophy (see May 2011). We need just a brief explanation for our purpose. Ontology is concerned with the nature of being and reality. Applied to you or me, the question is: do we have independent existence? The paradigm informing the scientific method assumes we do. But, according to some social science paradigms, that would apply to us only as a physical body. That means as a collection of bones and tissues, or cells or, at an even deeper level, a collection of chemicals, molecules and atoms. Looked at as a person with a name rather than as a body, a social science paradigm would suggest that our existence is not independent of the other people in our lives who respond to and interact with us as a person. In other words, Jim Stewart as a person exists only because I and others give meaning to the idea of Jim Stewart. So, my body may have independent existence but Jim Stewart does not. This difference can be described as that between a realist and non-realist ontology. The scientific method adopts a realist ontology which is appropriate to studying bodies. Some social science paradigms adopt a non-realist ontology which are appropriate to studying persons. So, my body has independent and objective existence in the material word but, as a person known as Jim Stewart, I have only interdependent and subjective existence in the social world.

Epistemology concerns the study of knowledge. This includes what constitutes knowledge and how we can and do know what we claim to know. There are clear connections between ontology and epistemology and so we can apply the terms realist and non-realist to epistemology as well as to ontology. A realist epistemology assumes that objective knowledge is possible and so we can establish truth and facts about the nature of being and reality. The scientific method is designed and intended to do just that. A non-realist epistemology might accept that this is possible in relation to the material world but argue that it is not possible in relation to the social world. This is because the social world is different and knowledge of that world is socially constructed. For example, I know I am Jim Stewart and many other people know that I am Jim Stewart. But that is only because I and those many other people share certain constructs; for example, the construct of names and their use to distinguish one person from another. I and those many other people also know that I am an academic. But again, that is because we share the construct of 'academic'. There are people in the world today who have no concept of 'academic'; for example, native South Americans living in the Amazon rainforests. So, saying to them that Jim Stewart is an academic would have no meaning; it would be literally nonsense to them. One reason for that is that their language will not have a word for 'academic'. Another reason is that they have no experience of the occupational role of academic. The role does not exist in their societies. And there was a time in history when the previous sentence was true of everyone in all parts of the world; for example, the occupational role did not emerge until around the sixteenth century. So, the concept of 'academic' as an occupational role and as a word to label that role is a social construction. Therefore, knowledge, rather than being objectively 'true' or a statement about 'facts' is actually socially constructed and so subjective. In the context of the place and time in which we currently live, we can claim to know that Jim Stewart is an academic, but in other places and in other times that claim would not be recognised.

THREE RESEARCH PARADIGMS

The different positions adopted in relation to ontology and epistemology are major factors in different paradigms informing research. Before we examine three of the most commonly applied paradigms it is important to make three introductory points. First, doing a research project in L&D means by definition that the project is within the social world and so is within the paradigms of the social sciences rather than the physical sciences. Second, that does not mean that the scientific method and the associated paradigm is rejected. As we will see, one of the commonly applied paradigms within social science is firmly rooted in the assumptions and traditions of the scientific method. This is because many social scientists still subscribe to the view that social science research should apply the same processes and meet the same criteria of rigorous research as those applied in the physical sciences. Third, whatever paradigm is adopted and applied, there needs to be both consistency in ontological and epistemological assumptions and rigour in the design and implementation of the research project (see Bryman and Bell (2015) for a fuller discussion).

Positivism

The first paradigm is that of *positivism*. This paradigm is in agreement with the scientific method. The name actually derives from logical positivism which is the philosophical position underpinning the scientific method (see Stewart *et al* 2011). Being associated with the physical sciences and with the scientific method, positivism adopts a realist ontology and realist epistemology. Thus, there is an assumption of an objective and independent reality, even in the social world. There is also an assumption that this objective reality can be independently investigated and known. Part of knowing is establishing truths and facts about the social world that apply in all places and all times. In other words, what is established as a truth or fact has universal application in all social contexts. An example of the positivist paradigm from the social science of psychology are the various learning theories such as experiential learning, behaviourism and social learning. In all of these theories, the claims to universal truth are based on research applying, with small variations, the scientific method and a positivist paradigm. They also illustrate, however, that there are problems with positivism being applied to the social world since each theory claims a different truth; each cannot be the final and absolute truth about how people learn since there are differences in the explanations provided by each theory. So, the theories are not 'facts' or universal truths.

Critical realism

The second paradigm shares some assumptions with positivism which is indicated by the term used to describe the paradigm. That term is *critical realism*. Critical realism accepts that there is, or at least that there may be, a reality in the social world independent of particular individuals in particular places and particular times. To that extent, they accept a realist ontology. But, in contrast to the positivist position, critical realism points out that social reality is capable of being changed. For example, I was born in the UK in 1950 at which point in time the UK was a democratic society and had what is known as a mixed economy. Russia at that time was at the centre of the Soviet Union and had a totalitarian political system and what is known as a command economy. These features were certainly independent of any actions of mine or anyone born in the UK or Russia in 1950 and so they were the social reality we were born into. However, in 2016 the UK has a liberal economy while Russia has some form of democracy as the political system and also has a liberal economy – a new social reality for me and for Russians. So, critical realism does not accept that social reality is fixed or universal. Therefore, it is capable of change.

Epistemologically, critical realism departs even further from positivism in rejecting the view that knowledge is objective and value free. For this paradigm, knowledge about the social world is coloured by the subjectivity of the 'knower' which in turn is shaped and influenced by many factors in their social environment and experience. For example, L&D professionals may commonly claim to 'know' that investing in L&D produces worthwhile returns. But, some in the private sector may associate 'worthwhile returns' with financial returns, some in the voluntary sector with individual returns such as improved skills and some in the public sector with community returns such as increased social cohesion. So, the 'knowing' is influenced by individual values and different employment contexts. And, other professionals such as accountants may disagree with the L&D professionals that investing in L&D produces worthwhile returns, whatever forms of evidence are produced to support the claims to knowledge. Because of these points, critical realism rejects the possibility of universal truth or fact. In this perspective, therefore, there may well be a single, albeit changeable, reality, but there will be multiple interpretations of that reality held by different groups and individuals. This informs what is judged to be possible in research. Establishing universal truths is not possible.

Interpretivism

The third and final paradigm is commonly termed *interpretivism*. This paradigm adopts both a non-realist ontology and a non-realist epistemology. The paradigm views the social world as socially constructed and so the paradigm is sometimes referred to as constructionism or social constructionism. These terms are associated with a sociological view of the world. An alternative view also associated with interpretivism derives from psychology and is known as constructivism. The key difference is that within sociology 'constructs' emerge from the patterns of interactions of people which construct, or make, shared meanings and understandings; for example, a shared meaning attached to and understanding of the value of L&D among L&D professionals. Within psychology the term 'construct' has a similar meaning but it is the result of the cognitive processing of a single individual and exists for that person alone. There may be many commonalities in the construct with many other people but there will always be differences. To use an earlier example, 'Jim Stewart' is a construct shared by many people and if we could examine each and every one we would find many similarities; for example, Jim Stewart is a male academic. In that sense, 'Jim Stewart' is a sociological social construction. But, we would also find slight variations and nuanced differences in meaning of 'Jim Stewart' in each person's understanding of the construct; for example, Jim Stewart is an excellent/ average/poor writer of textbooks! Those nuances come from variations in the psychological constructs of individuals.

The essential assumption of interpretivism is that the social world differs from the material world. The social world has no independent existence and is infinitely variable depending on the decisions and actions of human actors, and their interaction within human collectives. Given that reality is socially constructed it is also the case that knowing that reality in an objective sense is not possible. The 'knower' is influenced by the common assumptions, beliefs and values of their social context; for example, by being an L&D professional working in the public sector. The 'knower' is also influenced by their individual, personal and unique collection of psychological constructs. And the researcher of the social world is also always a part of that world and so cannot be detached and objective in investigating any aspect of the social world. All of this has clear implications for designing and conducting research projects in any social context, including L&D.

SUMMARY

Table 9.1 summarises the main points describing and distinguishing these paradigms. The main points to make are first that different paradigms influence but do not determine the design of research projects. Second, and more importantly, paradigms do determine what researchers claim that their research projects can achieve and the status of their results. Positivists will aim for and claim universal truth, critical realists will aim for and claim provisional and contextual truth, and finally interpretivists will aim for and claim deeper understanding of specific social contexts and issues. Whichever paradigm is adopted, small-scale research projects will follow the same, or at least similar, stages in the research process and so we will now turn our attention to that.

 REFLECTIVE ACTIVITY 9.3

Assess the advantages and disadvantages of each of the three paradigms for small-scale L&D research projects.

Table 9.1 Three research paradigms

		RESEARCH PARADIGMS		
		Positivism	Critical realism	Interpretivism
ASSUMPTIONS	Ontology: the position on the nature of reality	External, objective and independent of social actors.	Objective. Exists independently of human knowledge. Is interpreted by humans through social conditioning.	Socially constructed, subjective, may change, multiple realities.
	Epistemology: the view on what constitutes acceptable knowledge	Only observable empirical phenomena can provide credible data. The focus and aim is on	Observable phenomena can provide credible data. Focuses on explaining in a given context or contexts.	Subjective meanings. Focus upon the particular details of the specific situation, the experienced

		RESEARCH PARADIGMS		
		Positivism	Critical realism	Interpretivism
		causality and law like generalisations.		reality behind these details and subjective meanings and motivating actions.
	Axiology: the role of values in research and the researcher's stance	Research can be and is conducted in a value-free way by an objective researcher who is independent of the data.	Research is value laden. The researcher is biased by personal world views, experiences and upbringing.	Research is value bound. The researcher is part of what is being researched, cannot be separated and so will be subjective.

Based on Wahyuni (2012)

CASE STUDY 9.1

Angie Bates is a full-time student studying for a CIPD Level 5 Intermediate Diploma in Learning and Development as part of her undergraduate degree in HRM at a university located in a busy town in the north of England. Angie has secured a short placement at a firm of solicitors. The Managing Partner has asked that Angie produce a report detailing the L&D needs of all non-professional staff in the firm. These include clerical and administrative staff as well as personal assistants to the senior partners and the paralegal officers providing technical support to the solicitors and clients of the firm.

Angie realises that producing the required report for the firm will require a small-scale research project. After much consideration and discussion with her university tutor, Angie has decided that her personal beliefs support a positivist view of the world. Angie also believes this is a viewpoint that will be shared by the Managing Partner and the other senior managers in the firm. That in itself seems to Angie to be a sound reason for adopting the positivist paradigm for her project. But, Angie also recognises that her findings will be limited in application outside the context of the law firm. It might be possible to say some something about the general training needs of some, perhaps all, of the occupational groups being investigated. However, Angie understands and accepts that most of the training needs she identifies will be particular and specific to firms of solicitors and no other kinds of firms, and some will apply only to her placement firm. So, Angie knows to take care with what she claims in the dissertation that she also needs to produce for her university course.

Design and implementation of a research project commonly follows a number of steps or stages. Some of these are associated more with what we can call the first 'phase' of a project; designing the project; and the others with the second phase of implementation. But, there are clear connections between the two phases and they often overlap. For example, a data collection method selected during the design phase may not work exactly as intended when implemented and so may have to be adjusted or redesigned. That is not an unusual occurrence and so it is an important point to understand. Research projects do not always go as planned and adjustments along the way of implementation do not mean failure. They are simply a normal part of the research process. We will examine the steps of a project under the two headings of design and implementation.

THE DESIGN PHASE

The design phase is clearly of critical importance as the final outcomes of a research project depend on the quality of decisions made at this point. The phase can be divided into the following steps:

Decide the subject

The starting point is to determine the broad area or *subject* of the project. We are concerned here with L&D and so that is naturally our broad area. However, it is too broad for the purposes of research. So, the subject needs to be narrowed down to something more specific. Two common examples in L&D where research is valuable are first to establish learning needs and second to assess the value of investment in L&D activities. The former is often referred to as Learning Needs Analysis (LNA) and the latter as evaluation. Either one of those would be more appropriate as the subject of the project rather than a broad heading of L&D. There are, however, many other possibilities; for example, researching the effectiveness of various learning methods before selecting one to use in a new L&D activity. As an example here, we will take evaluation as the subject of an assumed project to apply in later steps.

Conduct a literature review

Step two in the process varies according to different views (see Fisher (2010), Bryman and Bell (2015), Saunders *et al* 2015). Some argue that step two is *deciding on a research paradigm.* That approach can work but it seems to me there are two problems with the approach. First, either paradigms reflect fundamental personal beliefs about the world or they don't. If they do, then there is no decision to be made as the researcher always adopts the same paradigm and so does not have to, perhaps even cannot, choose any other paradigm except the one that reflects their personal beliefs. The second problem arises if paradigms do not reflect personal beliefs and choice is possible. In that case, it is more appropriate to make the decision later in the process. So, an alternative view on the second step is to *conduct a literature review.* This will provide two outputs of relevance and value. First, it will inform you of what is already known about the topic. To continue our example, assume the focus of the project is to evaluate the outcomes of a leadership development activity provided as part of a graduate development programme. The literature review will inform you of what has been previously found on the outcomes, value and benefits of similar activities. Second, the literature will also be a source of information and ideas on how to do similar research.

Conducting a successful literature review involves three main steps. First, undertake a search to find relevant literature. This requires selecting or formulating search terms and second applying those terms in searches of appropriate databases of publications. Access to appropriate databases is easy and free if working through a university website and associated online resources. If this is not possible then Google Scholar is a search engine freely available to everyone and one which is highly effective. Another valuable resource is the CIPD website which has its own resources and also provides access for CIPD members to relevant databases of academic journals, as well as that of *People Management* magazine. The second step is to deal with the results which are likely to be too many in number for all to be included in the review. So, an initial review is necessary to identify the most relevant and appropriate material. The titles of articles and reports can be useful for an initial sift to select and reject material. Where available, abstracts, which are always included in academic journal articles, are the next useful feature to help select and reject material. Finally, a quick skim read of the introduction and conclusions will help make a final decision on whether to select or reject each remaining piece of material for the review. The second step includes recording details of and then reading each of the selected material. It is important to read with a critical mind and to make judgements of the validity as well as the relevance of each piece of material. The third step is to produce the literature review. This involves analysing similarities and differences in the results reported in the material. This summary of the steps in a literature review is too brief to do justice to this stage in a research project, even if the project is small in scale. Therefore, the additional guidance in the recommended texts should also be used in guiding any review. A specialist text by Chris Hart on how to do a literature review is also suggested and recommended (Hart 2009).

 REFLECTIVE ACTIVITY 9.4

Select a possible topic for a project. Do a search for relevant literature using Google Scholar or a database of academic articles you can access. Set a target of identifying a minimum of five and a maximum of ten relevant articles. Read and review the articles and summarise the main points you would include in a literature review.

Formulate research questions

Once the literature review is complete and current knowledge on the topic is established, the next step of *formulating research questions* can be completed. It is useful to do this step after the literature review because it is a waste of time and effort to undertake a research project to answer a question to which the answer is already known. So, the literature review supports narrowing the focus of the project by informing more specific and precise research questions. For instance, and to continue our example, much might be already known about leadership development in graduate programmes. But, little or nothing is known about those activities in particular industries; for example, in games development or entertainment or health services, or perhaps for graduate programmes for particular occupations; for example, engineers, or systems analysts. What is probably almost always the case is that a leadership activity as part of a graduate development programme has not been previously evaluated in a specific organisation. Naming that company therefore is one way of narrowing the focus of the research questions.

Research questions reveal the paradigm being adopted by the researcher in the research project. They indicate the ontological and epistemological position adopted by the way they are formulated. For example, the question 'what is the value of the leadership development activity in the graduate development programme in X organisation?' implies a belief that the value has objective existence and can be independently established by being measured. That in turn implies a positivist paradigm. Alternatively, the question 'what value is perceived and attributed to the leadership development activity in the graduate development programme by senior decision makers in X organisation?' suggests an interpretivist paradigm. In this question, value is seen first as subjective and second as variable according to the subjectivity being investigated; that is, groups such as middle managers or participant graduates may perceive and attribute different value to that of senior decision makers. So, if not previously decided, the step of *deciding on a research paradigm* is now taken and is informed by the nature of the research questions.

We will at this point make a slight but significant digression. The majority of textbooks on research in business and management, including L&D, use terms such as quantitative and qualitative research. This use also commonly implies an association with different paradigms; positivism is directly linked with quantitative research and interpretivism is directly linked with qualitative research. The same links are also applied when the terms are applied to research methods: quantitative methods are associated with positivism and qualitative methods are associated with interpretivism. However, attaching the words quantitative and qualitative to either of the words research or methods is a misuse of language. The terms quantitative and qualitative make sense only when applied to the word data. For example, the leading management researcher Tony Watson consistently and exclusively adopts an interpretivist paradigm in his work (see, for example, Watson and Harris (1999), Watson 2010). Yet, and as he has often pointed out, his work is peppered with words such as none, few, some, many and all; or never, sometimes, often and always. These words are all quantitative concepts which are also perfectly acceptable within an interpretivist paradigm. So, research projects cannot be classified as either quantitative or qualitative and those terms cannot be exclusively associated with a single paradigm. As we will see soon, the same is true of research methods. These too cannot be exclusively associated with either quantitative or qualitative, or with a single paradigm, despite what is claimed in most textbooks on research in business and management.

Types and sources of data

There are two linked steps next in the process. These are to first determine the *type of data* needed to answer the research questions – quantitative or qualitative or both – and second to determine the *sources of data.* The first of these is usually fairly straightforward. The research question in the positivist paradigm given earlier will require quantitative data while the interpretivist research question is likely to require qualitative data. Data sources are also likely to vary. Senior decision makers are the obvious and clear source of data for the second formulation of our research question. A variety of sources may be relevant for the first formulation. These will include performance data from secondary sources which may include financial data. Other secondary sources may include performance management/appraisal records of the participant graduates. Opinions from line managers and colleague co-workers of graduates may be an additional source of data but, given the positivist paradigm, these are likely to be treated as facts (see also the section on Populations and samples).

Select research methods

Once the types and sources of data are decided, the next step is to *select the research methods* to be used to collect the required data. There are many options in this step including experiments, questionnaire surveys, interviews, focus groups and documentary analysis. As indicated above, methods are commonly classified as either quantitative or qualitative in research textbooks. This is a mistake since it implies that individual methods are restricted in the type of data they can collect. In fact, probably all methods can be used to collect either or both types of data. A more accurate classification is that there are four methods of collecting data of any type. These methods are asking questions, observation, experiments and documentary analysis. These methods are applied through a variety of techniques. One common technique of asking questions, for example, is through interviews. Table 9.2 provides a summary of three modes of interviewing and three means of applying each of the modes. Modes and means are independent of each other; for example, any mode can be used in telephone or face-to-face interviews.

Table 9.2 Interviews

Mode	Means
Structured	Face to face
Semi-structured	Telephone
Unstructured	Email

Another common technique of asking questions is through questionnaires. Table 9.3 provides a summary of four different designs of questionnaires and four means of distribution to research participants. Design and means are independent; for example, closed or open questions can be used with any means.

Table 9.3 Questionnaires

Design	Means
Closed questions	Self/researcher administered
Open questions	Postal
Mixed mode	Email
Biographical data	Electronic

Any given research project can utilise either or both of these techniques and any single or mix of modes/design within each technique. It is not uncommon for projects to use both interviews and questionnaire surveys, for example. And it is not uncommon for questionnaires to be mixed design; that is, to have both closed and open questions, and to ask for biographical details of respondents. The latter often include details such as age, gender, qualifications, years of experience and years in current post. A word of caution is relevant here. Biographical detail should be asked for only if it is relevant to answering one of the research questions, or if it is necessary to substantiate the sample of respondents. It should be clear from Table 9.2 and Table 9.3 that both techniques can be used to collect either or both of quantitative and qualitative data. For example, and using our example research questions, a mixed-mode questionnaire may be sent to participant graduates and ask questions which rate the quality of the leadership development activity. These questions may have a rating scale for the response; for example, 'I was satisfied with the pre-activity briefing' rated on a five point Likert scale (see Fisher 2010) from 'Fully Dissatisfied' to 'Fully Satisfied'. Responses to this and similar questions will be converted to quantitative data in the form of statistical analyses. The questionnaire may also ask open questions such as 'What in your view was the most effective part of the leadership development activity, and why?'. This and similar questions invite personal and narrative responses which provide qualitative data. This illustrates that the technique of a questionnaire survey is not restricted to a single data type. Responses of both data types can also be considered and treated as either perceptions and opinions or as facts and truth. The status of responses in those terms, and not the methods or type of data, are determined by and reflect the paradigm being applied. So, we can say that methods, techniques and data type are all paradigm neutral. That is, any method, technique and data type can be and are used within any research paradigm. This argument can be further illustrated and supported by considering the method of observation.

REFLECTIVE ACTIVITY 9.5

Access a relevant source; for example, one of the recommended texts at the end of the chapter. Read more about the use of interviews and questionnaire surveys in research projects. Produce a summary of the relative advantages and disadvantages of each technique. Using the summary, assess the relevance and value of each technique for use in your research project.

Table 9.4 shows the various approaches to using observation as a research method. Broadly, observations can be carried out as a participant or non-participant and in each case the observation can be declared to those being observed and so be overt, or not declared and not made known to those being observed and so be covert. In all of these cases, both quantitative and/or qualitative data can be collected. For example, the number of conversational exchanges between different pairings in a team of employees can be observed, monitored and recorded. In our example project, different forms of behaviour such as initiating decisions by different individual members of a team can be observed, monitored and recorded. This will generate quantitative data; that is, the number of times each team member initiates decision making. Actual verbal responses by each of the other team members to each occurrence of the target behaviour can also be observed, monitored and recorded. Different verbal responses by different individuals, and variation in response to different team members displaying the target behaviour, will be of interest. These verbal responses will generate qualitative data. So, the method of observation is data type neutral; it can be used to collect either or both quantitative and qualitative data. The way in which either or both types of data are analysed and used, and the nature of the conclusions drawn and claims made on the basis of the analysis, will be determined by the paradigm adopted and not by the method or type of data. The conclusions and claims made will also reveal, or 'betray', the paradigm.

Table 9.4 Forms of observation

Participant	Non-participant
Overt	Covert

Populations and samples

This consideration of research methods nearly closes the research design phase. There is, however, one additional issue that needs to be mentioned and that is the *notion of a sample*. This issue is most significant if a positivist paradigm is adopted because it is most relevant if generalised truth or fact is believed to be possible and is aimed for in the research project. It is also most relevant to the positivist paradigm since the claims to truth or fact commonly rest on following strict rules of statistical analysis. Some of these rules apply to formulating statistically valid samples.

The books by Fisher (2010) and by Saunders *et al* (2015) provide much detailed advice on sampling and certainly much more than can be included here. The basic advice is first to distinguish between populations, samples and response rates. A population is all of those individuals of relevance and interest to the research project. For example, research is often carried out to predict the outcome of political elections – a UK general election, for instance. In those cases, the population consists of all of those citizens entitled to vote. In our example project, and when researching the second formulation of the research question, the population is all senior decision makers in the organisation. A sample is a selected subgroup of the population. In the case of research to predict election outcomes, the size of the sample is determined by statistical rules since the claim will be a prediction, or true claim, of the actual result. In practice, the size of the sample in such research is tiny compared to the population; hundreds of individuals in the sample out of many millions in the population. But, that is acceptable as we will see shortly. In our example project, the number of senior decision makers is likely to be small and so the sample can in fact comprise the whole population.

There are varying types of samples. The most common are representative and random samples. Both of these are commonly applied in constructing samples in the positivist research paradigm. In the case of general election projects, the key aim is to have a representative sample. This means that the significant characteristics of the population are represented in the sample in the same proportions as they occur in the population. Three examples of such characteristics are gender, age and social class. Researchers working on predicting election results ensure that they meet this requirement by controlling their response rates. They do this by interviewing enough people so that they end up with the right sample to analyse for their prediction. A useful analogy of representative samples, and one which illustrates why only a few hundred out of a research population of millions is a valid sample size, is that of a bowl of soup. A single spoonful of the soup contains all of the ingredients of the soup in the same proportions as in the whole bowl. So, the size of the bowl is irrelevant. Because the spoonful is representative of the soup in the bowl, I need just a mouthful of the soup to decide whether I like the taste or not and whether I will eat the whole bowl or not. I don't need to eat the whole bowl to decide if I like the taste. So, the bowl is the population and the mouthful is the sample. Constructing a representative sample might be one reason why biographical detail is sought in a questionnaire survey. If the responses cannot be controlled, then the data may be needed to check how representative the respondent mix is once all responses are received, and to demonstrate representativeness when doing the analysis and reporting the results.

A random sample differs from a representative sample in that all members of the population need to be known in advance; known in the sense of knowing who they are rather than known personally. In our example project, that is likely to be the case; i.e. the names and contact details of all senior decisions makers will be known. That being the case, a random sample is possible. The first decision is what size the sample will be. There are statistical formulae for making that decision (see Saunders *et al* 2015). Once how many is known, each member of the population has an equal chance of being selected to be in the sample. So, a random method of selection is applied. Let's assume there are 150 in the population of senior decision makers and that the sample has been determined to be 50%, or 75 individuals. A roll of a die will give a random number; assume it is three. That number is then applied in selecting individuals from the population to be in the sample by selecting every third individual from a list of the whole population. Depending on the number rolled, the dice technique may not provide the required 75 names by the end of the list. In that case, simply return to the beginning of the list and apply the same number to those names not selected until 75 names are selected.

At this point we have a research paradigm, a literature review, research questions, data types, data sources, research methods and techniques and, if relevant, research respondent sample. This completes the design phase and so we now move onto the implementation phase.

THE IMPLEMENTATION PHASE

Research ethics

The next step in the process and the first of the implementation phase is to consider the important topic of *research ethics*. This has always been important but has come much more to the fore in recent years. Ethics can and should of course be a factor when doing the research design phase. But, that applies to thinking about and anticipating the ethical issues and dimensions associated with the design. It is at this stage and step that the thinking is applied in ensuring an ethical project. So, this step means preparing material to achieve and demonstrate an ethical project whether or not ethical *approval*, as in a university for example, is a requirement for the project. There are three common issues that arise in L&D projects that have ethical dimensions. These are potential harm to human research participants, informed consent and health and safety. The first two apply exclusively to research participants and the third to all involved, especially the researcher. We will consider each in turn.

It is very unlikely that any L&D research project will have the potential to cause physical harm to research participants. However, it is good practice to consider the potential and to satisfy yourself and be able to satisfy others that this is the case in each specific project. Experiencing psychological harm is more of a possibility, although still unlikely. It is though worth giving more thought to the potential for this to happen. For example, asking personal and sensitive questions about life experiences may cause distress. So too may asking questions that provoke unhappy memories. In our example project, the leadership development activity may have included time at an outdoor development centre where physical activities such as abseiling and orienteering at night happened. Some individuals may have had negative experiences at the centre and of these activities. So, the researcher will have to be sensitive to that possibility. The potential for harm does not necessarily exclude use of a method, technique or question. But, the risk of harm needs to be assessed and justified, and measures planned and put in place for dealing with it if it occurs; for example, referral to a psychological counsellor if needed.

Informed consent is always necessary when implementing research projects with human participants. This usually requires two things. First that research participants know the purpose of the project, what is required of them, what will be done with the data they provide and their right to withdraw from the project if they wish to do so. Two additional issues often arise here and these are confidentiality and anonymity. These two concepts are often confused. Confidentiality refers to who will have access to the data provided and the resulting analysis. Usually this will be confined to the researcher, any supervisor and/or assessor involved if the project is part of a qualification programme, and the project sponsor(s) who will read the report. A related issue is how the data will be kept secure so that confidentiality is maintained. In the case of hard copy questionnaires for example, a locked filing space is usually enough. In the case of electronic questionnaires, a password-protected computer or similar meets the requirement. If confidentiality cannot be assured, then participants have to be informed that is the case as part of their informed consent. Anonymity means that participants and/or their individual responses will not be made known to anyone other than the researcher. In some research designs, participants may not even be known to the researcher; online questionnaires for example can be accessed and completed anonymously unless contact details are also requested. Such a request can be and often is optional. Anonymity is not of itself an ethical requirement of research projects. What is required is that research participants know and agree to the position adopted. A final word of caution on anonymity. Often researchers maintain anonymity by not using names of participants. They then make the mistake of using job titles. To exaggerate the point, there is little anonymity in using Chief Financial Officer if there is only one in the organisation, or HR Manager 1 and HR Manager 2 if there are only two; it won't be hard to work out which HR Manager said what! All of the issues discussed in this paragraph are included and explained in what is commonly termed a Participant Information Document (PID) which is given to, or access provided for, every participant. Such documents do not need to be very long and are often a couple of sides of A4 at the most.

The second part of informed consent is securing confirmed consent. This is usually a separate document with a statement confirming consent to the particular project which each research participant signs and returns to the researcher. In online questionnaires and other forms of electronic techniques, there will be a statement to the effect that participating in the project, for example, completing the online questionnaire, confirms consent. The key requirement is that the researcher can demonstrate that consent has been sought and received from each participant. There are some circumstances where consent is a more difficult issue; where children or adults with learning difficulties are the research participants for example. This though is unlikely to arise in the vast majority of L&D projects.

The final issue to be considered is that of health and safety (H&S). Again, this is unlikely to be a significant issue in the vast majority of small-scale L&D research projects. However, most ethical approval systems require the issue to be addressed and usually through completing a H&S risk assessment. Many of the items identified in most of these assessments will not apply. I can think of only one occasion when such a risk required amending a research design and that was when travel restrictions to Africa were in place because of an epidemic of a particular disease being experienced in many countries on that continent at the time of the project.

 REFLECTIVE ACTIVITY 9.6

Identify the main ethical issues in your research project and consider how you will deal with each of them.

Data collection

The next step in the process is *data collection*. This simply means implementing the methods and techniques decided in the design phase. The main points to be aware of are first that this step rarely goes exactly to plan. In our example project, some senior decision makers may decline to be involved in the project. Others will agree, also agree to be interviewed and also agree a date, time and place. But, with varying notice and because by definition they have lots of demands on their diary, some will cancel agreed arrangements. So, they will have to be rearranged. As with all research interviews, some will be talkative and forthcoming in interviews and some will be more guarded and reticent in responding to questions and expressing their views. It is also very common to have lower response rates to questionnaire surveys than anticipated and this often has to be dealt with as it happens; for example, by sending out reminders and extending completion/cut off dates. So, do not be surprised or disheartened if and when you have similar experiences. A second point is that participants often surprise you with their responses. It is nearly always the case for example that some completed questionnaires are unusable. This is often because they are incomplete or because the responses given to questions do not relate to the intended meaning of the questions. Finally, and related to the previous points, amendments sometimes have to made to the design during implementation because when applied in practice, the planned methods and techniques do not deliver the expected and required data.

CASE STUDY 9.2

Ahmed Hussein works as a Talent Development Officer for a large multinational company in financial services. He has particular responsibility for IT staff across all divisions and operations of the organisation. These number over 2,000 in 15 different countries in all the main continents. Ahmed's current focus is applying the newly revised and updated equality in employment policy and procedures adopted by the main Board, which has to be implemented in all business operations. Much online training has been provided by the group level equalities and L&D teams but Ahmed is not sure how far this has been taken up or been effective for the IT staff he is responsible for.

Ahmed clearly needs to gain data from this group of employees. Being large in number and also widely spread geographically, Ahmed understands that his options are limited in relation to collecting data. There will not be time or budget to visit all of the work sites of the IT staff. Perhaps fortunately for him, Ahmed knows that all of the staff are internet savvy and very comfortable with using ICT-based solutions. That should also make it likely that the online training has been popular but that cannot be taken for granted and neither can its effectiveness. So, the most effective, including cost effective, way to collect data will be to set up an online questionnaire. Ahmed considers himself doubly fortunate working for the IT department since he can call on expertise to help with the task of setting up the site for the questionnaire. He also has a full email group distribution list of all the staff in the department to use to send a request to staff to visit the site and complete the questionnaire. Ahmed also decides that the email can be used to provide the Participant Information Document as an attachment and the questionnaire site can include a statement explaining that completion of the questionnaire confirms informed consent to participate in the research. These two actions will help ensure the research is conducted in an ethical manner.

Data analysis

Once the data is collected it is time for the penultimate step which is *data analysis*. Techniques for this will vary depending on whether you are analysing quantitative or qualitative data. Quantitative data is usually analysed using statistical techniques. These can vary from simple descriptive statistics; for example, converting responses into percentages; to highly sophisticated inferential techniques such as structured equation modelling (see Saunders *et al* 2015). Analysis of qualitative data commonly uses techniques such as content analysis, discourse analysis and approaches such as template analysis. The aim in all forms of data analysis is to identify relationships, connections, similarities, differences and patterns in the data which provide full or partial answers to the research questions. Using our example project and the first formulation of the question, relationships between successful completion of the leadership development activity and subsequent performance may be tested to see if they are statistically significant. If they are statistically significant, that does not prove a causal relationship, but one could be inferred. Differences in that effect could also be tested to examine factors such as gender or, because it is a graduate development programme, which university participants gained their degree from, or the subject discipline of their degrees. These factors are possible intervening variables in the relationship between successful completion of the activity and subsequent performance. For example, it turns out that female graduates with science degrees perform better than male graduates with arts-based degrees. In this case, the gender of participants and the subject of their degrees 'intervene' in determining the relationship between completion of the leadership activity and subsequent performance. Again, unarguable causal relationships cannot be claimed. But, the evidence provided by the analysis may be judged strong enough to prioritise certain universities or certain degree subjects in future graduate recruitment.

Analysis of qualitative data commonly looks for themes in the data and uses forms of coding of words, phrases and other content. In the second question of our example project, connections between functional departments or senior managers' own previous experience for example, and views on the value of the activity may be found. More detailed advice on techniques of data analysis can be found in the recommended texts. One final piece of advice here is to decide on and prepare the data analysis techniques before data collection and, as far as possible, record the data in a form which is ready to analyse using the chosen technique. It can be very off-putting to be faced with a large dataset if the means of analysis has not already been decided and prepared.

Reporting the results

The final step in the process is *reporting the results.* This is usually, but not always, in a written document. The form that reporting takes will vary according to the context of the particular project. In the case of a qualification, the form of a written document will be specified – a dissertation, for example. In a work context too there may be a house style to follow, whatever the form of reporting. Sometimes in a work context a presentation of the results to a meeting of decision makers may be required, perhaps supported by a written document. Because of these variations in context it is not possible here to prescribe the form of reporting. What can be said though is that those reading and/or hearing the results need to be in a position to judge them. That means the methods and techniques chosen to collect and analyse the data need to be fully described, explained and justified. This enables the users of the results to assess the worth of the findings and conclusions. The whole of the research process is summarised in Figure 9.2.

Figure 9.2 The research process

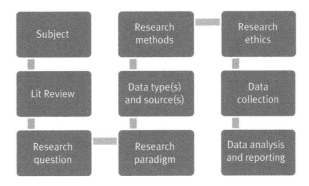

REFLECTIVE ACTIVITY 9.7

Using Figure 9.2 as a series of headings, produce a project plan showing how you will apply each step in the research process in your project.

SUMMARY

Small-scale L&D projects will, by definition, have some limitations. Because they are small in scale, they are likely to have corresponding small datasets. The small datasets will be a limitation. A related limitation arises from the varying contexts of small-scale L&D projects. Populations and samples are likely to be restricted to a single organisation. This limits the generalisability of the findings and conclusions. Finally, and again by definition, small-scale L&D projects will have few resources available. This will limit what can be done and achieved in the project. Some methods and techniques may not be feasible; for example, the time and expense in conducting interviews will limit the number possible. As with most areas of life, conducting research has to be pragmatic and compromises between what is ideal and what is possible often have to be made. This is likely to be particularly the case in any small-scale L&D project.

While recognising and acknowledging these limitations it is also important to recognise and acknowledge that small-scale L&D projects need to be as rigorous as possible and so need to follow the well-established research procedures and protocols which have been shown to be effective in reaching informed and evidenced conclusions. Applying the broad advice provided here, and in particular the research process explained above, will help achieve well-designed and well-conducted research projects. Additional advice will be needed on the detail and specifics of individual projects and the texts recommended at the end of this chapter will prove a valuable and perhaps essential resource for achieving a successful project.

CASE STUDY 9.3

Amanda Nwankwo is a recently appointed Talent Development Manager in Spellman Engineering Ltd (SEL). Her appointment was made by the Chief Executive Officer of SEL, Ella White, who herself has been in post for only six months. SEL is a wholly owned subsidiary of the Humber Group, a UK-based world leader in all forms of engineering. The approach of the Humber Group is to leave its operating companies to manage in their own way and control primarily through financial targets. This suits Ella White very well as she was taken aback at what she found in SEL on taking up her appointment. While SEL has been very successful in recent years and

consistently meets or exceeds income and operating profit targets set by the Humber Group, the approach to managing the company left by the previous CEO does not suit Ella. The approach is best described as command and control and a culture of fear. The incumbent Director of Manufacturing believes in wielding the 'big stick' as the best way of achieving performance. This has naturally been adopted by middle managers and supervisors as their preferred approach.

The HR function in SEL is the responsibility of Peter Jones, the long-serving HR Manager. Jones too took his lead from the previous CEO and from the

Director of Manufacturing. The purpose of HR in Jones's view is to control the behaviour of staff on behalf of senior management. This is achieved in his view by careful recruitment, training and development and strict application of performance management and disciplinary policies and procedures.

Ella White is convinced that the approach to management and the current culture in SEL need to change. The market for SEL's precision-engineered products is becoming more competitive with customers' expectations and demands on price, quality and delivery schedules becoming increasingly challenging. Ella believes that meeting this challenge will require support and commitment from all employees, and such support and commitment will not be forthcoming under the current management approach. While understanding that change will be easier to achieve when she is able to replace current members of the senior management team, which will be over the next 18 months, a start has to be made now. Talent Development Manager is a new post created by Ella White as part of that initial change process. The post is also part of a small reorganisation with training and development being separated from HR and the new post reporting directly to the CEO.

Amanda Nwankwo is aware of the big job facing her as she was fully briefed by the CEO when she was offered the post of Talent Development Manager. Amanda's immediate priority in her first three months is to establish the current view of the workforce on the management style adopted to date by managers and supervisors in SEL. She believes that will signal a change in approach as well as provide some evidence on what style employees will respond to best. Both of these will begin to change the culture and also provide an evidence base for designing some L&D for managers and supervisors. Amanda has agreed with the CEO that changing the management style of middle managers and supervisors is both a possible and desirable priority. But, she prefers to proceed with an evidence base rather than to adopt generic and generalised solutions and has the support of Ella White for that approach.

Questions

1. What ontological and epistemological assumptions, and associated research paradigms, are informing Amanda's actions?

2. How would you translate Amanda's aim and decided approach into a set of research questions?

3. What data types and data sources will be most appropriate for answering these research questions?

4. What methods and techniques will be most relevant and effective to gather and analyse the required data?

5. What ethical issues will the research project Amanda plans raise and how should Amanda deal with them?

FURTHER READING

Anderson, V. (2009) Research methods in human resource management. 2nd ed. London: CIPD.

Bryman, A. and Bell, E. (2015) Business research methods. 4th ed. Oxford: Oxford University Press.

Fisher, C. (2010) Researching and writing a dissertation: an essential guide for business students. Harlow: Pearson Education.

Hart, C. (2009) Doing a literature review. London: Sage Publications.

May, T. (2011) Social research: issues, methods and research. 4th ed. Maidenhead: Open University Press.

Saunders, M.K., Lewis, P. and Thornhill, A. (2015) Research methods for business students. 7th ed. Harlow: Pearson Education.

REFERENCES

BRYMAN, A. and BELL, E. (2015) *Business Research Methods.* 4th ed. Oxford: Oxford University Press.

FISHER, C. (2010) *Researching and writing a dissertation: an essential guide for business students.* Harlow: Pearson Education.

HART, C. (2009) *Doing a literature review.* London: Sage Publications.

MAY, T. (2011) *Social research: issues, methods and research.* 4th ed. Maidenhead: Open University Press.

NOLA, R. and SANKEY, H. (2014) *Theories of scientific method.* Abingdon: Routledge.

SAUNDERS, M.K., LEWIS, P. and THORNHILL, A (2015) *Research methods for business students.* 7th ed. Harlow: Pearson Education.

STEWART, J., HARTE, V. and SAMBROOK, S. (2011) 'What is a theory?', *Journal of European Industrial Training,* Vol 35, No 3, pp221–229.

WAHYUNI, D. (2012) The research design maze: understanding paradigms, cases, methods and methodologies. *Journal of Applied Management Accounting Research.* Vol 10, No 1, pp69–80.

WATSON, T. J. (2010) In search of management: culture, chaos and control in managerial work. Andover: Cengage Learning.

WATSON, T.J. and HARRIS, P. (1999) *The emergent manager.* London: Sage Publications.

Conclusions and Future Directions

JIM STEWART AND PATRICIA ROGERS

OVERVIEW

Our closing chapter has two purposes. First, we will attempt to identify some significant themes that emerge from the chapters of the book. Second, an attempt will be made to predict how these themes may develop in the future and to anticipate some consequences and implications for the professional practice of L&D. These purposes therefore have direct connections. Given the speculative nature of the purposes, we have not formulated or stated specific objectives for the chapter. We have also not included any reader activities. However, we hope readers will join in our speculations and that those provided here will inform and stimulate both thought and debate.

It needs to be acknowledged that as an edited text we cannot include the views of all of our contributors. Therefore, what we write here are our views and not necessarily those of the authors whose chapters we draw on for these conclusions and speculations. We hope none of our contributors will object to what we say here. But, they may well disagree and wish to dispute or debate our views. That will be perfectly healthy and no doubt some of you will have similar reactions as you read on. The important point to make is that we make our own arguments and not those of our contributors.

SOME SIGNIFICANT THEMES

Drawing out significant themes from the book is both a difficult and an arbitrary task. This follows from the range of topics covered and from the range of writers involved in authoring the chapters. We are aware therefore that our ideas are simply that. However, we can use the broad structure of the book and its associated logic of the L&D intermediate core units to organise speculation on some significant themes. These are first the professional practice of L&D, second the organisation and other contexts in which that practice occurs and finally the role of data in L&D practice.

THE PROFESSIONAL PRACTICE OF L&D

There are a number of points to make under this heading. First, L&D professionals rarely if ever achieve results alone. L&D practice requires collaboration with managers, employees, other professionals as well as, often, with external partners. This is a theme evident in other sections of the book – when doing research projects, for example. Second, L&D professionals need to stay current in their own knowledge and skills. This will be examined again in the next section. But, continuous professional development (CPD) is an activity in which all professionals need to be competent. Again, there are reinforcing points on this need in other sections and chapters, for example in relation to varying and different contexts of practice. We are reminded here of a clichéd but nevertheless relevant analogy in the phrase 'doctor, heal thyself'. This is often used in jest but it is also meant to indicate the tendency of medical doctors to neglect their own health. So, we might say a clear theme of the book is 'L&D professional, develop yourself'. Third, although not directly addressed throughout the book, the issue of continuous developments in L&D practice is an additional important factor in creating the need for L&D professionals to engage in CPD. One of the most pressing examples of this is the application of information and communication technology (ICT) in enabling and supporting learning and development.

Many terms have been used to characterise such ICT applications; technology-based learning, e-learning and m-learning for example. Perhaps the most accurate all-encompassing term is digital learning; there are many technologies, platforms and forms of hardware/software that are included in digital learning which are not all included in e-learning or m-learning. Whatever term is used, the main points that ICT provides fast and easy access to content and to social interaction and social learning, facilitates the use of a variety of media to present content and also tends to broaden access remain true. Additional factors are also always associated with ICT applications to L&D; for example, removing full direct control from organisations on the what and how of learning, reducing L&D costs over time and enabling delivery of learning at times and places that suit learners rather than L&D professionals. The final point is that changes in ICT occur almost daily and new opportunities, and challenges, are created for L&D professionals. If nothing else is the focus of CPD then developments in ICT, and their implications for L&D, have to be on the agenda of every professional. As we will see in the next section, there is much uncertainty about the future. We can though be certain that there will be both new ways of using current new technology and new forms of technology that will have significant implications for L&D professional practice.

THE CHANGING CONTEXT OF L&D PROFESSIONAL PRACTICE

The first point about the context is that it is ever-changing. This is not necessarily new but developments in ICT discussed above, for example, illustrate the increasing rate and impact of change. So too does the related impact of data and information sources discussed in Chapter 9. A recent addition to the management lexicon is the acronym VUCA. This stands for Volatile, Uncertain, Complex and Ambiguous and these adjectives are argued to describe the context within which all organisations now operate. Given that the organisation context is such, it is also the case that the context for L&D professional practice is the same; that is, subject to VUCA environments. One significant example is the changing organisation designs being adopted with related changes in the nature of employment and work. These changes, and the new levels of uncertainty we all now experience, will demand different responses from and changes in the role and contribution of L&D professionals in the future.

Changing organisation forms and fast-moving operating environments will produce both opportunities and limitations for L&D professionals. An example of the former is that business strategies based on differentiation arising from the skills and abilities of employees, as explored earlier in the book, will lend support to the business case for investment in L&D. This in turn will lead to increases in resource allocations for L&D activity. However, this will only happen if valued returns of the kinds discussed in Chapter 9 can be demonstrated from that investment. Or, perhaps it is more likely to happen if it is the case that valued returns can be demonstrated. Another example is when L&D professionals keep up to date with developments in research and practice relevant to L&D practice. For example, new knowledge arising from research in neuroscience and related understanding of learning processes. This can and does lead to improvements in learning methods and techniques which make L&D interventions and activities more successful. Adopting and applying new techniques requires constant attention to CPD by L&D professionals.

Limitations will also be experienced. New organisation forms and ways of working for example will produce limits on the use of traditional and established ways of doing L&D. An illustration of this is that arranging face-to-face delivery of learning and development will be difficult for temporary, casual and transient employees. All of these are increasing forms of employment across all industries. In addition, the rise of myriad approaches to flexible working, and location free-working, also creates similar difficulties for such delivery. L&D professionals will need to adjust to new roles and new ways of facilitating learning in order to respond positively to these limitations.

Globalisation is another significant element of the VUCA operating environment examined in the book. At least one positive outcome of this phenomenon of value to L&D is a widening source of ideas to inform professional practice. It is reasonable to claim that Anglo/US ideas have shaped management thought and practice in and since the previous century. Globalised product and labour markets, however, have and are surfacing different ideas and theories. This is happening not least because of the problems experienced by multinational corporations (MNCs) in applying single models of management practice in the new and emerging markets. The additional and related problem of managing multi-cultural workforces is another driver of new and different approaches to organising and managing. These different ideas include approaches to and methods of L&D professional practice.

THE ROLE OF DATA IN L&D PROFESSIONAL PRACTICE

As with contextual change, the use of data in L&D professional practice is not new. Data has always been required and used in the identification of training/learning needs, for example. But, and again as with contextual change, the situation now and in the future will be very different from that in the past. There have been and will continue to be changing opportunities for the use of data arising from new sources of data, new forms of data and new ways of analysing data to inform decision making.

New sources and forms include those associated with developing ICT platforms, especially but not exclusively those collectively named 'social media'. We are reminded of a story told to near graduating business students by a senior HR professional from a telecommunications MNC. The story concerned the MNC's standard practice of doing an online search of the names of job applicants; in this case, those applying for the company's graduate training programme. The results for one applicant revealed a Twitter account and a particular tweet of interest from three months previously. The tweet content consisted of disparaging comments about a talk being given to near graduates by the same HR professional, and similarly disparaging comments about the graduate training programme being described; the very one the applicant was now attempting to join! This story has some direct relevance to L&D practice since graduate training programmes are a common L&D intervention in medium and large-sized-organisations. It is also relevant as it illustrates examples of both new sources and new forms of data now available to L&D professionals. It is though perhaps more relevant as a salutary lesson to final year business students!

Social media platforms are just one example of new sources and forms of data. They are likely to become more and more significant in the future. One of the reasons for this is that they also represent a new tool and range of techniques for actually designing and delivering L&D interventions and activities; to facilitate social learning, for example, among groups of employees without the need for face-to-face interaction. One advantage of using social media, not easily available to some other forms of social learning, is the ability to produce a range of data on the processes and outcomes of the techniques applied. These data can be used first to assess the effectiveness of the method and make adjustments to improve the learning, and second to analyse the success of the intervention to demonstrate valued returns in the associated investment.

Social media and other sources and forms of data will continue to develop and change and so produce even more opportunities for data use in L&D professional practice. An additional development will be access to and use of what is termed 'big data'. Social media sites are just one example of where big data can and will exist in the future. There are debates on the meaning and definition of the term and also uncertainties about access and use. That is why the idea of big data receives little attention in the book; there is little of value to say currently about using big data in L&D practice. However, the notion will undoubtedly be of more and more relevance and value in the future and so of importance to L&D professionals.

The existence of and access to datasets, whether big or small and whether internal or external, will not always satisfy the need for accurate, valid and reliable information. So, L&D professionals will, as now and in the past, need to continue to be able to generate original data themselves in order to tackle some of their individual and unique L&D problems. Hence, a key ability is conducting effective research projects. Our view is that the important word in the last sentence is 'effective'. A feature of management thought in the previous couple of decades is the rise of interest in and value attached to 'evidence-based management'. An example from L&D is the use and application in design of L&D activities of research into learning conducted within neuroscience. Such research is based on 'effective' research projects. Similarly, the rise of interest in and use of HR and L&D analytics is based on sound understanding of the nature of data and the status of data analysis. Hence we believe that L&D professionals will increasingly need a full understanding of research design and the claims to knowledge that can be supported by original data. Because of evidence-based management and the increasing use of analytics, decision makers in organisations will become increasingly sophisticated in assessing and judging analyses and arguments based on internal research projects. So, L&D professionals will have to match that sophistication in their use of their own research.

SUMMARY

To summarise, we have argued in this chapter our own views on what factors will affect and influence L&D professional practice in the foreseeable future. We have also suggested some implications that will increasingly face and occupy the attention of L&D professionals in their work. We hope our speculations provide food for thought and a basis for debate. However, we offer our thoughts with little certainty. This is not because of a lack of confidence in our knowledge base or in our ability to analyse what we know. Rather, our lack of certainty springs from a view of the nature of the future. We do not believe it is a given and waiting for us to discover as time passes. That is not the nature of the future. We believe the future has to be and will be created by human choice; by the choices you, we and others make. So, to the extent that what we speculate here is possible, they represent choices. And the speculations can be judged as more or less desirable than alternatives. The key question to close this chapter and the book is what kind of L&D professional practice do you, we and others want to promote and work to accomplish?

Index